To Relish the Sublime?

Were their views on some points divergent?

Stephen dissented openly from Bloom's views on the importance of dietary and civic selfhelp while Bloom dissented tacitly from Stephen's views on the eternal affirmation of the spirit of man in literature.

James Joyce, *Ulysses*

Contents

Introduction: To relish the sublime?

This book is prompted by an understanding of culture that many today are likely to reject as anachronistic and politically regressive. In referring to Matthew Arnold's conception of culture as offering 'sublime' experiences from which all could in principle benefit, we hark back to an ideal that is seldom invoked now except as exemplifying the elitism and ethnocentrism of nineteenth-century cultural commentary. Here, we take Arnold's views about culture's potential social and individual benefits altogether more seriously. We also take seriously, and affirm, the view that some cultural works can be defended as better than others, and that engagement with better works is likely to prove more rewarding. We do so, however – as the query in our title suggests – in a spirit of interrogation that acknowledges the contradictory dimensions and contestable relevance of any such view of culture as a universal good and repository of value. We know that such claims are problematic. They were when Arnold first made them, and have perhaps become still more so in our own postmodern times.

To defend them may therefore seem wishful and idealist. However, modern industrial democracies have been committed to the idea that cultural education is a general good, enabling people to realise themselves more fully and to become more autonomous and reflective. They have made material and institutional provision for it (as Raymond Williams observed,

Arnold's cultural essays are not properly comprehensible except in the context of his active work as an inspector of schools).[1] To be sure, this commitment has been compromised, if not confounded, by the persistence of socio-economic divisions; and it is at odds with the narrower vocational priorities of the workplace. But for these very reasons, an ideal of cultural development cannot but imply a critique of the social conditions pre-empting its fulfilment. Keeping open the idea of culture as a universal good in turn keeps open the space for critical reflection on the tensions between our society's endorsement of non-instrumental values and conceptions of the self, and their actual marginalisation in what is nowadays significantly called the 'real world' of the economy.

Moreover, it is not only those (like us) who speak openly in terms of cultural value who sustain its idea. Whether acknowledged or not, presumptions of value and an associated ideal of self-development are implicitly at work in any project of cultural education. The specialised engagement with culture in the school and the academy is defensible only on a broadly Arnoldian view that cultural self-realisation comes with difficulty and usually with the aid of some instruction. Those who do the instructing may be loath to offer any form of cultural evaluation, but we shall argue that in their role as specialised teachers they implicitly endorse an overarching project of selection and discrimination. The special attention accorded to cultural ideals within education (a consequence and analogue of their marginality in society at large) is problematic, tending to subvert the very claims for culture's general importance which justify its educational dissemination; but one does not escape this social contradiction by disowning cultural value.

This aspect of our argument engages directly with themes in academic cultural and literary studies today. Much of the book is devoted, however, to philosophical and literary texts of earlier periods (the majority of our authors wrote between 1750 and 1930); and most of these are more or less canonical works in the European and English tradition. This too may seem merely old-fashioned, and certainly reflects the authors' educational formation. But aside from any question of our own expertise, there are two reasons why we have chosen this historical–cultural focus. First of all, the texts we discuss allow us to set the Arnoldian claim about culture in a dual historical perspective: we trace some of its roots in European philosophical conceptions of the self, and note some of the ways it was represented and called into question, both before and after Arnold, during the formative period of the liberal democratic state. Secondly, we are defending a project of cultural education which stresses the value of historical perspective and of engaging with less accessible texts and less familiar ideas. Our own critical and expository readings are offered as evidence for the claim that an engagement with works of the past can still throw light on the contemporary.

Arnold's cultural 'sublime'

'The taste of the bathos is implanted by nature itself in the soul of man; till, perverted by custom or example, he is taught, or compelled rather, to relish the sublime'. Matthew Arnold quotes this sentence from an obscure satire by John Arbuthnot, a contemporary and associate of Swift and Pope.[2] As often in *Culture and Anarchy*, some irony appears to be intended, directed (it almost seems) at the educational values Arnold holds and the conception of *Bildung* or cultural self-realisation implicit in his entire argument. Arnold is often regarded as a complacent liberal humanist, but his tone here suggests defensive anxiety rather than assurance.

Of course there were, and are, reasons for scepticism about the scope and pertinence of the cultural ideal. We have already noted these and will return to them shortly. For the moment, we can paraphrase Arnold's and Arbuthnot's sentence, given the context, as follows: 'Most people, left to themselves, will prefer cultural works that make few demands and yield only trivial pleasures; but, encouraged by education, they can be brought to appreciate more demanding works that ultimately offer deeper and more complex satisfactions'. Put like this, Arnold's claim still raises a host of questions: Who will do the educating? How do they derive the authority to pronounce on what is 'bathetic' and what is 'sublime'? What relation exists between these educational–cultural hierarchies and differences of social status and power? However, it is by no means self-evidently untenable. Indeed, it sums up the underlying rationale for the programmes of cultural education that many industrial democracies have instituted and in which all likely readers of this book will have been involved. Even those teachers whose hostility to 'sublime' or élite culture leads them to work only on popular texts will discuss these in terminology that breaks with everyday understandings: far from being allowed to enjoy the pleasures of *Bridget Jones's Diary* or *Lara Croft, Tomb Raider* unreflectingly,[3] their students will probably be made to give an account of signifying practices, constructions of gendered subjectivity, the evolution of genre. And the purpose of all this will be to help them acquire a more complex understanding of culture than they would have arrived at left to their own devices.

Arnold's essay has acquired its own canonical status, not least as a starting point for critiques of canonical culture,[4] because it marks the moment where 'culture' comes to denominate not just an inherited tradition of texts and an associated ideal of self-development, but the endeavour to make these current through education beyond a restricted leisure-class audience. Arnold wrote at the moment of the Second Reform Bill; within sixty years of its passing, all citizens of Britain would enjoy formal political and civil equality.[5] The largest question *Culture and Anarchy* raises, explicitly and implicitly, concerns the uses of learned culture, historically the preserve of a small élite, in these new conditions whose coming Arnold foresaw. It is problematic to assume that everyone will benefit from engaging with 'the best that has been thought and known'[6] as this has been defined in a history of privilege and inequality, and disingenuous to pretend that everyone, even in rich countries, is in a position to do so. However, is no less problematic to say – as, for instance, Nietzsche in effect does[7] – that the health of culture depends on most people remaining excluded from it. The ideal of a common culture is in tension with socio-economic division and self-ascribed cultural difference, but the persistence of cultural hierarchy troubles democratic principle. Thus, if from one point of view the universal, normative claims of the cultural ideal are hypocritical and oppressive, from another they are grounds for an immanent critique of societies that proclaim in the domain of culture the equality of persons while in their economic and social life they reproduce and rely on structural inequality. These twin perspectives, and their representation, acknowledgement or disavowal in works of culture and cultural reflection, provide the framework for our argument. They are divergent, even opposed, perspectives; but neither can be relinquished if we wish to understand the historical meaning of the cultural ideal.

The term 'culture', in the post-Arnoldian anglophone tradition, connotes these tensions, ambiguities and educational ideals, as well as denoting a body of texts and commentaries. Our denotative usage is in one sense restrictive: by 'culture' we refer usually to 'the works and practices of intellectual and especially artistic activity', to cite one of the definitions given by Raymond Williams;[8] and especially to the more or less canonical literary texts that have been widely studied as exemplary instances. We sometimes use the phrase 'learned culture' to remind readers of this restricted usage. This is a culture that depends doubly on education, both to equip us to engage with many of its works and also because the works often retain currency mainly because they are taught in courses. However, we adopt this seemingly narrow focus on learned culture, rather than taking 'culture' in the wider semiotic and anthropological sense usual in cultural studies, because we intend to sustain a broad engagement with the social and educational contradictions that the Arnoldian project has involved. When we discuss contemporary critiques and contexts, our main concern is with how these contradictions continue to make themselves felt. To claim that nothing has changed since Arnold would be as absurd as to defend his views in their original formulation. But one thing that has not changed is the tension between the provision of cultural education offered as a means to universal self-development, and an economic system that values people instrumentally rather than as ends in themselves and allocates them very different and unequal positions in the division of wealth and labour.

The project announced by Arnold has been revised, rather than abandoned. A society that had indeed abandoned it – that no longer expected works of culture to be studied in schools and universities – would be very different from the contemporary anglophone liberal democracies. Its conceptions of value, selfhood and progress deserve critical interrogation, rather than simple endorsement or dismissal. In Chapters 1–5 of this book, we illustrate and discuss them in a somewhat wider register than that of recent literary and cultural theory and metatheory, drawing on works of philosophy and fiction to provide this. The critical perspectives we develop derive from the inherently self-questioning nature of our texts, as well as from the new kinds of scrutiny they are nowadays subject to. By the nature of its object, our account dwells much on antinomies and lacunae, as these are both represented in and exemplified by the texts we consider. Our central focus is on the period of emergent and newly established political democracy in Britain and western Europe, where philosophy, literature and critique highlight both the supposed or potential universality of the cultural ideal and its actual limitations and restrictions. At this time, ideals of cultural democracy drew energy from their links to movements for the political and legal equality of citizens, and from the tension between the progress made on those fronts and the persistence of social and economic inequality. If universalist cultural ideals are in eclipse today, this reflects our greater awareness of the exclusions that universals may camouflage and the homogeneities they may enforce; but it reflects also the eclipse of social democratic and socialist ideas. Postmodernist celebrations of the eclectic, the partial, the demotic and the incommensurable may make us lose sight of kinds of 'difference' – in the nature of tasks done at work, in wealth and income, in educational opportunity and experience – of which a more universal language was more forcefully critical.

Our Conclusion, developing themes opened in the body of the book, focuses on recent and current contexts and arguments. Acknowledging the pressures exerted on the cultural ideal by the instrumental conceptions of the person implied in the still-dominant (in some ways, newly dominant) work-ethic, we argue that there is a dialectical linkage between the ideal of the developing and autonomous self and the expansion of free time – an expansion which the productivity of social labour makes possible in principle, but which has been realised only to a limited extent in European societies (among which Britain has been conspicuous by its backwardness). We then turn, in a discussion of 'cyberculture' and some of its implications, to the distinction between cultural forms that mirror and extend an existing sense of selfhood or identity and those that offer a less individualised (not to say narcissistic) address and response. Finally, we return, in a discussion of academic critiques of canonical values, to the tension between culture's universal claims and its particular instances.

Before offering a more substantial overview of the topics covered in Chapters 1–5, we should draw attention to some other general bearings and boundaries of our project. Our emphasis is on the value of learned culture. But this should not be taken to imply that we consider that this alone offers fulfilment and self-realisation – either in the sense that we would most admire a sensibility formed only through such culture (far from it), or in the sense that we think everyone will or should enjoy it. We do, however, stress the universality of the ideal, even while recognising its always partial application, because the specificity of its historical development, as well as its dimension of immanent critique, depend precisely on the rejection of older ideas that saw learned culture as the exclusive preserve of particular castes or élites. Speaking more empirically and from our experience as teachers, we would also emphasise what sometimes gets lost in purely theoretical debates, namely the continuing desire of students to make their way over still-existing barriers to engage with cultural education and critique.

We discuss philosophical arguments and literary representations, and it is to the novel that we turn in illustration of the claims made for cultural self-realisation. This is not to deny the importance of music, painting, poetry and other kinds of high or learned culture. The general argument about cultural self-realisation, in our own sense as well as in some of the literature of *Bildung* on which we draw, takes it as axiomatic that these other kinds – requiring an element of work and learning and then rewarding this in deeper appreciation – can also give the sort of pleasure that Arnold calls 'sublime'. However, we recognise that other parts of our argument depend more definitely on the particular kinds of reflection and self-reflection that socially embedded discursive and narrative genres (such as philosophy, the novel, and film) afford.

Our understanding of the idea of culture as contributing to self-realisation presupposes a view of the individual as formed by culture but also actively responsive to it, and capable of self-change in the light of its influence. A third point, then, concerns the attention we pay to defending the conception of the self as a reflective and existentially determining agent against those critics who are hostile to any 'humanist' approach to the theorisation of the subject. This emphasis distinguishes our approach from the narrower focus on texts and canons alone that is more usual in accounts of culture and its study, and involves an engagement with recent theoretical debates about the subject. Critics (we contend) cannot target what they see as the inevitable bias and partiality of value discriminations without being tacitly committed to their own prescriptive views on what counts as self-realisation and the role of culture in promoting it. Pedagogy depends on some positive ideal of subject formation: this poses a challenge at the level of their own practice to academic theorists and teachers who say they reject inherited (humanist, Enlightenment) ideals, but are unwilling to articulate what their own might be.

The subject realised in culture

It is to this question of the humanist, Enlightenment subject that the historical and critical exposition of our first two chapters is devoted. The idea that culture promotes something we are calling self-realisation is less often discussed than the idea that it depends on aesthetic canons and evaluations. However, the general association of personal development with access to culture is implicitly accepted as a rationale for education. The more specific view that culture has a distinctive contribution to make to the realisation of one's humanity has also been widely held: it is involved, for example, in Arnold's injunction to realise the 'best self' through a developed 'relish for the sublime', and it is certainly central to the German tradition of *Bildung* or cultural self-realisation by which Arnold himself was partly inspired and whose contours and problematic dimensions we trace in Chapter 1. Here we shall confine ourselves to some remarks that will clarify what we see as distinctive to the form of self-realisation promoted by learned culture, while also signalling some of its conflictual aspects.

Cultural self-realisation requires intellectual effort, and may come about only under a certain duress or, in Arnold's terminology, 'compulsion'. It depends on resisting or deferring easier and less exacting types of engagement or gratification in the interests of an ultimately more memorable and cherishable satisfaction. This satisfaction, moreover, has to do with attaining to a self-transcendent mode of understanding: with gaining access to a more comprehensive and nuanced sense of things than one would have attained left to oneself. In all these respects, parallels can be drawn with the quest for personal salvation through religion. Religion is comparable in its spirituality, in the demands it can make on the devotee, and in its structure of gratification, which requires the deferral or transcendence of more immediately pleasurable satisfactions in the interest of ultimate rewards. (Historically, moreover, it is arguable that the transcendent value ascribed to culture by Arnold is in part a compensation for the vanishing transcendence once offered by a religion which he and his contemporaries were finding it more and more difficult to believe in.) However, in several other respects cultural self-realisation differs profoundly from religious salvation. Religious belief may provide solace, insight, even revelation in this present life, but the form of fulfilment specific to religion is offered in essentially redemptive terms – in terms of the promise of salvation in an afterlife. Works of culture, on the other hand, though they may be placed at the service of religion, provide aesthetic pleasures or fulfilments attained and enjoyed in this world rather than the hereafter. They may help us come to terms with mortality, but they neither require belief in anything transcendent to their own forms of exaltation or fulfilment nor offer any guarantees of ultimate bliss. Moreover, and of especial relevance to our concerns here, religious and cultural self-realisation have very different educational conditions and implications. The spiritual gains offered by religion are available to all and do not require a specialised training. It is true that individuals can be more or less schooled in religious doctrine, that many religions require their followers to undergo forms of initiation, and that only a select few attain positions in which they can officiate at religious rites or interpret theology. Nonetheless, religion's promise of salvation is in principle available to all who believe, regardless of their level of education and socio-economic standing: in Christian teaching, the least advantaged in worldly terms are closer to the Kingdom of Heaven. Cultural self-realisation, by contrast, as a secular matter, is limited by socially imposed constraints on educational participation and correlated with the nature of people's work. Culture's sublime rewards, moreover, come not through faith and obedience to doctrine but rather through the suspension of safe and comforting forms of conviction and self-understanding.

As with so many of the ideas contributing to the Western ideal of cultural self-realisation, this has an analogue and mythic register in the philosophy of ancient Greece, in this particular case in Plato's image of the Cave and the pain of its shadow-obsessed occupants on being forced to turn around to confront the world not of illusory reflections but of reality, and thus to begin the slow process of adjustment to the pure light of the Sun.[9] The analogue is not exact, but it captures the sense of a truer vision gained only with difficulty. Plato, we may recall, also requires that those compelled to see the Sun should then return to the Cave to serve their fellows as philosopher Guardians, a role for which they are all the more qualified by their reluctance to assume it. This aspect of the image is pertinent too, for it highlights the tension between the individually gratifying and the socially valuable dimensions of cultural self-realisation; and indicates, perhaps, something of the form of political accountability that might be expected to follow upon it. In our understanding, and for much of the tradition we draw on, what is gained through culture is a good in itself for the individual. But we also interpret it as having a social orientation in the sense that it goes together with a more historical, intersubjective and critically-honed sense of one's own identity and society. Cultural self-realisation may thus far be associated with the fostering of a political consciousness or the development of republican virtue. However, there is no denying that a self-formative project directed at the development of an inner core of being, and justified (as it often has been) in virtue of its 'other-worldliness' and abstraction from the concerns of politics and commerce, can also generate what may be seen as culpable indifference to the fate of society at large. In Germany, as we note in Chapter 1, Thomas Mann was inclined to associate the lack of resistance to the rise of National Socialism with the political quietism of *Bildung* as self-discovery through culture.

We recognise, too, that culture in itself offers no guarantee of political understanding or tolerance. The culturally developed person is not immune to evil or incapable of cruelty, and cultural sophistication may even in some situations enable people to behave more woundingly and contemptuously to others. Nor do we claim that the transcendent perspective encouraged through learned culture – although it may be inflected in ways that indicate political critiques and agendas – is directly analogous to that offered in political analysis and discourse. We suggest, in discussing novels of cultural self-realisation in Chapter 4, that 'culture' and 'politics' as denominating some holistic perspective or view from outside emerge synchronously and are both counterposed and interconnected.

We are not, then, making a case for any necessary link between cultural self-realisation and politicisation of the individual, still less politicisation along any particular ideological axis. For our argument here, the essential link between the individual and social aspects of cultural self-realisation lies along other lines. Only in another kind of society, where people were no longer subordinated as means to the ends of 'the economy', would the space for autonomy and for a diversity of autonomously chosen forms of self-realisation expand freely. Cultural reflection helps to awaken forms of sensibility which are immanently in contradiction with instrumental economic 'ends'. We have made it clear already that this book is committed to the holding open of that contradiction, to the defence of an idea of culture that retains rather than collapses its tensions, and ultimately to a critical perspective that sees capitalist economic rationality as a culturally destructive force.

In its reliance on what Charles Taylor has referred to as the 'inward' self (a self conceived as possessing and reflecting upon its own individuality and inner depth), cultural self-realisation is essentially a project of European modernity; and it only begins to be conceived and promoted as a universally applicable goal and rationale of education in recent times (from the later nineteenth century). However, as our reference to Plato indicates, it draws on ideas or ideals about the distinguishing features of the human that may well be coterminous with Western written culture. According to these, it is the possession of reason, essentially, that divides us from other creatures. It follows that the pursuits most proper to the realisation of our humanity are those which engage our powers of rational contemplation. It also appeared to follow (at any rate, it was conveniently assumed) that anyone not socially positioned to develop the life of the mind must be by nature a little less than fully human. The story of cultural self-realisation as an ideal is the story, essentially, of this 'humanist' double-bind and its gradual unravelling from the period of Enlightenment, and it is this that we first discuss in Chapter 1. We focus there not so much on the overt and aristocratic élitism of Classical and pre-modern views on the life of the mind (although we trace their survival in a Nietzschean strand of cultural commentary) as on the more troubled and contradictory discourse that emerges in societies affected by ideas of political democracy in which the ideal of cultural self-realisation begins to be conceived as if it did have universal application. It is here (as we have noted) that the ideal starts to function as immanent critique of economic and social divisions. It is in this context, too, that we review the shifts in thinking that take place over time as to what most properly constitutes the life of the mind, noting in particular the move away from the emphasis on reason and philosophical contemplation to a view that focuses on the importance of aesthetic mediation. In contrast to the Platonist view of a self-realisation fully attained only in the vision of the Sun (the cognition of the Forms), we find here, in this Enlightenment engagement with the idea of the aesthetic and its mediation of sensory and cognitive dimensions (we focus in particular on the contribution of Kant and Schiller), a philosophical discourse more immediately relevant to the idea of a distinctively cultural self-realisation.

We must emphasise that our engagement with the aesthetic is limited, being intended specifically to illuminate and critique the way in which that category in Kantian philosophy is grounded in the presumption of a common human sensibility, which under certain conditions disposes us to pleasingly harmonious responses. The category thus registers – if only in a wishful and purely formal mode – something of the aspiration towards a common culture and its universal appreciation. We here emphasise the equivocal status of the aesthetic as both ideologically confirming the status quo of bourgeois society and gesturing towards its redemption. Although presented as the realm in which social divisions are harmoniously reconciled, it also inevitably points to the lack of any truly collective and reciprocal mode of being – and so gestures towards a future in which intellectual fragmentation and the division of labour will have been overcome in reality. In exploring these ambiguities, and their vulnerability to materialist critique, we draw on some recent contributions to philosophical aesthetics and engage at a number of points with critics working in the Marxist tradition, notably Adorno. However, we are not offering any historical survey of aesthetic theory, nor seeking to defend or contest any specific position within philosophical aesthetics. Broadly, we agree with Adorno that the autonomy of art in bourgeois society (and hence its critical potential) has been inextricably bound up with its purely aesthetic status. However, we are critical of his tendency to confine any 'promise of happiness' to be found in art to works of modernism. More generally, we take issue with the position within philosophical aesthetics which so insists on the deformation of existing society, including its very categories of thought, under the dominance of instrumental rationality that it denies or overlooks the socially constitutive dimension of cultural work and its often countervailing influence. For our part, we question whether society is 'one-dimensional' even in capitalist (post)modernity, and insist on the ongoing tension between systemic and symbolic values as registered in the overall antithesis between economic and cultural–educational domains.[10]

By and large, however, we support the dialectical position on subjectivity developed within Critical Theory against Nietzschean and neo-Nietzschean attacks on the idea of a self-reflecting subject. In Chapter 2, we seek to defend the ultimate coherence, and political credentials, of the idea of cultural self-realisation against post-structuralist positions in social and cultural theory that would condemn it for its humanist illusions and ethnocentric understandings of culture. Unreconstructed Arnoldian–Leavisite formulations of the cultural ideal have merited feminist and postcolonial criticism and revision; but we dispute the idea that these critiques themselves can be consistently sustained from within a relativist and anti-humanist framework of thinking on culture and subjectivity. In pressing this case, we distinguish between more and less radical (and respectively less and more sustainable) challenges to Enlightenment views on the 'autonomous' individual, illustrating the distinction by reference to recent feminist criticism and controversy. The limitations which in our view undermine the more radical constructivist position within feminism equally undermine (we argue) the attack on the 'tyranny of the subject' found in some postcolonial theory.

In this second chapter, then, we defend the formal coherence of the subject of cultural self-realisation by exposing the self-defeating nature of the neo-Nietzschean opposition to its categories. In a concluding section, we also seek to answer some more general criticisms of the continued viability of its project in a period when the demotic and eclectic impulse of post-modernity makes it increasingly difficult to defend any definition of the good life as preferable to any other. Here we consider the objection that the fulfilments of cultural self-realisation are inherently or necessarily a matter of competitive self-distinction. Rejecting this, and sketching arguments elaborated more fully in our Conclusion, we here link the democratic potential of the pleasures of learned culture to the wider aspirations intimated in contemporary society's continued commitment to the values of the 'symbolic' domain. Culture, we argue, is a source (we do not claim it is the only source) of fulfilments which, unlike expensive material goods and resource-hungry leisure activities, do not depend on unequal wealth or run up against ecological limits.

Fictions of cultural self-development

Culture, wrote Arnold, 'seeks to do away with classes; to make the best that has been known and thought in the world current everywhere . . . This is the *social idea*; and the men of culture are the true apostles of equality'.[11] In the decades following *Culture and Anarchy*, a number of novels explore the claim made by Arnold, and this body of work (discussed in Chapter 4) is the central focus of our engagement with literary texts.[12]

Our main emphases are those which derive directly from the novels. These can be read as documents both because they set out to portray contemporary cultural aspirations and circumstances and because they are themselves examples of the cultural discourse they explore. They are realist novels whose protagonists seek self-development in culture even though they are not from the well-to-do classes. New ideas of cultural democracy encourage these aspirations, which are thwarted by inadequate or inaccessible educational provision and the pressure of material needs. These themes, central in *Jude the Obscure*, are echoed to a greater or lesser extent in several other works of the period 1890–1910. Hardy's comment that when Ruskin College was founded some people said it 'should have been called the college of Jude the Obscure' suggests that his novel was read as social criticism and may have had some practical effect.[13] One emphasis of the books we discuss is of that kind: elements not just of *Jude* but of E.M. Forster's *Howards End* and H.G.Wells' *The Wheels of Chance* (for instance) can be read as deploying the cultural ideal in a critique of the society which professes to uphold it but which cannot satisfy the educational and cultural desires of its citizens.

Even in *Jude*, however, we can detect alongside the critique of society in culture's name a scepticism about the cultural ideal: about its capacity to survive in marginal lives, and about the extent to which it demands revision in itself. A more radical scepticism is voiced by George Gissing, who focuses, in *New Grub Street* and the less well-known *In the Year of Jubilee*, on how ideas of culture were implicated in changing forms of status and newly commercial definitions of leisure and free time. Gissing conceives culture in sociological as well as evaluative terms, and displays how cultural attitudes and self-conceptions are involved in people's striving for social status and in the striving of authors for authority. Like the Californian novelist Jack London, whose autobiographical *Martin Eden* we also consider at some length, he shows us how difficult it is to hold literary value apart from the monetary and social values to which it is conventionally opposed. Yet for both Gissing and London, the position of authorship sustained by their commitment to an autonomous literary standard is indispensable to the critical and analytical perspective they develop. Culture is social, but to those who pursue it as their life's ideal it appears to afford the privilege, or entail the penalty, of a position somehow above or outside society.

Several of these narratives in this sense support Raymond Williams' affirmation that the 'basic element' in 'the idea of culture' is its 'effort at total qualitative assessment'.[14] However, their presentation of the value and fate of this 'effort' is complex and equivocal: the transcendent perspective that culture supposedly affords runs up against culture's this-worldly meanings and determinations. In some of them, political discourses and engagements appear (albeit episodically) to complement or challenge this uncertain literary–cultural transcendence, and we discuss how the oppositions and analogues between these two forms of critical perspective are represented.

We explore throughout Chapter 4 the deployment in fiction of the idea of culture as conferring a consciousness (ultimately, a 'writerly' consciousness) which knows itself to be marginal but speaks for that reason with critical intensity. In Chapter 5, we consider from this perspective the increasingly specialised and self-conscious forms and discourses of modernist fiction, by virtue of which 'the content of the work of art, its "statement", recedes ever more as compared with the formal aspect, which defines itself as the aesthetic in the narrower sense'.[15] Our discussion, centred on *Ulysses* and referring to some recent critical discussions of modernism (including those of John Carey, Andreas Huyssens and Marshall Berman), assesses the equivocal claims of literary modernism to offer cultural emancipation. The foregrounding of text and language as mediation and representation offers readers new kinds of reflexivity and new possibilities of self-realisation; but many potential readers will be repelled by modernism's difficulty, which is part of a strategy of explicit self-differentiation within writing and culture. This can be seen as reasserting and re-establishing divisions and hierarchies that had been challenged in the proto-democratic post-Arnoldian moment. We conclude by inviting readers to consider whether this modernism, subsequently so influential on literary-critical and culturally evaluative practice, depends intrinsically on a binary counterposition of petty-bourgeois reader and culturally self-differentiated writer (between Leopold Bloom and Stephen Dedalus, in the terms of *Ulysses*), or whether we can endorse the gesture it makes beyond the present towards a recognition that both identities are positional, partly contingent, and implicated in one another.

The relevance of these themes to the project of our book will be clear. The novels discussed in Chapters 4 and 5 allow us to expound some dimensions of the idea of 'culture' as it developed in the decades after Arnold and to develop critical perspectives on it. Chapter 3, which draws on recent feminist criticism and scholarship in offering a review of fictions by women published during and after the 'revolutionary decade' of the 1790s (especially Mary Hays' *The Memoirs of Emma Courtney* and Jane Austen's *Sense and Sensibility*), has a more tangential relation to our overall argument. Here too, in their ambiguous representation of formative influences on women's consciousness and conduct, there is a metacultural aspect to the novels we consider, which depend on and assess the culturally formed and mediated concept of 'sensibility'. Our primary aim in this chapter, however, is less to consider how novels represent cultural ideals than to suggest ways in which their reading may offer opportunities for self-reflection and self-development. We draw a distinction between readings that revolve around identifications with character and those focused on the transcendent position of the author. Writerly transcendence (we argue) is imaginary, created only within the text, but this does not negate the value of the vision which it affords. A further aim of this chapter is thus to substantiate our contention that critical approaches to culture should be evaluative as well as historical and contextual, and that the terms of evaluation must engage with the substantive and formal properties of texts. The sophistication that makes Austen's work canonical is a condition of the possibility of writerly transcendence that it offers. Hays' novels are not canonical in that sense (though they, more so than Austen's, are available today only as part of learned culture); but they are very interesting, as we acknowledge.

We begin our consideration of literature, then, by seeking to juxtapose historical and evaluative approaches, and to exemplify some possible, and competing, terms of evaluation. Neither here nor later, however, do we suggest that cultural criticism and teaching should restrict themselves to a canon, however defined. What matters is that complex evaluations of cultural works and reasoned arguments about cultural forms of self-realisation should be sustained. It is these kinds of evaluation and argument that we offer in the body of the book and whose terms we defend in the Conclusion.

Philosophical Conceptions

1

Philosophy and self-realisation

However we view cultural self-realisation, whether in terms of the Arnoldian perfection of the 'best self',[1] in terms of the role culture plays in personal fulfilment, or in terms of the individual's quest to become a 'cultured' person – and all these mutually implicating aspects are reflected in this work – we are dealing by reason of its understanding of subjectivity with an essentially modern idea, of European origins. Inhering in the project of cultural self-realisation are conceptions of selfhood, self-making and self-expression that really only begin to emerge (and converge) in the early modern period (from Descartes onwards), and are arguably not fully established prior to the mid-eighteenth century. This modern self is radically reflexive and autotelic: a self conceived as possessed of a particular and unique identity, whose fulfilment will be a matter of realising or giving expression to potentialities or aspirations that at the same time remain the object of continuous interest, monitoring and readjustment. It is thus both an inward and a doubled identity: inward in the sense that its various qualities or facets are located within the individual, and doubled in the sense of combining a self conceived as the object of understanding, scrutiny, discipline, reformation, expression, and so on, with the subjective self who is the agent of such reflection and creativity. It is also unstable, restless and without final identity, meaning by this not so much what the postmodernists mean by 'fragmented' (an idea to be discussed later), as that the modern self is conceived as both perennially in quest of its essence (as if this were in some sense attainable) and, by reason of that very quest, always transcendent to it.

Most historians of the Western subject will agree that this conception of the self and its realisation was a long time in the making, required scientific revolution and Enlightenment as preconditions for its full development, and was more or less absent in its main delineations prior to those developments. We would therefore claim that the most significant conceptual mutation for the project of cultural self-realisation – and it is a mutation which is in constant dialectical involvement with the various other shifts of focus to be discussed in this chapter – is that which establishes, in Charles Taylor's term, the 'three-sided individualism' central to the modern identity: a view of the individual as combining self-responsible independence, recognised particularity and personal commitment.[2] This is a conception which over time tends to link the idea of the 'good life' ever more closely with the pursuit of private ends rather than the service of the larger community; and which progressively comes to view the purposes of individual cultural participation in personal terms, as a means to self-expression, the development of critical autonomy and the project of discovering and giving voice to one's distinctive identity. This focus on private self-formation rather than public service is not without its tensions, some of which we shall discuss below, but it is indisputably an essentially modern and seemingly irreversible development.

But if the idea and project of cultural self-realisation belong in this sense to modernity, the most formative influences upon their development and understanding date back much earlier, to the Classical period, and in particular to the arguments of Plato and Aristotle. In the form it took in Germany from the eighteenth century onwards, cultural self-realisation, or *Bildung*, is essentially a revitalisation of the humanism of ancient Greece and Rome and steeped in reference to its philosophy. Aristotle is the presiding genius over Matthew Arnold's hugely influential defence of culture, in *Culture and Anarchy* (1869), as a kind of transcendent 'mean' distilled from the excesses of all social classes, and the work concludes its tribute to Hellenism with a rhetorical appeal to the Platonism in all of us:

> In his own breast does not every man carry with him a possible Socrates, in that power of disinterested play of consciousness upon his stock notions and habits, of which this wise admirable man gave all through his lifetime the great example, and which was the secret of his incomparable influence?[3]

Here we shall distinguish between two overlapping and often imbricated modes in which the 'Socratic' influence has been at work. Classical thought and culture have clearly been of paramount importance in promoting the idea that the life disencumbered of material interests and concerns and dedicated to intellectual pursuits, especially philosophical contemplation, is the most worthy and humanly fulfilling. In Plato's argument, the only truly human life is one spent in erotic quest for the enlightenment that comes from the contemplation of the Forms, especially the Forms of the Beautiful and the Good. The good life is here construed in terms of freedom not only from everyday desires and concerns, but also from the duties and interferences of public life (Plato's philosophical Guardians are depicted in his Republic as the most reluctant of statesmen). Aristotle is less inclined than Plato to think that the good life for the individual is achievable by means of philosophical devotion alone, differs in the emphasis he places on the balancing of a variety of goods as a condition of well-being, and is altogether more worldly in the importance he attaches to such contingencies as wealth, good health and congenial friends in attaining happiness in life.[4] He nonetheless fully agrees on the superiority of intellectual pursuits, especially those of contemplation (*theoria*) and the acquisition of deliberative reasoning power (*phronesis*).

However, Plato and Aristotle, and indeed Greek and Roman culture at large, have exercised their influence not only through the conception placed on the idea of the best or most properly human forms of occupation, but also through their conviction that humanity itself is by nature hierarchically stratified in such a way that only a privileged minority are endowed with the mental qualities essential to the highest form of self-realisation. Although Plato allows, somewhat surprisingly, that women may become Guardians of his ideal city state, he presupposes a tripartite division within humanity (his men of Gold, Silver and Iron), each order of being having their respective functions and responsibilities, and hence modes of being or doing well in life, and only those of Gold being suited to philosophy, hence guardianship of the polis.[5] Aristotle, for his part, argues that the purpose of all living beings is to fulfil their 'nature' (*physis*) and readily allows that different types of human being (citizens or slaves, men or women) will, by virtue of possessing separate natures, have differing functions to fulfil and differing modes of succeeding in life.

This naturalisation of social class came in, of course, for a good deal of subsequent criticism, and rather few by the late eighteenth century would have explicitly defended such rigid formulations of the division of human types (although Schopenhauer comes pretty close with his psycho-physical distinctions between inferior, good and eminent minds).[6] Yet the legacy of the Classical hierarchy and its particular form of humanism continued to be felt throughout Western culture in the modern period, and nowhere more so than in assumptions about the innate inability of any but an élite of male citizens to participate in the life of the mind. Well into the nineteenth century (and even beyond), many writers on culture and its role in self-formation continued to assume that the lower orders and women were effectively excluded, not for want of education, but because they lacked the innate capacities and 'germs' of inner wealth essential to cultural self-enhancement. These assumptions are particularly noticeable in some of the German commentary on the cult of *Bildung*, focused as that is on predisposing talents and the fostering of natural endowment. Described by Herder as a 'reaching up to humanity', and subsequently developed through the arguments of, among others, von Humboldt, Goethe, Hegel,

Schleiermacher, Schopenhauer and Nietzsche, *Bildung* is the concept of a distinctive project of self-formation centred around the idea of the duty of the individual to develop the seeds of 'inner wealth' with a view to realising what is proper to humanity as such: the break, as Hegel put it, with the immediate and the natural, and the promotion of the universal intellectual being.[7] We may describe such conceptions as *emphatically* élitist whenever they rest on the explicit claim or tacit presumption that most human beings are deprived of the necessary 'germs', and are thus incapable by nature of self-formation through culture. Associated with this type of élitism we find an aristocratic line of argument running from Plato and Aristotle through to Schopenhauer and Nietzsche, which views the restriction of culture to a minority of men as indispensable to its health, and expressly advocates the continued toil and relative impoverishment of the many as essential to the enjoyment of the elect. *Culture and Anarchy* is influenced by German thought on *Bildung* (though that of Goethe and von Humboldt rather than Schopenhauer) and it contains a Nietzschean vein of argument in its opposition of a Hebraism that is moralising and self-punitive in tendency to the hedonistic intellectuality of Hellenism. It is also strongly anti-democratic in its sentiments on mob-rule and the necessity of quelling riots (which express Arnold's response to the working-class demonstrations taking place in London at the time he was writing the essay). But in arguing that a 'best self' is discoverable in everyone, and that education could foster it as a collective benefit, Arnold leans away from aristocratic élitism. He writes:

> Because all men are all members of one great whole, and the sympathy which is in human nature will not allow one member to be indifferent to the rest or to have a perfect welfare independent of the rest, the expansion of our humanity to suit the idea of perfection which culture forms, must be a general expansion.[8]

So it is that culture 'does not try to teach down to the level of inferior classes . . . It seeks to do away with classes; to make the best that has been thought and known in the world current everywhere; to make all men live in the atmosphere of sweetness and light.'[9]

Philosophy likewise in the modern period has by and large run against the grain of the blatantly patrician tendency, although at times its commentary has been partial and prejudicial. Certainly, it has remained hugely influenced by the view that the most fulfilled life, that given over to intellectual pursuits, is a life spent in a certain abstraction from the more appetitive and materially driven everyday concerns,[10] and for this reason it is caught in irony and contradiction: irony in the sense that self-realisation is here conceived as demanding a lofty indifference to the 'getting and spending' and material provisioning without which there would be no leisure to pursue it; contradiction in the sense that what is being advocated as the universally applicable route to human self-realisation demands and recommends means (mental pursuits, the acquisition of culture, free time) which for long remained available only to a privileged élite, and have never become a truly collective property.

It would nonetheless be misleading to present the history of philosophical thinking on the issue of cultural self-realisation as monolithically obtuse to its own ironies and inconsistencies, for there have been a number of shifts worth noting, both in how the quality and mode of function of the 'life of the mind' has been understood and in how philosophers have thought about its range of applicability. In this sense, there is another story to be told about philosophy and cultural self-realisation, and it is the one to which we shall devote more attention here. In this story what is charted is not the emphatic élitism of those who have continued in the Platonic–Aristotelian tradition of aristocratic cultural commentary, but the more apologetic, ambivalent and fractured discourse that results from the philosophical adoption of the ideal of cultural self-realisation as if it did indeed have universal validity. This story acknowledges, of course, that even when philosophy has broken with an emphatically élitist commentary on cultural participation, and has presented the acquisition of culture as the condition of a more collective human fulfilment, it has all too often been blind both to its partial assessments of intellectual significance or aesthetic merit and to the economic and social barriers that have stood in the way of extending the cultural franchise. It acknowledges, too, that impercipience of this type is still evident today in the numerous well-meaning academic texts on the history and role of Western culture that continue to refer us to a 'we' that, although no longer so blatantly white and masculine in outlook as it once was, remains presumptive of 'our' collective access to this culture and more or less comfortable positioning within it.[11]

But in the very making of these acknowledgements, we are registering some features (and their effects) that are specific to the philosophical engagement with self-realisation in Western culture. For this culture has not been alone in privileging the intellect and endorsing the spiritually preoccupied life as the most humanly worthy. Nor has it been alone in tacitly accepting the mental–manual division of labour as the precondition for its pursuit. But it has placed a distinctive emphasis from a relatively early date on the contribution of intellectual pursuits to the realisation of the individual person; and the apologetics to which it has so frequently had recourse have consequently had a distinctive tenor. Western culture has arguably been both especially obsessed with individual development and self-expression, and especially hypocritical in its attempts to conceal its failures to provide for this in any truly collective sense. But to grant this is also to allow that this obfuscation testifies to a certain guilt; and in tracing, in this second story, what Western philosophy (or some significant voices within it) have had to say on cultural self-realisation, we are at the same time tracing some disruptions to its earlier complacencies and a growing critical awareness of its own repressions.

'The life of the mind': mutations and contradictions

Despite the influence exercised by Plato and Aristotle on the idea of cultural self-realisation, it has to be said that the promotion of the self as a complex of unique aspirations and sensibilities is not the primary goal either of Plato's ascent to the Good or of Aristotle's advocacy of the life lived in a proper proportioning of all goods. This was not because these gurus of antiquity were consciously preaching the virtues of abstraction from such a focus on the self, after the manner of some contemporary advocates of the 'self-loss' to be gained through certain types of meditation. It was rather because neither they, nor the culture of antiquity at large, conceived of selfhood on the inward and self-reflexive model. They did not possess the modern Western notion of a self-significant and self-interpreting subjectivity. As Charles Taylor has persuasively argued:

> It is probable that in every language there are resources for self-reference and descriptions of reflexive thought, action, attitude . . . But this is not at all the same as making 'self' into a noun, preceded by a definite or indefinite article, speaking of 'the' self, or 'a' self. This reflects something important which is peculiar to our modern sense of agency. The Greeks were notoriously capable of formulating the injunction 'gnothi seauton' – 'know thyself' – but they didn't normally speak of the human agent as 'ho autos', or use the term in a context which we would translate with the indefinite article.[12]

The continuous stress on culture as expression of (or condition of fulfilling) a uniquely existential project is in fact in some tension with the recourse to the humanistic model of antiquity. What its advocates have read back into Classical culture to make it serve as the inspiration for a more contemporary self-realisation is an anachronistic Enlightenment individualism. Yet Taylor has also instructively charted the influence of Plato, and the Augustinian tradition in Christianity he inspires, in generating the turn to a more inward – Cartesian – conception of the self. Without Plato's articulation of the unified self conceived in terms of a rational self-mastery of lower impulses or desires, suggests Taylor, the modern notion of interiority would never have developed. For Plato, rationality is a vision of order in the cosmos at large and the standard of reason is set 'externally' by the Forms rather than defined in terms of internal cognitive procedures. Yet in emphasising rational control and the disposition of the soul rather than worldly success, Plato also initiates a tradition in which the internal is exalted over the external, and reason viewed as the essential adjunct of personal autonomy.[13] In Augustine's Platonist conception, the moral source is still located outside the self in the divinely ordained order of the cosmos, but the 'inward' turn is further encouraged by the doctrine of the inner light as revelatory of God. With Augustine's 'proto-cogito' – his stress on the idea that God lies within as well as without, and on the importance of a 'radically reflexive' first person standpoint in establishing the truth of God's existence – a crucial step is taken towards the idea of the self we find in Descartes, and thus to the establishment of the more recognisably modern self-realising self: the self subsequently elaborated and reflected upon in the thought of the major architects of Enlightenment and post-Enlightenment thought.[14]

These developments opened up new forms of thinking about the constitution of intellectual existence and participation in it. We are talking here in part about changed perceptions of the sovereignty of reason and the role it should play in the properly human life; and also in part about the place of an aesthetic sense within the life of the mind and the role of aesthetic response as a component of the cultured life. But we are also referring to changing conceptions about the rightful constituency for cultural self-realisation: to the varying degrees of insight that philosophers begin to show into the forms of social exclusion that have restricted access to cultural self-realisation – and have latterly been responsible for its dismissal (by some) as an inherently élitist form of fulfilment.

Under the first set of concerns, one crucial move is from viewing the exercise of reason as a matter of assent to certain external forms of order or authority, to viewing it in terms of autonomy and inner self-direction. Rather than the right function of the mind being seen in terms of its coexistence with, and confirmation of, an existing cosmic arrangement (whether the source of this is understood in Pagan or Christian terms), the mind comes to be be viewed as self-reflexive: as both aware of and concerned with its own activities, but also, correlatively, as disengaged from the outer world in the sense that it confronts it as a reflecting – and potentially critical – subject. Knowledge is less and less viewed in terms of agreement to a pre-existing Logos, whether scriptural, Platonic or Aristotelian, and more and more as a matter of constructing accurate representation; and for that reason it also comes to be viewed increasingly in terms of the exercise of independent judgement. This goes together with a new sense of ethical and moral accountability. The individual is the main maker of the self – with all that that implies in terms of the choice of life-style and the responsible exercise of will – but is also conceived increasingly as the arbiter of the moral – as only acting in a truly moral way when acting on the authority of an inner sense of rightness, rather than in obedience to any external authority or compulsion.[15]

Two of the most important early architects of this shift are Descartes and Locke – Descartes in virtue of his programme of radical scepticism towards the Scholastic legacy and his establishment of certainty in a founding performative act of personal self-reflection (the *cogito ergo sum*); Locke in virtue of his instrumental view of the individual as the agent of self-making, and his rejection of what he saw as the manipulative doctrine of innate ideas. (For Locke, this doctrine puts people 'off from the use of their own reason', encouraging a 'posture of blind credulity' through which they might more easily be governed and 'made useful to some sort of men, who had the skill and office to principle and guide them'.)[16] But it is of course Kant who does most to further the ideal of the autonomy of reason, and who is most zealous in establishing the philosophical conditions of its possibility. It is Kant, too, who memorably sums up the Enlightenment message as '*sapere aude*' ('Have courage to use your *own* understanding!').[17] The Enlightenment subject is no longer in thrall to received ideas and externally imposed rules of comportment, but thinks and acts in accordance with self-ordained principles. Such an individual prescribes the law unto the self in the light of an inner freedom (or as Lessing put it, 'no man need say "I must"'). The Enlightenment subject in this conception is central to a normative theory about what it is to be a fully realised, liberated human person. It also, in an important sense, refers us to a historical category: to one who comes to be as a result of the new rationality and scientific understanding illuminating the times. As Cassirer has pointed out, this reflects a distinct change of view, for now reason 'is no longer the sum total of "innate ideas" given prior to all experience, which reveal the absolute essence of things. Reason is now looked upon as rather an acquisition than a heritage.'[18]

It is true, of course, that whatever progress it made in throwing off older forms of tutelage, religious bigotry and superstition, the thinking of the Enlightenment was hardly as emancipated or autogenetic as some of the rhetoric might suggest. With the benefit of hindsight, we can see how deeply steeped many of the Enlightenment thinkers were in the traditions and cultural values of their time. Such advance as is made in the move to the 'autonomous' subject is not, in reality, to a form of thinking that is literally freed from its cultural formation and boundedness, but to a thought that reflects more clearly than ever before on the nature of cognitive authority and the degree of its own powers of self-direction.[19]

It is also true, relatedly, that all the commentaries on and injunctions to the 'human thinker' are paradoxically concealing their own prejudicial and partial conceptions of the human community. But they do also collectively mark a move within philosophy to a mode of thinking about the role of reason which in principle, if not in practice, is more socially comprehensive ('democratic') in conception. Where the sages of the classical and pre-modern period consciously and explicitly regarded the life of the mind as a role or function discharged only by a small élite fitted to it by nature, the modern equation between exercising reason and thinking for oneself is inherently more egalitarian in its logic, since it implies that all acts of autonomous thought, whatever their origin, must equally be credited with rationality; and if 'being Enlightened' is defined as using one's own understanding, then it is defined in terms which would allow any and everyone in principle to participate in its form of self-realisation. There are also some signals of recognition of what this new logic might imply for cultural practice. Descartes writes his *Discourse on Method* (1637) in French with the express purpose of being accessible to female readers uneducated in Latin.[20] Kant acknowledges that the culture of learning depends on the division of labour: 'The majority take care, mechanically as it were and without particularly needing art for this, of the necessities of life for others, who thus have the ease and leisure to work in science and art, the less necessary ingredients in culture.'[21] Moreover when Kant remarks in his essay on Enlightenment 'that the step to competence is held to be very dangerous by the far greater portion of mankind (and by the entire fair sex) – quite apart from its being arduous – is seen to by those guardians who have so kindly assumed superintendence over them', the implications of his irony are quite consistent with the argument of Mary Wollstonecraft and others concerned in the period with enhancing female autonomy.[22]

Aesthetic mediation

The evolution and theorisation of the Enlightenment view of the quality and role of reason proceeds in the course of the eighteenth century *pari passu* with a new emphasis on the importance of feeling and sentiment. This is reflected in various ways both in the philosophical writings of the period, notably those of Shaftesbury, Hutcheson, Hume and Kant himself, and also in much of the fiction (indeed this is the period of the rise of the modern novel); it is dramatically illustrated in the reception given to Rousseau's *La Nouvelle Héloïse* and Goethe's *The Sorrows of Young Werther*. We shall see in Chapter 3 that in England, 'sensibility' was a central, and contested, term, in fiction and more generally. Hence the corrective proposed by some commentators to the conventional view of the Enlightenment as the 'Age of Reason'. The Age of Reason 'distrusted Reason,' writes E.L. Tuveson, 'as it had been understood for many centuries – far more deeply than did any preceding period.'[23] Another commentator goes so far as to claim that

> it would be mistaken to think of reason as the rallying cry of the Enlightenment except in so far as it was opposed to faith, and the Age of Reason opposed to the Age of Superstition. If one's gaze shifts away from the battles with l'Infame, then the 'Age of Sentiments', 'Sentimentality', 'Feelings', 'Passions', 'Pleasure', 'Love' or 'Imagination' are apter titles for the movement of ideas in the eighteenth century.[24]

This may be to overstate the case somewhat, but there is no doubt that another major shift of thinking about the quality and function of the life of the mind and the cultured self is importantly influenced by the eighteenth-century turn to sentiment (even if some of its origins are traceable earlier). This leads, via a critique of the repressive and one-sided aspects of the focus on rational self-control, into the Rousseauan–Romantic re-engagement with Nature and opposition to instrumental rationality, thus establishing the set of tensions (between nature and culture, materialism and idealism, positivism and anti-positivism) which are at work in one way or another in all subsequent social and cultural theory up to our own times. Also relevant here is the weight that comes to be placed in the eighteenth century on the aesthetic as a means of reconciling sense and reason and the respective claims of mind and body. In the aesthetic theory of the period which evolves under the influence of Alexander Baumgarten's 'philosophical poetics',[25] especially that of Kant and Schiller, the aesthetic is assigned a tempering or fusing role whose effect is to balance the claims of a too repressive reason on the one hand against those of a too crudely materialistic sensuality on the other. Artistic beauty is seen as incorporating and transcending both poles of the reason versus sense opposition; and in the appreciation of it, individuals supposedly themselves attain to a comparable harmony and equilibrium of their mental faculties. None of this reduces the importance attached by these philosophers to the life of the mind as the vehicle of self-realisation; but what counts as proper to that life comes to include rather more than the arid exercise of reason or philosophical contemplation. The engagement with art and literature and the development of aesthetic appreciation are thus seen as the means of transcending an overly narrow commitment to rationality without abandoning the distinctively human vocation for higher (Socratic rather than pig-like) gratifications. The fully spiritual self is the self in touch with the senses, and culture, in the sense of great works of art, literature and music, provides the objects of engagement for this materially rooted exaltation and lofty sensuality. In Schiller's estimation,

> man is meant to be a human being. Nature is not meant to rule him exclusively, nor Reason to rule him unconditionally. Both these systems of rule are meant to co-exist, in perfect independence of each other, and yet in perfect concord.[26]

Yet one can miss out on this destiny in either of two ways: undue surrender to sensual nature results in self-loss; too much rationality means one is never 'outside' oneself. In the first instance man 'will never be himself; in the second he will never be anything else; and for that very reason, therefore, he will in both cases be neither the one nor the other, consequently – a non-entity'.[27]

Although calls for a tempering of reason are encountered quite early on – in Aristotle's refusal to share Plato's disdain for art and his insistence on the balancing of goods essential to *eudaimonia* (well-being), in Renaissance satire and its ideals of the multifaceted cultural self, in Montaigne's writing on the 'excesses' of wisdom[28] – only in the 'turn to sentiment' that accompanies Enlightenment are they framed in terms of the mediating, and socially harmonising, role of the aesthetic. Kant opens the way here with his account of the aesthetic, not as challenging rational and moral cognition or substituting for their truths, but as providing for a community of feeling, an experience of quasi-objective solidarity, in an otherwise atomised and hierarchically divided social milieu. It is of the character of aesthetic judgements, according to Kant, that although subjective, they are at once both removed from the particular desires and interests of those who make them, and made with a presumption that everyone else must agree with their verdict. In this they are unlike mere statements of preference for this or that flavour or colour, matters in which we readily agree to disagree. Pure aesthetic judgements ask and expect an agreement in taste whose source is neither in the object occasioning the judgement nor in any personal liking or interest, and for this reason must be rooted in some universal cognitive structure linking us all as human beings and disposing us to a pleasurable harmony of our faculties in certain situations. Aesthetic appreciation, in this Kantian account, gives us access, as Terry Eagleton has put it, to a 'precious form of intersubjectivity', whereby we establish ourselves

> as a community of feeling subjects linked by a quick sense of our shared capacities. The aesthetic is in no way cognitive, but it has about it something of the form and structure of the rational; it thus unites us with all the authority of a law, but at a more affective intuitive level. What brings us together as subjects is not knowledge but an ineffable reciprocity of feeling.[29]

The aesthetic offers what Kant terms a 'common sense' (*sensus communis aestheticus*) – a solidarity of feeling distinct from ordinary 'common sense', or the forms of understanding and sundry opinions which govern thought in everyday life, and quite removed too from the divisions and abrasions of the political sphere. In its domain, where consent is given without constraint and on the basis of a common structure of subjectivity, 'we compare our judgement not so much with the actual as rather with the merely possible judgement of others, and thus put ourselves in the position of everyone else, merely by abstracting from the limitations that may happen to attach to our own judging.'[30] In thus being projected as the site of a kind of democratic reconciliation, an aesthetic Kingdom of Ends, beyond the real world of invidious commerce and political discrimination, 'culture' does indeed figure for Kant as a source of supposedly universal self-realisation. It is his utopian apology for the harsh realities of competition and social antagonism which, under the hat of political commentator and moral theorist, he presents, in classic liberal style, as the result of the 'unsocial sociability' of man and as the indispensable vehicle of all actual civilised human progress.[31] This is a doubly problematic move however, in part because of its complacent acceptance of the blessings of culture as merely cosmetic or reconciliatory, in part because the idea of a *sensus communis* must remain entirely formal where the majority are denied access to the cultural education and experiences of art that might allow it to acquire any concrete content. It is true, maybe, that there is wide if not universal agreement as to the beauties of the rose, the sunset or the humming bird, but Kant himself allows that some measure of 'culture' will in fact be necessary to the appreciation of nature's more sublime attractions. As he himself implies in the quotation cited earlier, where he speaks of the minority who have 'the ease and leisure to work in science and art', this is even more true of the conditions of aesthetic responsiveness to high art, music and literature; in other words, to the kind of works that alone counted properly as culture for Kant.[32]

Schiller, although much influenced by Kant, and ultimately still giving priority to the disciplining powers of reason, differs markedly in two respects. Unlike Kant, he is concerned less with analysis of the preconditions of actual human sense perception and aesthetic experience than with how, hypothetically, the human psyche would have to have been constructed for the tensions between Form and Matter, reason and sense, to find harmonious resolution – with no implication that this has necessarily obtained.[33] Yet the political argument that can reasonably be extrapolated from this thought experiment is also more radical than anything found in Kant, in the sense that it aspires to a society from which actual social divisions would be absent, and views art as a possible means of achieving some kind of real economic and social reconciliation as opposed to a merely aesthetically based solidarity. At the present time, he argues, humanity is everywhere degraded by the 'tyrannical yoke' of material needs and utility, the 'great idol' to which all powers are in thrall and all talents must pay homage.[34] For Schiller, in fact, the capitalist division of labour is the main obstacle to human culture. 'The mental state of most men', he writes, 'is, on the one hand, fatiguing and exhausting work and, on the other, debilitating pleasure', and from this arise two dangers: that of viewing art as existing only to provide pleasure and relaxation, and that of thinking it should serve only to ennoble mankind morally.[35] It also means that political revolution is impossible, since those who might be charged with its making cannot be so by reason of their cultural under-development. As Peter Bürger has pointed out, for Schiller the division of labour in class society cannot be abolished by political revolution because the revolution could be carried out only by those who, stamped by a society in which the division of labour prevailed, have for that reason been unable to develop their humanity. Art is supposedly the solution.[36] Or, in Fredric Jameson's account, 'Schiller's is indeed one of the first meditations on the antinomies of cultural revolution'. Post-acquisitive human nature can come into being only after revolutionary change, but the Terror (and in our own time, Stalinism) stand as warnings that purges cannot complete a process for which objective social conditions are not yet ripe.[37] But at the same time, argues Jameson, Schiller's remains a political system in the sense that aesthetic experience affords a practical apprenticeship for the real political and social freedom to come:

> In art, consciousness prepares itself for a change in the world itself and at the same time learns to make demands on the real world which hasten that change: for the experience of the

> imaginary offers (in an imaginary mode) that total satisfaction of the personality and of Being in the light of which the real world stands condemned, in the light of which the Utopian idea, the revolutionary blueprint, may be conceived.

And if we cannot today take this seriously, Jameson continues, sounding a note of late 'sixties Utopian speculation himself, what if that reflected more on us than on Schiller's imaginings? What if our judgement were itself 'a symptom of our incapacity to support such thinking, of our own repression of the principle of futurity . . .?'[38]

Jameson was here endorsing Herbert Marcuse's Schillerian recourse to the regenerative powers of art and the 'play drive', in a reading which presented Schiller as a precursor of the Romanticism represented in Surrealism.[39] Others, notably Lukács and, more recently, Eagleton, have placed greater stress on the vacuity of the still purely potential 'achievements' of the aesthetic in Schiller's argument,[40] and see it as all too compromised by its idealism:

> His aesthetic programme is on the one hand positive and constructive – an hegemonic strategy for which culture is no solitary contemplative dreaming but an active social force . . . But this resourceful social project is in partial contradiction with its author's aestheticist idealism . . . The brave effort to refine matter into spirit, while somehow preserving it as matter, founders on the intransigent appetitive life of civil society, and can turn at crisis point into an aestheticizing away of this whole degraded domain.[41]

We may add that insofar as Schiller can be said to be materially concerned with a concrete programme of aesthetic education, his focus is entirely on correcting the philistinism of middle-class males. No more than those who preceded him can Schiller conceive of culture as in fact a socially shared and universally available means of achieving personal harmonisation or self-fulfilment. ('As a need,' he writes, 'it exists in every finely attuned soul; as a realised fact we are likely to find it only in some few chosen circles.')[42]

Yet the promotion in the Enlightenment of the aesthetic as intellectual mediation, and the emphasis on its educative role in the period of bourgeois ascendancy, must nonetheless be related to the formal commitment to universal equality and freedom. Rather as the work of art is conceived in Kantian terms as 'lawfulness without law', so the aesthetic figures a self for whom self-determination has (supposedly) reached the point where obedience to the moral law has become entirely customary, an unthinking impulse of the will rather than a matter of conscious obedience to rule, and hence the act of a subject who is both 'free' and responsibly committed. Aesthetic education will purportedly 'convert a "first" and philistine nature of appetites and desires, to a second spiritual one which will then become customary.'[43] There is a wishfulness about this whole conception: not only are dispersed and class-divided individuals supposed to discover a source of collective harmonisation in the aesthetic, but this latter will also provide the social cohesion that will prevent the mass of atomised 'free and equal' wills from dissolving into anarchy. In these respects, the role of the aesthetic has to be viewed instrumentally as the vehicle for sustaining bourgeois hegemony, and thus as overtly ideological. Yet it remains ambiguous: supposed both to harmonise and to integrate society, it at the same time inevitably operates as an immanent critique of the failure of the market to provide the material means of any such universal reciprocity.[44] The Kantian *sensus communis* is both ideological aspiration and utopian gesture towards a society where the necessarily non-coercive quality of aesthetic judgement might find itself reflected in the non-oppressive nature of social and economic relations themselves. Or as Lukács says of Schiller:

> Like so many important poets and thinkers of this period, [he] reveals the obscure, confused, never fully conscious notion of a negation of the contradictions of bourgeois society to take place

> beyond bourgeois society itself. These presentiments and illusions, however, are inseparable from the bourgeois–humanist hopes of Schiller for the realization of the ideas of the bourgeois revolution. Despite his sharp opposition to the Jacobin illusions, Schiller still shares the most essential of these illusions: the hope that the 'pure' form of bourgeois society would lead to a negation of these contradictions of capitalism.[45]

Let us note, too, that the emphasis on individuality of judgement, whether aesthetic or cognitive, is necessarily always in tension with any pressures to bourgeois conformity: the same developments which tend to project culture as a harmonising and socially unifying force are also those which for the first time emphasise the extent to which the development of individuality (the realisation of personal uniqueness) depends on the 'audacity' to think for oneself. That which promotes the free-thinking individual as the model of 'self-realisation' also inevitably condones the emergence of the more critical, and hence potentially rebellious, spirit.

After Schiller

We have seen that Schiller's legacy is equivocal. One current runs on into Romantic expressivism where it becomes absorbed in a focus on the individual creative imagination of poet or painter and on the specific artwork as a symbolic combination of form and matter. In Coleridge's argument:

> The poet, described in *ideal* perfection, brings the whole soul of man into activity . . . He diffuses a tone and spirit that blends and (as it were) fuses, each into each, by that synthetic and magical power, to which we have exclusively appropriated the name of imagination. This power, first put into action by the will and understanding, and retained under their irremissive, though gentle and unnoticed control reveals itself in the balance or reconciliation of opposites or discordant qualities: of sameness, with difference; of the general with the concrete; the idea, with the

image; the individual, with the representative; the sense of novelty and freshness, with old and familiar objects; a more than usual state of emotion, with more than usual order; judgement ever awake and steady self-possession, with enthusiasm and feeling profound or vehement.[46]

Elsewhere in his *Biographia Literaria*, Coleridge summons the image of the water-insect's progress as emblem of the both active and passive self-experience of the mind in its mediation by the imagination; or in illustration of the reader's activity of mind in response to the poem, that of the serpent which at each step 'pauses and half recedes, and from the retrogressive movement collects the force which again carries him onwards'.[47] The reconciliation of form and matter is also central to the achievement of the Romantic ideal of the symbol that Coleridge evokes through the image of 'translucence': the perfect symbol, he tells us, 'lives within that which it symbolises and resembles, as the crystal lives within the light it transmits, and is transparent like the light itself'.[48] The Schillerian project of integration is kept alive, then, but now viewed as achievable primarily or only by means of the poetic imagination and within the individual poem or painting, and hence in abstraction from any utopian project of aesthetic harmonisation founded in the breakdown of the division of labour. The critique of the industrial 'system' is manifest in the Romantic turn to nature, both inner and outer, as redemptive resource, and in its conception of the imagination's role in producing expressive rather than mimetic art; but what is less in evidence (although obviously finding some voice in the argument of Blake and Shelley) is the concern with the social causes and effects of a more general aesthetic deprivation.

Schillerian conceptions of aesthetic wholeness and reconciliation were also at work in the argument of the writers on *Bildung*, though here, too, in a manner almost entirely disengaged from any concerns with democratising aesthetic education or opening cultural self-realisation to any but select individuals. The tradition of *Bildung* was from its origins apolitical in tendency since the inner core of sensibility it hoped to realise was thought to be incapable of full development except through seclusion from public life. The attitude is captured in Friedrich Schlegel's injunction: 'Do not squander your faith and love on the political world, but offer up your inmost being in the divine world of scholarship and art to swell the sacred fiery stream of eternal culture.'[49] This quasi-Stoical suspension of involvement was justified by von Humboldt and Goethe on the grounds that self-development ultimately did more for the world than meddling in it. Unsurprisingly, there are echoes of this argument in John Stuart Mill's case in *On Liberty* for the greatest diversity of individual development.[50] The mutually complementary nature of the project of an inward-looking self-cultivation and Millian style liberalism, is, after all, quite patent, since the 'negative liberty' and minimal State defended in the latter provide ideal conditions for focusing on one's own personal daimon, in all its isolated eccentricity.

Arnold, in contrast, makes rather more of the morally and socially beneficent potential of a developed relish for the sublime. Mocking the ideal of a State designed to ensure that 'no man's taste for bathos shall tyrannise over another man's', Arnold offers instead a republican (though also clearly problematic) defence of culture's role in establishing the State as an 'organ of our collective best self' and 'national right reason'.[51] In Germany itself, we might note, Thomas Mann came to regard the anti-republican tendencies of the cult of inwardness (which he traced back to a long tradition of Lutheran disdain for the external order) as deeply problematic and even inculpated in the disaster of National Socialism. In 1923, Mann was already arguing that

> the culture of a German implies introspectiveness; an individualistic cultural conscience; consideration for the careful tending, the shaping, deepening and perfecting of one's own personality or, in religious terms, for the salvation and justification of one's own life; subjectivism in the things of the mind, therefore, a type of culture that might be called pietistic, given to autobiographical confession and deeply personal, one in which the world

> of the objective, the political world, is felt to be profane and is thrust aside with indifference . . . What I mean by all this is that the idea of the republic meets with resistance in Germany chiefly because the ordinary middle-class man here, if he ever thought about culture, never considered politics to be part of it, and still does not do so today. To ask him to transfer his allegiance from inwardness to the objective, to politics, to what the peoples of Europe call freedom, would seem to him to amount to a demand that he should do violence to his own nature, and in fact give up his sense of national identity.[52]

As Hitler becomes Chancellor in 1933, Mann writes that 'it is not admissible in a world as anti-divine and bereft of reason as ours, to represent man's metaphysical, inward and religious activities as inherently superior to his will to improve the world. The political and social is one aspect of the humane.' This sense that a purely individualistic and intellectual *Humanität* was a danger for the development of a truly humane (social and political) *Kultur* informed many of Mann's speeches after his move to the USA in 1938.[53]

At this point we should return to the nineteenth century in order to resume a further thread of the Schillerian legacy – that which leads not into Romanticism or the evolved forms of Hellenistic humanism in the nineteenth century, but towards the dialectical materialism of the Marxist critique. It is often said, with some justice, that Schiller's 'dialectic' of reason and sense mediates between the subjective and objective accounts of Kant and Hegel respectively.[54] But in his registering of the strains placed on a purely idealist aesthetic theory in the age of capitalism, it is as if Schiller also stands between Hegel and Marx – or perhaps comes closer to Marx in his ambitions for the realisation of the 'whole' man, in the 'totality of his powers', and free from any specific determinations. Hegel, after all, quite in contrast to Schiller, regards the aesthetic as both too ethereal and too removed from individual self-interest to be able to function in its putative role as harmonising force. Indeed, for Hegel, such possibilities for art are essentially a thing of the past, and the times are not favourable to them. 'Art', he argues, 'is no longer able to discover that satisfaction of spiritual wants, which previous epochs and nations have sought for it and exclusively found in it' in the world in which 'universal forms, laws, duties, rights, and maxims hold valid as the determining basis of our life and the force within of main importance.'[55] Hegel, then, both questions the spiritual compulsion of art in the bourgeois era, and is more of a pragmatist in the emphasis he places on the role of the established ethical conventions and institutions of civil society in securing a measure of social cohesion. He is also rather closer to Kant than to either Schiller or Marx in his acceptance of the inevitability of social divisions and abrasions. No more than Kant does Hegel think the allocation to class can be justified by the accident of birth, but he does, as he puts it, view the differences of class as 'essential to the notion of state-life, and . . . founded on reason, for they are caused by the inevitable articulation of the organic community'.[56] And his advocacy of education as the means whereby everyone will be able to attain to the level of their competence and thus to determine to which class they shall belong is very much in contrast to Schiller's would-be transcendence of the mental–manual division of labour in the utopia of an 'Aesthetic State' in which, as he puts it, 'everything – even the tool which serves – is a free citizen, having equal rights with the noblest; and the mind, which would force the patient mass beneath the yoke of its purposes must here first obtain its assent'.[57] Admittedly Marx did not quite share in this Schillerian romance either, since not only did Marx see all too clearly that this was a purely imaginary or formal solution to economically derived social contradictions, he also sustained a rather un-Schillerian view of the seriousness of labour ('life's prime need') and its indispensable role in supplying for material needs. (Hence Lukács' stern rebuke that criticism of the destructive effect of the capitalist division of labour on culture becomes in Schiller a condemnation of work itself as a principle hostile to culture.)[58]

What plainly divides Marx from all the thinkers who precede him (and many who come after) is his understanding that the alienations of the class system and the division of labour cannot be overcome conceptually or by the purely 'superstructural' means of 'cultural revolution' and political reform, but require economic transformation: socialist relations of production that guarantee economic parity (and hence a genuine rather than purely formal equality of opportunity for and access to the means of self-realisation). It would not be appropriate here to pronounce on the ultimate viability of Marx's communist vision, or to dwell on the problems of any transition to it. The point, rather, as far as our survey is concerned, is that here for the first time we have brutal acknowledgement of the mismatch between social reality and its representation in liberal-humanist philosophy. In Marx's analysis, immanent critique is activated: the cat is entirely out of the bag. Society is not the realm of universal 'freedom and equality' and cannot be rendered so by the magic wand of 'culture' and aesthetic integration. Among the nineteenth-century philosophers only Nietzsche will see this as clearly, albeit to draw entirely different conclusions about what is to be done.

On the other hand, Marx plainly shares Schiller's aspiration to transcend the division of labour, and sounds a very Schillerian note in his denunciations of its stunting effects on the individual. Where Schiller complains that man, who ought to put the 'stamp of humanity' upon his own nature, has become nothing more than the 'imprint of his occupation' or 'specialised knowledge', Marx rails against the squandering of human lives and argues that 'it is only by dint of the most extravagant waste of individual development that the development of the human race is at all safeguarded and maintained in the epoch of history immediately preceding the conscious reorganisation of society'[59] – that is, in the epoch of capitalism. Moreover, even if Marx is always somewhat dismissive of the utopian imaging of work as play (hence his attack on the naivety of Fourier's views on work, and his insistence on the 'damned serious' hard work even of artistic activity),[60] his whole critique of capitalism is in an important sense directed against the life of labour and towards the restoration to the labourer (and ultimately to the collectivity), in the form of free time, of the time currently devoted to the production of further surplus-value. It will be seen that our own arguments in the Conclusion to this book draw on this line of critique.

Marx also follows Schiller in seeing the meaning of life and its overall goal as more to do with the development and gratification of aesthetic sensibility than with materialistic consumption, and places a comparable emphasis on what might be called the dialectic of plenitude and indetermination deemed essential to this project of self-fulfilment. But whereas for Schiller human wholeness is to be restored by means of the unboundedness of art, for Marx it is the disembedded and indeterminate existence of the worker in capitalist society that becomes the condition of unlimited self-expansion. Thus Marx argues that whereas the pre-capitalist individual enjoyed an objective extension of selfhood in the immediate and naturally given community, with its presupposed structure of needs and personal ties of dependency, the worker under capitalism has no other 'community' than that formed through the indifference and generality of monetary exchange, and hence lives in a condition of 'objectlessness' or 'naked subjectivity'.[61] But this lack of a fixed and presupposed objective mode of existence is also the springboard for unlimited self-development, since it frees the worker from 'all traditional, complacent, encrusted satisfactions of present needs, and reproductions of old ways of life . . .'[62] 'Objectlessness' is the *sine qua non* of an infinitely varied objectification; deprivation of a pre-given form of self-reproduction is the basis of an unlimited personal transcendence; and what appears as self-loss is in reality emancipation of the self from the constraints of parochial existence:

> In bourgeois economics – and in the epoch of production to which it corresponds – this complete working-out of the human content appears as a complete emptying-out, this universal objectification as total alienation, and the tearing-down of all limited, one-sided aims as a sacrifice of the human end in-itself to an entirely external end. This is why the childish world of antiquity

> *appears on the one side as loftier.* On the other side, *it really is loftier* in all matters where closed shapes, forms and given limits are sought for. It is satisfaction from a limited standpoint; while the modern gives no satisfaction; or where it appears satisfied with itself, it is vulgar.[63]

In founding his ideal of the 'all-round development of individuality', as its enabling condition, on the indeterminacy of 'naked subjectivity' that only the full-blown capitalist market can generate, Marx makes very plain his resistance to any backward looking and nostalgic conceptions of the means of self-realisation.

Yet the imprecision of his vision of communist 'abundance', with its indefinite development of needs, is not without its problems. Marx resisted blue-printing for communist gratification for fear of confining its potentials to those conceivable from a merely bourgeois perspective on the psychology of satisfaction. The world of communist self-realisation is for Marx one freed of all previous presuppositions about needs and modes of self-expression, and is thus in an important sense 'unmeasurable' and beyond representation. 'What is wealth', he famously asks, 'other than the universality of individual needs, capacities, pleasures, productive forces, etc . . . the absolute working-out of all creative potentialities with no presupposition other than the previous historic development, which makes this totality of development . . . the end in itself, not measured by a predetermined yardstick?'[64] But this vision is also problematic in its implication that all human powers are positive in their potential, and all individual capacities deserving of development.[65] Given his obvious concern that self-realisation should become democratically available to all, we should no doubt at least credit Marx with supposing that this can take place only on a reciprocal basis: in other words, individuals would only develop those powers and capacities that are consistent with others doing likewise. All the same, Marx is not as insistent as he might be on the point. Nor does he say nearly enough about the possible conflicts and incompatibilities between differing forms of self-realisation, or about the strains placed on any project of universal fulfilment in virtue of the inherent alterity of many of the more gratifying forms of personal success and self-expression (where one individual's achievement must very often come only at the cost of another's disappointment). The problems created by what Rousseau referred to as *amour propre* with its *fureur de se distinguer* ('passion to be distinguished') hardly seem to figure for Marx – who appears to have assumed that all competitive urges and sources of factitious feeling were products of bourgeois existence and would disappear with it.[66]

Above all, in this context, we might note that Marx offers very little guidance on the role to be played by specifically cultural forms of activity and participation in universal personal fulfilment. We intuit that Marx intended that a significant role would be played by the engagement with the cultural sublime in the achievement of the post-capitalist society of 'abundance', but he never in fact says so quite explicitly, and his views on what happens to culture and its role, socially or individually, after the breakdown of the mental–manual division of labour are left entirely under-developed. (We cannot know what Marx would have made of subsequent 'Marxist' cultural criticism, or how he would have regarded twentieth- and twenty-first-century mass-cultural forms.) If, then, Marx is the first fully to expose the wishfulness of any project of universal aesthetic education within the framework of bourgeois economic relations, it is in the context of a narrative about self-realisation that is entirely vague about the role to be played by the aesthetic in the 'rich development of individuality' that supposedly follows the transition to a socialist mode of production.

We might also note here that Marxism cannot expose the ideological dimensions of art and the bourgeois discourse on the aesthetic without bringing into focus a new and difficult set of questions about its own distinctive conception of (and provision for) 'cultural democracy': questions which are in part about the emancipatory role of culture, in part about the quality of socialist existence itself, including the role of cultural consumption therein. How, to put it crudely, can a theory which tends, through its immanent critique of bourgeois culture, to expose the domain of the cultural as inherently ideological in its fostering of ruling class ideas, at the same time present 'high' art as a (relatively) autonomous bulwark against the degradation and reification of commodity society, or see it as a potential vehicle of universal self-realisation in a post-capitalist order? The various arguments that can be assembled under the heading of a 'Marxist aesthetics' can all be seen as attempts to preserve art (and aesthetic education) as a means of emancipation and site of collective self-realisation without on the one hand collapsing art into politics or on the other endorsing an ultimately ineffectual aestheticisation of the political.

It is important to recognise how divergent these arguments in fact are. In particular we should note the contrast between those theories which (despite other differences) have explained the emancipatory potential of art in terms of its connecting with or giving expression to needs for liberation that are thought of as already existing, albeit latent and inarticulate, and those which have regarded monopoly capitalism, and particularly its 'culture industry', as eliminating any felt sense of oppression or revolutionary need. Among the former, one may include Lukács' faith in the potential of realist fiction to expose the 'false appearances' of capitalism, Benjamin's hopes for sudden, galvanising moments of disruption to the catastrophic and repetitive sequence of normal history, or Brecht's championing of epic theatre as occasioning changed evaluations and heightened forms of political awareness. To Marcuse and Adorno, on the other hand, there seems no obvious reason to privilege the working class as the agent of revolution, since proletarian needs have been in their eyes just as warped by processes of capitalist commodification as those of the bourgeoisie; nor, therefore, have they attempted to defend some form of Marxist cultural practice as a means of awakening the oppressed to the 'falsity' of their existence and their 'real' need for radical change. Adorno has argued that if art, as opposed to the entertainments provided by the 'culture industry', retains some kind of counter-cultural or redemptive role, it does so only in a deeply compromised and contradictory mode. In its very provision of an aesthetic dimension to existence, avant-garde work, however critical and abrasive, must affirm the society against which it seeks to retain its autonomous distance. Artworks that keep open the promise of another form of existence (and for Adorno, these are essentially works of modernism) cannot, in virtue of their rebarbative character, speak of it to any but the critical elite, and must, in any case, pre-emptively subvert their possible political potency by acknowledging their merely aesthetic status. Art can only retain its utopian promise in virtue of its autonomy, but it is just this autonomy that preserves art from any entanglement with the real business of existence.

Something similar holds for the 'critical theory' that informs us of all this, since it cannot but acknowledge the exceptional status of its own insights into the processes that have blinded others to the truth of their condition. Adorno is honest enough to tell us that 'direct communicability with everyone is not a criterion of truth . . . It is up to those who, by a stroke of luck, are not quite adjusted to the prevailing norms to say what the most cannot see.'[67] But this leaves it somewhat unclear how those in a position to speak came by their good fortune, or why, if their words can only fall on deaf ears, it remains so important to give voice to them. The only way out of this impasse is to argue, as indeed Adorno does in effect, for the necessity of cultural education. For art to intervene in social consciousness it requires the interpretative mediation of philosophy, and this is particularly true, he claims, for non-discursive artworks, whose import can only be disclosed through various forms of discourse, commentary and criticism. Yet to argue this is also, of course, as Adorno sees, to accept the continued critical importance of the mental–manual division of labour that has led to the impoverishment of life in the first place.[68] That which classical Marxism analysed as the main obstacle to any more collective cultural self-realisation, and which it plainly saw was irremovable by purely aesthetic means, has to be recognised by later Marxist critics as the only means of keeping alive the flicker of interest in what might follow from its own dismantling.

The Nietzschean turn

Marxist sympathisers, socialist critics and others concerned with promoting cultural democracy may be caught in the contradictions of their own cultural elitism, but it is not clear that the alternatives are any more compelling or intellectually coherent. The liberal-humanist vein of argument running from Arnold through to Leavis and into some of the more mainstream academic commentary of our own times can reasonably be viewed, in its essentials, as continuing in the tradition of the earlier Enlightenment aspiration to aesthetic harmonisation, and as suffering from similar limitations. Thus it is that even as the Marxist-socialist theorists have continued to fret at the antinomies of their own arguments, they have also persistently sought to expose the weakness of the reformist trust in the extension of the franchise and educational opportunity to issue in any genuine 'common culture', often enough backing this with critiques of the still too partial and restricted conceptions placed on this notion of 'communality'.

Yet for all their differences of views over the best means of promoting cultural democracy, the Marxist-socialist and liberal-humanist traditions have shared some common commitment to it as an end, and this distinguishes both from the overtly anti-democratic individualism of the Nietzschean commentary on culture. Nietzsche, like Marx, is a non-conformist, and a debunker, like him, of the eternal verities of religious and moral thinking. In virtue, moreover, of his anti-Platonist urge to bring philosophy face to face with the history of its repression of the body, he has to count as a refreshingly cynical critic of the hypocrisies associated with the 'life of the mind' and its obsession with 'truth'. But Nietzsche deplored the socialist political agenda as pandering to proletarian resentment, and had little patience with the moralising humanism of those who sought to extend education or culture to the masses. Such moves, he thought, themselves gave evidence of a philistine view of the arts, and could only issue in a culture of mediocrity to which all genuinely original and transcendent initiatives would inevitably be sacrificed. In *Twilight of the Idols*, Nietzsche presents all great periods of culture as periods of political decline, and suggests that one can view the 'culture-state' as a civilising influence or socially therapeutic instrument only on the basis of a philistine view of culture.[69]

To give priority, moreover, to an egalitarian politics over the promotion of individual distinction was for Nietzsche to privilege the goals of self-preservation over those of aesthetic creation, and thus mistakenly to accord more means–ends rationality to human existence than is warranted by its actual, sublimely purposeless, contingency. If there is a point in politics, it does not lie in advancing the collective well-being of the species as if thereby some telos of universal happiness would finally be realised, but rather in immediate provision of the conditions of exceptional aesthetic achievement: a vocation requiring a social hierarchy which, in *Beyond Good and Evil*, Nietzsche compares to the division of labour provided by nature for the Javan sunflower, which can only ascend to the ethereal heights above the jungle where it can finally blossom by way of the support provided by the sturdy proletarian tree-trunks below.[70]

One of the paradoxes of Nietzsche's elitist position on cultural self-realisation is that it can be seen as the culmination of a turn against culture in favour of nature. It is central to Nietzsche's teaching on the all-encompassing nature of the 'will to power' that it affirms the bodily appetites and natural impulses against the repressions of social convention and moral doctrine and their internalisation in the form of the rational control exercised by the self-policing and supposedly autonomous individual. This is a paradox, however, perhaps more apparent than real, since in the end Nietzsche is no more lamenting the 'humanising' forces of culture than Rousseau is seeking to reinstate the 'noble savage'. Indeed rather as the strongly anti-cultural theme developed by Rousseau at the beginning of Romanticism has to be seen as looking towards a future society that can only be built by those (like his character Emile) who have been insulated from the decadence of present culture,[71] so Nietzsche, at the far end of the movement, is looking to the truly aestheticised culture of the 'Overman' as that which will finally emerge in all its glory from the painfully restricting and distorting chrysalis of what currently passes for 'civilisation'.

Nietzsche, then, views the overly rationalist, coercive and self-punitive aspects of Enlightenment culture as a kind of purgatorial process of humanisation without which there could be no ultimate 'revaluation of values'. It is his emphasis on the association of Enlightenment with the dominance of instrumental rationality and suppression of 'inner' nature that is carried forward into the argument of Critical Theory, especially that of Horkheimer and Adorno on the dialectics of Enlightenment. At the same time, of course, Nietzsche's views on female education and his disdain for any collective good or common culture render his thought profoundly at odds with any democratically motivated critique of Enlightenment.

Yet herein lies a further paradox, since it is in the name of furthering a less Eurocentric and more democratically sensitive tenor of cultural commentary that so many contemporary theorists and critics invoke the Nietzschean legacy. This paradox, too, has a kind of rationale or explanation – even if this is not ultimately entirely compelling. It lies in the stress placed by Nietzsche on the resistance of the 'chaos' of the world to any decisive representation or conceptual ordering. For Nietzsche, any conceptualisation involves 'identity thinking': it means bringing always naturally differentiated items or forms of being under a common universal that must inevitably ignore the endlessly ramifying plurality of differences. Transferred to post-structuralist cultural commentary, this 'anti-dialectical' resistance to conceptual assimilation has issued in an important and significant body of anti-canonical and deconstructive readings, all of them challenging in one way or another not only the legitimacy of the idea of culture we have associated with cultural self-realisation, but also the coherence of the self-reflecting subject around which it is based. It will be one of our concerns in the following chapter to consider the power of this neo-Nietzschean relativist and anti-humanist perspective on culture, selfhood and self-realisation.

2

Cultural self-realisation: countervailing forces and sceptical voices

As the survey of the last chapter reminds us, modern Western society – and this is a paradoxical feature of it that has persisted into our own times – has tended always culturally to disown its exchange system and commercial activities even as it has defended the market as the only economic system of any real merit. Throughout its history capitalist society has been deplored for its philistinism, utilitarianism and cash-nexus reduction of all social bonds even as it has been vaunted for its efficiency, freedom of choice and expansion of wealth. The history of its materialistic triumphs can be said to have been shamefaced to the degree that its consumerist paradise has been gained only at the cost of sinning against the values that were (and, we shall argue, to a significant degree still are) supposedly to be held most dear.

Marx told a version of this story in his dialectical account of capitalism as both alienation and 'civilising influence'. From a somewhat different angle, we can view it as the continuation of the ideological conflicts between aristocratic paternalism and bourgeois entrepreneurialism: a tale of political overdetermination and décalage that has been recounted on any number of occasions and in a variety of accents. In its largest and most over-arching sense, and in the terms in which the story is most usually related, we can see it as the tension between instrumental and intrinsic value commitments: an opposition starkly registered in the stand-off between utilitarianism and Romanticism in the nineteenth century (and epitomised at the level of individual experience in the 'crisis' of John Stuart Mill), but which has continued to run on ever since both in the oppositional strands to be found in later artistic and intellectual movements, and in their overall aesthetic or philosophical countervailing force within the 'system'.

'System' and culture

If we revert to these contradictions here, it is not to repeat Marx, since Marx himself, of course, condemned the capitalist mode of production *in toto*, even as he recognised its importance in expanding the conditions of wealth production. Nor are we remarking here on a clash of values confined to the differences between two social estates, or felt and made manifest only within artistic and intellectual circles and movements. Our point, rather – and it is close in spirit to Habermas's distinction between the 'systemic' imperatives of power and money and the 'symbolic' values of the 'life-world'[1] – is that capitalist society in the West, and particularly in Europe, has embedded ethical ideals and cultural values in its educational system (including, importantly, ideas about the indispensable role of culture to the full realisation of the individual), and has sought to promote these in its institutions, from the primary school to the university, even though they are directly confounded by the principles to which its economic life defers. The goods extolled by society are not those by which it is ruled. It teaches altruism, but depends on egoism, approves social responsibility but rewards financial self-interest, advances goals of critical autonomy and all-round personal development while endorsing the system that condemns the majority to long hours of dull and undemanding labour. The bad faith or system of double standards involved in this, whereby the instrumental rationality and utilitarian calculus which rule in the economic domain are supposed happily to coexist with the intrinsic value commitments of the cultural sphere, is tacitly acknowledged and reproduced by all those committed to the continuation of the free market economy.

From an orthodox Marxist point of view this mismatch between cultural values and economic imperatives would be explained as a clear instance of that form of ideological distortion whereby the minority ruling-class interest in sustaining structures of direct exploitation is masked by discourses of moral and cultural universalism. Yet to ask why the concealment might be necessary in the first place is to come up directly against the system of double values on which we are remarking, and Marx himself and later Marxists are nowhere more products of bourgeois society than in their explanatory appeals to the necessity of representing as a 'free and equal' system of contractual arrangements what would otherwise be exposed as 'naked slavery'.[2] It is only to those who have been educationally shaped, as Marx and his readers have, by the counter-slavery ethic of Enlightenment with its endorsement of individual development that this 'explanation' will prove immediately compelling. On the other hand, it is an explanation that inevitably tends to subvert its own wisdom since an appeal is made to a system of cultural values presented as essential to commodity society, and without which there would be no need to mask its wage-slavery, but only in a manner which must present these values as mere adjunct, secondary or inessential except for their ideological screening function – or even as a dispensable form of false consciousness.[3] In either event, the domain of culture and the values it sustains are treated inconsistently as being both of the nature of bourgeois society and mere addendum or supplement to it. Here our argument is close to that of Adorno when he points out that wherever Marxism presents culture (meaning authentic works of art and literature rather than mass entertainment) as a kind of 'functional lie' creating the 'illusion of a society worthy of man which does not exist', it also, in its implication that all lies should be denounced, tends to develop an anti-cultural, anti-aesthetic momentum.[4] Adorno also warns against dislocating art from its socio-historical context, thus abstracting from its mediation of that context. 'The historical moment', he writes,

> is constitutive of artworks: authentic works are those that surrender themselves to the historical substance of their age without reservation and without the presumption of being superior to it. They are the self-unconscious historiography of their epoch; this, not least of all, establishes their relation to knowledge. Precisely this makes them incommensurable with historicism, which, instead of following their own historical content, reduces them to their external history. Artworks may be all the more truly experienced the more their historical substance is that of the one who experiences it.[5]

Adorno here registers the immanence and entrenchment of culture, although we would dispute the suggestion (if it is there?) that where it is 'authentic' it must exclude artworks that are expressive of their conditions of production and produced in consciousness of their own impact on their time. For Adorno, the critical ('political') role of culture within the society where it is first produced is limited to the 'promise of happiness' carried within all art in modernity in virtue of its aesthetic status: fully authentic art is efficacious primarily in its exposure of the disaster from which it emerges, and by which it is always compromised, and in its glance towards a utopian future where art in its quasi-autonomy and 'alienation' from the socio-economic would no longer be needed or would be replaced by something needing another name.[6] We argue that cultural work is critical not only by virtue of its abstracted aesthetic status, and hence otherness to and gestured transcendence of its context of production, but also in actualising the ongoing self-critical dimension intrinsic to bourgeois society itself.

Relatedly, we are not of a mind to restrict 'good' culture, or its intrinsic value and critical potential, to its least accessible forms, or to privilege the difficult works of modernism as necessarily the most progressive (or least compromised) in their political implications and effect. Modernist artists and writers are certainly to be valued for their principled stance on art: in their commitment to produce to a certain aesthetic standard, even though it seldom helped to line their pockets and always exposed them to the charge of intellectual snobbery, they both resisted the pressures of commodification and helped to keep alive a sense of values alternative to it. But the paradox, of course, is that there is nothing very new or modern about this since the defence of culture and its potentially redemptive role has throughout the bourgeois era been made in terms of its opposition to the cash nexus. Matthew Arnold would have been deeply perplexed (and probably affronted) by most modernist literature but, by his own lights, he would have had to applaud the resistance to the bathos of either 'barbarians' or 'philistines' found in modernism's view of culture.

There is nothing, therefore, about modernist work as such that makes it inherently more oppositional to 'systemic' priorities than art and literature in previous periods. Nor can its inaccessibility in the present be defended as an essential aspect of its critical perspective and promise for the future. The case for viewing the difficulty of modernist texts as integral and indispensable to their redemptive critical powers cannot be based simply on their face-setting against the 'system', since this is a feature shared to a greater or lesser degree with earlier and other more accessible works of culture. Nor even can it be defended solely in terms of the dialogic complexity of vision it allows these texts to open up for their recipients upon the world within which they have been produced. For this, too, is a discrimination that comes into play in assessing the value of earlier and relatively straightforward narratives: in the next chapter, for example, we defend the more comprehensive – 'writerly' – perspective opened to the reader by the conservative Jane Austen over the more immediate identification afforded by the more radical Mary Hays. The case will have to be grounded, rather, in the way in which difficulty may be employed as an ironic signal or register of the continuing limitations, even within modern democracies, on access to the world of high cultural texts and on what such texts may themselves legitimately claim to represent. At issue here is the differently situated nature of modernist cultural production relative to earlier work: the modernist text differs from Austen's in its specific social context, in having been produced, that is to say, in a society significantly more democratic than that of the eighteenth century. Yet for all its democratic advances, this society was then and has remained very divided in respect of the possession of the cultural sophistication needed to appreciate modernist texts. One might thus argue that the only modernist texts that are really holding the line open to a more democratic culture are those in which difficulty works in such a way as to remind their (educated) readers of these anomalies of modernity, and thus of the limits of the reader's, and the text's, positioning within the world. Some modernist works also open up a space of ironic reflection on the absurdities and pomposities of 'high' art, and the supposedly universal need for or aspiration to it, even as they continue intransigently to affirm their commitment to art. Thus Joyce, as we seek to show in Chapter 5, is proclaiming the 'eternal affirmation of the spirit in man' even as he invites us to share the self-irony of his doing so.

Modernist texts, then, do not secure specific immunity to bourgeois ideology nor guarantee their critical perspective upon it simply in virtue of their relative inaccessibility to the ordinary reading public. Nor, conversely, is realist fiction necessarily given over to the creation or reproduction of false consciousness, or more prone to conceal the conflict within capitalist society between 'systemic' and 'symbolic' values. On the contrary, it is arguably through their pedagogically prescribed engagement with the 'bourgeois' novel in school and university that many people have received their fullest exposure to the mismatch between economic rationality and humanist value and the ideological quality of the attempts at its concealment. Austen, for example, pragmatic and unsentimental chronicler though she is of the benefits of private property and mercantile activity, is an immensely eloquent and subtle observer of the moral tensions and hypocrisies of her home counties middle classes. Many canonical novels of the nineteenth century dwell on aspects of the social and economic disruption caused by the industrial revolution and the rise of entrepreneurial capitalism in ways that invite the reader directly to sympathise with those who have fallen victim to its turbulence and oppressions. When, moreover, the space is opened up, as later for example in Gissing or Lawrence or Joyce, for presenting the alienating and deracinating impact of capitalism or commercial activity in a different and more positive light – as counter to cultural élitism or patriarchy or as pointing the way to less confining modes of subjectivity – it is almost always in a narrative context that preserves, explores and leaves ultimately unresolved the tensions that arise. Marxist critics will have little difficulty in nailing the conservatism of Austen, or the specific ideological lapses or symptomatic silences of Hardy or Dickens or Gissing, but the more sensitive the critic, the more likely he or she will be to recognise the limitations of any analysis that dwells only on the socialist shortcomings of such writing rather than acknowledging its contribution to the making of the complexity and problematic being of its own cultural context.

Our argument sketched here (some of whose themes will be elaborated, and qualified, in subsequent chapters) is to the effect that 'culture' as manifest in much post-Enlightenment art and writing can be treated neither simply as functional illusion masking truth (whether by instilling 'false consciousness' of reality or by positioning recipients as if they were autonomous subjects), nor as consciously seeking to preserve a distinctive aesthetic domain, nor even as immanent critique exposing the illusion of its own pretensions to that autonomous status and message, but must also be recognised in its own non-specular substantiality: not as mirror but as the material bodying-forth of the self-reflecting and partially self-critical and self-ironic being of the class-divided market society in which it has been produced. Had it not been produced and consumed in the ways it has been, capitalist society would not simply have been deprived of a medium for expressing critical distance and utopian promise. It would also, in a significant sense, have been other than itself (and therefore open to other forms of critique or despair); and the same point holds formally, we would maintain, at any and every phase, including that reached in our own 'late capitalist' and postmodern times – a point whose implications we shall return to shortly.

Moreover, even as it creates some of the more reflexive and complex textures of the social whole at any moment, culture can also expose its limits or forms of blindness, and hence prefigure the society in which those limits will be overcome, and the unseen made visible. This is so where fiction becomes the vehicle of 'excessive' or (to invoke Richard Rorty's term)[7] 'crazy' forms of critique – as in the case, for example, of early feminist novels (and theory), which were not simply exposing an obviously apparent gap between social practice and values professed, but highlighting the absence of any professed commitment to the equality of women. Culture here figures as the place where frustrations or emancipatory demands begin to find some expression before their time, in other words, prior to the provision of grounds for immanent critique within the existing discursive formation. Something similar applies in the case where literature and art give voice for the first time, or in a new register, to previously unheard or culturally stereotyped identities. Work such as this initially challenges existing canons, even if it may subsequently gain a canonical status itself. We shall come back to the question of how these texts – which may be privileged by critics today as providing the most liberating narrative opportunities for reader identification – figure in cultural self-realisation. Suffice it to say here that narrative forms, particularly the novel, provide potent means of emotional expression for those identifying with figures represented in the text and perhaps most especially when their representation highlights previously unremarked forms of insensitivity, neglect or distortion, or focuses on the existential conflicts experienced by particular subjects in virtue of the constraints placed on them by their social milieu.

However, we would argue for the superiority of those narratives which, in virtue of their form, allow or require readers to transcend imaginary identification by inviting critical participation in the act or arts of representation itself. In such critical participation, the insight of readers both into their own positioning *vis-à-vis* those imagined in the text and into the historically varying conditions on the formation of subjectivity and the 'positions' open to it is necessarily extended. The best cultural works are 'sublime', not quite in the sense that Longinus gave to that term of inducing in their readers or audience the proud feeling of having created them themselves[8] but in the more limited sense of giving them access to a more comprehensive authorial or writerly perspective.

Culture and 'one-dimensionality' in the present

We have argued that the cultural works we are primarily engaged with here are important because in registering the opposition between 'system' and 'life-world', they also actively reproduce and keep open a sense of the tension between them. However, the argument is open to objections concerning its contemporary relevance. Some may argue that although capitalist society was indeed caught in the tensions of its contradictory complexity throughout the nineteenth and into the first half of the twentieth century, this has been much less true of the more 'one-dimensional' world that came into being with the era of monopoly capitalism (when Marcuse and Adorno first coined the term 'one-dimensional society') and is now fully consolidated in the age of intensive privatisation, transnational corporatism and globalisation. For in these conditions, where the commercial ethos has been altogether more openly espoused, and neo-monetarist governments have blatantly encouraged aggressive economic self-assertion and unashamed entrepreneurialism, the force of the moral or symbolic domain has dwindled to the point where it no longer figures as any serious dialectical counterweight, and the space and function we have accorded to cultural mediation have been progressively squeezed out. Some may further argue, updating an essentially Adornian argument on the 'culture industry', that given the dominance today of TV and new media, other cultural forms, particularly literature, have been displaced, in ways that have resulted in a general decline of cultural standards and erosion of a more reflexively critical cultural domain.

It is certainly true that we now live in a more one-dimensional world in the sense that professed values have come increasingly to coincide with economic dictates. Particularly in the most recent period the combined effects of new right politics, the collapse of 'actual existing socialism', the weakening of social democracy and the ascendancy of postmodernist forms of irony, relativism and anti-foundationalism have brought about a social context in which the economic rationality of capitalism is both more openly acclaimed and more cynically accepted for what it is and does. In such circumstances, where the gap is significantly narrowed between what society does and what it projects as admirable, culture loses its potency as a source of immanent critique. As contemporary Western society has come to feel less need to conceal its dominant rationality, so it has disarmed criticism of its hypocrisies. It has also freed itself from the pressures to summon forth some ideologically comforting bonding or harmonising role for the aesthetic level and function. No cultural ideologue is likely today to cling to the utopian promise of a Kantian *sensus communis* or Arnoldian 'common culture' as the fig-leaf for the 'original sin' of the mental–manual division of labour.[9] Indeed, whether in the form of the new-right resistance to the idea of the social collectivity or in the left-wing form of the academic postmodernist's insistence on respecting cultural difference and particularism, the impulse today is not to seek for harmony and reconciliation but to celebrate individuation and diversity. If the aesthetic is still charged with a bonding role it is at the sub-cultural level rather than as the source of any more general social integration.

These developments have gone together with the emergence of new, more assertive and narcissistically or voyeuristically directed forms of popular culture, especially on television. Some ('Big Brother' and kindred programmes) make a drama of *taedium vitae* itself, others (the quiz shows and lotteries) of the risks of money-making and competition, yet others centre around catastrophic disruptions to the mundane round: illness, hospital operations, violence, death in all its forms, especially accidental. Such programmes, which are sometimes quite distressing to watch, and frequently embarrassing, even humiliating, for the increasing numbers of 'ordinary' people upon whose active participation they depend, are at some distance from the banal and anodyne provision condemned as 'culture industry' pap by the Frankfurt School. This is not to say they are any better, or offer any more in the way of fulfilment for their viewers, but it is to recognise the degree to which popular culture – or at any rate some forms of it – might be analysed not too much as escapist distraction from everyday life but rather as obsessively dwelling on some of its nastier and more stressful dimensions. What is compulsive here, it seems, is the registering of the vulnerability and even the futility of existence: what one is invited to acknowledge is the quasi-sublime attractions of the narcissistic and appetitive spirit itself, both in its successes and in its victimisations.

On this kind of evidence, one might agree that society has become more unapologetically one-dimensional or that its one-dimensionality has taken a new and more aggressively self-sufficient direction. But there is a dialectic here, too. For the clearer recognition and readier acceptance of the extent to which society is functionalised and commodified also in a sense testifies to its still less than totally administered status – to the existence of a cognitive space of reflection. To recognise oneself as a cog in the 'system' is at the same time to be something other than its creature, even if it is no very comforting form of intellectual transcendence. Some time ago now, Christopher Lasch pointed out that

> as more and more people find themselves in jobs that are in fact beneath their abilities, and as leisure and sociability themselves take on the qualities of work, the posture of cynical detachment

> becomes the dominant style of everyday discourse. Many forms of popular art appeal to this sense of knowingness and thereby reinforce it.[10]

Lasch himself viewed this as an essentially negative development in blunting the will to change social conditions. Yet self-awareness of this type is inherently ambivalent: it may lead to despairing or Stoical resignation, but it can also on occasion prove the ironically powered catalyst for new and imaginative forms of resistance.

There are, in any case, other kinds of evidence to be placed in the balance. The very rich and commercially successful are certainly glamourised as never before, yet there is also extensive moral disapproval of greed and overt profiteering, the 'fat cat' remains a reviled figure, and the tension between human needs and moral values on the one hand and economic imperatives on the other continues to make itself felt. TV soaps may not offer complex critical argument, but it would be mistaken to overlook their engagements with issues of identity politics or their various challenges to establishment thinking. To argue this is not to make strong aesthetic claims on their behalf: they often lack irony, and queer their critical pitch by an excess of moral didacticism. But in a sense this is the very point, and only goes to confirm their occupancy of a certain kind of sentimental high ground, where humane values of tolerance, sympathy, ritual bonding and conviviality still battle on (as indeed they do in real life) against the depredations and disenchantments of the ruling economic logic.

A case might also be made for claiming that the openness of popular culture to multiple signification allows it to provide complex quasi-mythic modes of differentiation-cum-integration, thus fulfilling something of the counter-systemic bonding role dreamt up for the 'high' aesthetic. Anthony Easthope has argued that what popular culture lacks in connotative complexity at the level of writing it can sometimes make up for in the plurality of what can be read into its 'narratemes' or epitomising images, where

> a seemingly univocal meaning, in virtue of iconic polysemy, opens into a shared collectivity, so that a narrateme whose denotation appears unitary and universal, a commonplace everyone knows the same way (or thinks they do) actually excites connotations everyone accedes to differently at the level of phantasy . . . It is via such narratemes that popular culture can sometimes speak with what Beckett calls 'the voice of us all on all sides', arising from and articulating as little else the intersubjective everydayness of life under late capitalism.[11]

Of course, this in itself does not indicate any collective response to the sources producing capitalist 'everydayness', but it does suggest that popular culture is more complex in its potentials and effects than is recognised by those presenting it as straightforwardly collusive with the drift towards one-dimensionality.

We might add that the evidence about people's relations to serious or learned culture does not seem to point in any one direction. There has been a growth in reading groups, and an expansion of the market for those same difficult high modernist texts of Joyce and Beckett that Adornian aesthetic theory presented as inherently so confined in their appeal. (Modernism, to add to the irony, has also now generated something of its own 'culture industry', with Woolf, Joyce, Beckett and other writers being enlisted in tourist promotion. A fair number of those Dublin bound will never, we can guess, read Joyce's work, but they will be glad all the same to cross the Irish sea on the *Ulysses*, enjoying a Guinness – or glass of Burgundy? – in the Leopold Bloom bar as they go.) In other areas, too, transgressions or confusions of the former divide between high art and popular culture might seem to be taking place: against the flop of the Millennium Dome must be set the new publics for art exhibitions and the unprecedented success of Tate Modern, a success which itself has to be linked to the challenge within art to older criteria of 'art' and the provision of gallery space for surrealism, conceptual or Pop Art, and other departures from the earlier canon.

These reflections are impressionistic, and do not warrant

definite conclusions about the direction of current cultural trends. We suggest only that the picture is not that of a relentless disengagement from learned culture. But even those who argue that it is would have to concede that in education there is still a commitment to serious cultural work as the best resource for promoting critical autonomy and self-realisation. Even as the universities have been obliged to adopt a more techno-pragmatic and vocationally oriented view of the purposes of higher education, they have also issued mission statements committing them to all the traditional non-instrumental goals of degree level study (the development of critical autonomy, cultural self-enhancement, ethical awareness, and so on) – thus acknowledging the contradiction between their 'culturally self-realising' provision and the narrow demands of the work world. If these recent professions represent a departure from past pieties, they do so only in their new Quality Assurance Agency idiom and in the fact they have been written down at all. In one sense, of course, as we are here implying, they are merely cosmetic, a papering over of the social contradiction of which their stated, but never economically and socially consolidated, aspirations represent one aspect. But this only goes to confirm our original point: that these aspirations have still continually to be sounded speaks to the incomplete triumphs of one-dimensionality. That economic rationality has still to be tempered by a logic or sense of worth which is not of its own making, and indeed runs directly counter to it, indicates the persistence of a need for its cultural antithesis.

In other words, whatever is inferred from the evidence on cultural consumption, there can be no disputing the important role still accorded to the critical study of learned culture in schools and universities. Even if society may have become more one-dimensional in the postwar period it remains caught up in a project of cultural pedagogy whose values and guiding principles are at odds with the motives and forces that prevail in the economic sphere. It is certainly true, however, that the complex of forces at work over the last fifty years has highlighted the contradictory dimensions of this commitment. It has also exposed the ideal of cultural self-realisation to new forms of criticism within the academy itself. Much of this has centred on the coherence and political credentials of the conception of subjectivity invoked in talk about self-realisation. To present the subject as if it were a relatively autonomous centre of agency and self-making is not only illusory in itself, say critics, but also promotes a partial view of the self – a view still tainted by its white, Western, and patriarchal construction – as if it had universal application. In this sense cultural self-realisation, even when freed of its explicitly Arnoldian outlook, is said to remain caught in dubious forms of humanist thinking. It is also associated with what some see as an unwarranted discrimination between different types of cultural production, particularly that sustained in the pedagogic privileging of canonical works over popular culture. Since these lines of criticism point to the breakdown of traditional conceptions of self-fulfilment and the role of culture in it, they have also created a context in which academics themselves have become more inclined to question the long held assumption that the most authentic forms of self-realisation lie by way of intellectual and spiritual gratification and development. In what follows, therefore, we shall consider the vulnerability of the idea of cultural self-realisation to charges of this kind concerning its constituency, philosophical consistency and social legitimacy, focusing in particular on the problems relating to its humanist paradigm and reliance on value discrimination.

The 'autonomous' self?

In the previous chapter we noted the extent to which the project of cultural self-realisation is indexed to a specifically modern sense of the person as possessed of an inner depth or meaning that is itself the focus of self-reflection and expression. Were it not for the emergence of this self-significant and self-directing sense of individuality, artistic production would have been very different (altogether more publicly oriented, cultist and mimetic) and would hardly have offered a medium for personal discovery or self-narrative on the part of its audiences. However, the story of how cultural works and artistic movements have at once reflected and provided for the 'inward' self is complex. In recent times it is certainly not a simple matter of cultural works providing expression for an already fully conscious sense of self or identity. This is in part because, through the dispersion of ideas stemming from Marx, Schopenhauer, Nietzsche, Heidegger and perhaps most especially Freud, a wide acceptance has developed that the self is not and cannot be a fully self-aware and self-directing self, but has to acknowledge that it is always 'in the world', with others, and formed by structures and forces (childhood experience, socio-economic circumstances, conceptual schemas, language, and so on) that transcend it and whose impact can never be entirely transparent. To the extent that we are self-knowing (self-making), and our depths consciously sounded, we know that we are not fully self-knowing (self-making). And to the extent that we acknowledge (as in differing ways Hegel, Lacan, Sartre and others have suggested we must) that a component of our selfhood is as others 'receive' us, whether intuitively, or linguistically, or by whatever other mode, then we also know ourselves to be in some sense 'alienated' – we do not suggest either removably or regrettably – in the other's constitution of us.

But the complications of expression stem also from that fact that culture itself shifts and turns in respect of the prominence or understanding given to the expressive role. Modernism, for example, breaks with the idea of the self as translucent unity, in a reaction against Romantically derived ideas of art as providing for an integral self through reconciliation of sensibility and reason. But in other respects, it remains equally if not more involved in subjectivity and its articulation. If in the work of such writers as Mann, Proust, Eliot, and Pound the centre of gravity is displaced, as Charles Taylor has suggested, to the flow of experience and new forms of unity across time[12] the aim is still to register modern experience in a more adequate and depth-sounding manner. If what is problematised here is the idea, more or less sanctioned in much realist fiction, of the self as a unified and self-contained plenitude, it is problematised in the interests of a more truly realistic reflection of the distinctive forms of experience of the modern self: its heightened self-consciousness (including of its own involuntary and uncontrolled formation), its troubled response to gender norms and their revisioning, its existentialist awareness of the contradictory aspect of notions of the 'life-plan' or of 'self-realisation', and so on. Moreover, to the extent that modernism is also caught up in a crisis of authorial authority regarding the capacity or legitimation of the cultural producer to offer any universally applicable message or representation, it falls back upon something more autobiographical and in that sense expressive of the artist's own vocation and problematised place in the world.[13] In fiction particularly, the emphasis comes to fall increasingly on the act of writing itself, and what can be transfigured through it; and this in turn prompts in the reader a sense of identification with the authorial place as the promise of self-realisation.

Some of these themes are pursued further in Chapters 4 and 5. If we touch on them here it is to bring out the extent to which a self-reflecting, even self-expressing, subject is presupposed in the production and reception of cultural work even where this has broken with more traditional conceptions of the unitary self and recognises – sometimes foregrounds – the constituting role of ideology, language or the unconscious and their 'theft' of the fully self-knowing, self-directing subject. That the self has depth, even unknown and irrationally driven depths (the Id that Freud sought to make ego, and so on), is no reason to doubt the applicability of a category of the subject as a self-aware and self-motivating social agent. If psychoanalytic readings have focused on the ways in which texts realise phantasies or wish-fulfilments for their readers (or, as Freud himself put it, allow them 'to derive consolation and alleviation from their own sources of pleasure in their unconscious which have become inaccessible to them'),[14] the reference is still to readers fully implicated in their own self-pleasuring. Even when Althusserian–Lacanian readings have presented texts in terms of their interpellations and positionings of subjects (with realist texts analysed as securing the appearance of autonomy for the subject and modernist texts as subverting that appearance and repositioning the subject as a misrecognising self), the theoretical analysis still depends on an appeal to that self that is interpellated, misconstrues the extent of autonomy, and thinks of itself as a subject.[15]

To the extent that this dependency is not explicitly acknowledged within their theory itself, these critical moves are obviously question-begging: for what can readers who are theorised as inherently so locked in ideology or *méconnaissance* be thought to gain from texts that purportedly reveal their incapacity for self-cognition? In this respect, they share in the difficulties which beset a further and more radical challenge to the notion of the subject as capable of self-realisation. This comes when depth is explicitly denied: in other words, when, as in various neo-Nietzschean forms of argument, doubt is cast on there being a self prior to interpellation, some 'doer' behind the deed, some intuitions, desires or compulsions that are not discursively constructed behind one's back and beyond one's ken, some 'truth' of the self or *jouissance* to be reached or restored by the psychoanalyst, some sexuality that is more than wholly conventionally instituted. One must take some account of these distinctions when considering the challenges that have been issued to the coherence and the desirability of any project of self-realisation conceived in terms of the promotion of the 'autonomous' self-reflecting individual subject of Enlightenment philosophy. For these challenges have not all been equally radical or subversively anti-humanist in their critique, and we need to make a broad distinction between arguments that have criticised the partial and socially biased preconceptions traditionally associated with the notion of autonomous subjectivity, and those which have challenged its very conception of selfhood.

This difference is probably best illustrated in the spectrum of feminist critique, where a division can be made between those who retain broadly Enlightenment commitments and those who denounce these as the legacy of an inherently masculinist and manipulative rationality. Within the first group, we can count those who, developing arguments first sounded by Mary Wollstonecraft and other feminists of her time, have objected to the arbitrary and unjustifiable exclusion of women as candidates for the autonomy and cultural transcendence said to be proper to humanity at large. For these critics, what is objectionable is not the formal appeal to an autotelic conception of self but the partial and gender-biased interpretation that has been placed historically on its content – the presentation of women as lacking the cognitive faculties or aesthetic sensibilities essential to become full human agents in this sense. Their quarrel, to select only a few of the more glaring examples from the nineteenth century onwards, has been with Hegel's privileging of male ethical capacity, or Schopenhauer's and Nietzsche's disdain for the female intellect, or the presumptions of phallic supremacy brought by Freud to his understanding of psychic development, or the masculine bias of Sartre's ontology, or Kohlberg's differential account of male and female moral understanding – and so on. In the argument of some feminists, these critiques have developed into full-blown attacks on the ideal of autonomy itself and the associated fetishisation of masculine attributes (or at any rate of those associated with male performance in patriarchal culture). This, it is said, has promoted a falsely abstracted sense of the individual as both disembodied and socially disembedded, and allowed men in particular to justify their detachment from the sphere of domesticity and reproduction.[16]

Yet even these critical elaborations, it can be argued, are questioning the cogency of a certain essentially Cartesian and solipsistic idea of autonomy, rather than quarrelling with an autotelic conception of selfhood as such. Indeed, they are primarily directed against the view that the individual could have any kind of consciousness of the distinctness of self in the absence of embodiment and social context, or develop any authentic autonomy not mediated through forms of dependency on others, rather than querying the philosophical coherence and political credentials of the very notions of selfhood and autonomy. Autonomy so conceived is never, of course, a final or fixed achievement, and any substantive interpretation given to it will be open to challenge. Feminists, in particular, have noted how equivocal and unstable its content can be in relation to their own agenda. As Jean Grimshaw puts it:

> When does need for another itself become a sign of undue dependence and lack of a necessary autonomy? When, in a sexual relationship, does the need for another's desire shade into a problematic kind of sexual objectification? If sexual desire is closely related to the desire of another person for oneself, to what extent and in what contexts does one's own desire for another's desire shade into a subordination of that desire to another's?[17]

But to recognise this instability at the psychological level is in no sense to undermine the conceptual coherence of claims to autonomy. To many feminists the development of personal autonomy in this conception remains an essential aspect of the emancipatory agenda, rather than a mark of co-option by modern power and what Foucault has termed its 'techniques of individuation'.[18] Seyla Benhabib, for example, in rejecting the model of fractured selves who 'joyfully deny their own coherence and relish their opacity and multiplicity',[19] has argued for a view that would

> situate the subject in the context of various social, linguistic, and discursive practices. This view, however, would by no means question the desirability and theoretical necessity of articulating a more adequate, less deluded, and less mystified vision of subjectivity. The traditional attributes of the philosophical subject of the West, like self-reflexivity, the capacity for acting on principles, rational accountability for one's actions and the ability to project a life-plan into the future, in short, some form of autonomy and rationality, could then be reformulated by taking account of the radical situatedness of the subject.[20]

A more post-structuralist influenced feminist criticism of the 'abstraction' of the Enlightenment subject, on the other hand, has been directed not only, or not primarily, at the discounting of the claims of female subjects and the illusions of a de-situated view of the self, but rather against the error of promoting a view of the self as in any sense transcendent to the forces engaged in its cultural construction. According to the currently influential neo-Nietzschean account of the subject offered by Judith Butler, we must reject any model which vests the subject with a capacity for reflexive mediation that remains intact regardless of its cultural embeddedness: for on such a model, she argues, '"culture" and "discourse" merely mire the subject, but do not constitute that subject.'[21] Hence the charge of evasion she levels at Benhabib:

> What does it mean to situate 'feminism' at the same time that one makes fundamental to that feminism a de-situated transcendentalized self? Is this the solace that the philosopher needs in order to proceed, problematically imposed from the scene of philosophy onto the scene of politics? Is it right to suggest that any theory of agency must evacuate the situation of being discursively constituted and enabled in order to proceed?[22]

According to Butler, discursive constitution in this understanding does not (counter to what one might suppose) imply determination, since to be constituted by language is 'to be produced within a given network of power/discourse which is open to resignification . . . "Agency" is to be found precisely at such junctures where discourse is renewed.'[23] Yet Butler never really makes clear how it is that subjects who are wholly constituted in language can at the same time discover within themselves the intentionality and element of relative autonomy that is prerequisite to resignification. Nor does she adequately explain how conventions are brought into being in the first place if subjects are always the effect of their enactment. It may be true, as she claims in explanation of her theory of performance (itself derived from J.L. Austin, Derrida and De Man), that 'to the extent that a performance appears to "express" a prior intention, a doer behind the deed, that prior agency is only legible as the effect of that utterance.'[24] But that it was not previously 'legible' does not mean it had no prior existence: it is not taking the marriage vows that constitutes the intention to get married. Indeed, Butler seems in effect unhappy with her own argument here, since no sooner has she told us that the category of 'intention' and the notion of the 'doer' have a place only in virtue of the enabling deed, than she reminds us that the 'subject' – a category within language – must be kept distinct from the 'self'. But if the implication here is that 'selves' are, after all, by contrast in some sense transcendent to language, it is no longer so clear how her position ultimately differs from the one she is opposing. Conversely, when Butler claims in polemical mood that to require the subject is an authoritarian ruse by which the political contest over the status of the subject is summarily silenced, or that to think of oneself as a subject is tantamount to claiming that one is one's own point of departure (a fantasy she associates with an inherently masculinist disavowal or primary repression of the maternal),[25] it is as if she has reverted to attacking a straw-woman feminism rather than those of her critics who have themselves been loud in denouncing such crudely Cartesian conceptions.

Butler is right, of course, to imply that the opposition is equivocally formulated, and faces its own difficulties of theoretical articulation: where do the determinants of 'situation' cease and where does the 'transcendent' self take over? Indeed, it is not clear that any theory is adequate to the task of registering the aporic nature of the constitution of the subject, where the ambivalence between actual and merely sensed autonomy, constituting and constituted dimensions, may be better illustrated by way of the more concrete and particular narratives found in literature (particularly the *Bildungsroman*, with its focus on the ambiguities of self-formation and the life-project). Yet it remains the case that both sides of this precarious dialectic have to be retained as the necessary condition of any coherent account of subjectivity: counter to the suggestion that agency has to be analysed either as a pre-discursive attribute of persons or as always implicated in discourse, we have to view it as an overdetermined exercise in both modes conjointly.

The tyranny of the subject

As we have suggested earlier, post-structuralist objections to the self-reflecting subject, such as those found in Butler's writing, are motivated philosophically by a Nietzschean resistance to any form of conceptualisation as inherently betraying the irreducible plurality of an always particular existence. But as its rhetoric makes plain, this philosophical argument is at the same time a political critique. Claims to truth, insofar as they are implicitly universal, are viewed as constraining differences within the concept of some sameness, and therefore as suspect.[26] Lyotard spoke in his *Economie Libidinale* of the 'white terror of truth', and presented any theoretical claim to truth as wilfully bent on the denial of cultural disparity and heterogeneity.[27] Foucault from the time of *Discipline and Punish* consistently sought to undermine the commitment to 'truth' by revealing its link to power, domination and the disciplining control of the subject. Butler herself speaks of the 'authoritarian ruses' and 'political offenses' at work in the invocation of the subject.[28] Post-colonial theorists have invoked a similar vocabulary and form of critique in their exposure of what they see as the essentialist suppression of cultural difference perpetrated by Enlightenment-influenced conceptions of selfhood and self-realisation.[29]

Yet wherever anti-foundationalist thinking is defended on the grounds of its more democratic or emancipatory potential, as it has been in so much recent cultural theory and criticism, it is seriously undermined. Foucault could develop his critique of 'truth' only at the cost of disallowing any special claims for the truth of the critique, and only by leaving unresolved the tensions in his account of subjectivity – which he presents both as wholly the 'construct' of power and as the site of resistance to its manipulative strategies. Moreover, as several critics have pointed out, the critique of 'disciplinary' power always remained implicitly reliant for its force on an acceptance of Enlightenment values of freedom and justice.[30] Lyotard is readier than Foucault to acknowledge the contradictory nature of making any claims to truth from a position of relativism and infinite ontological plurality, but he too runs up against the inconsistency of denouncing the 'tyranny' of truth as if to imply the desirability of freedom from it: for whence comes the critical force of the condemnation if not from an implicit and unacknowledged appeal to a universal understanding of what constitutes 'tyranny' and what is wrong with it? In the absence of any conception of a feeling, suffering, self-asserting subject why should we even worry about discursive 'tyranny' and its 'authoritarian ruses'?

It may be true that there is no opposition to power that is entirely outside the workings of power, but there is a considerable difference between allowing this and agreeing that power is entirely a matter of discourse and linguistically constituted subject places. There is also a difference between claiming that all agency is caught up in power relations or that 'emancipation' will never be the transcendence of power, and claiming that all acts are on a par and all emancipatory discourses equally tainted by authoritarian zeal. Could Butler, for example, even begin to give an account of what is wrong with authoritarianism that does not invoke some more universal idea of what it is to be human than she would ever explicitly avow?

One line of response to these charges might be that they mistake the strategic purposes of the emphasis on 'difference' and in the process take too literally an anti-foundationalist argument that was never intended to be construed as a denial of a minimal human identity of needs and aspirations. The advocates of difference have the edge over their opponents, it might be said, because they have recognised more clearly that there can be no cultural politics which does not invoke an identity of needs in its very attempt to represent the 'other' – and have in consequence become that much more cautious about the act of representation. In Gayatri Spivak's argument:

> Contrary to the received assumption, it seems to me that the non-foundationalist thinkers are suggesting that you cannot have any kind of emancipatory project without some notion of the ways in which human beings are similar, but that there are practical-philosophical problems that attend on this assumption. Historically, the people who have been involved in emancipatory projects from above – slave-holders and proponents of Christianising the natives and so on – are the ones who have produced the discourse. The contradiction can be avoided only if the principles of a universal humanism – the place where indeed all human beings are similar – is seen to be lodged in their being different. So that difference itself becomes a name for the place where we are all the same – a 'name for' because difference is not something that can be articulated, as a monolithic concept. But if difference becomes a name for the place where we are all the same – if difference becomes the name for that – then it stands as a kind of warning against the fact that we cannot not propose identity when we engage in actual emancipatory projects.[31]

Yet there is surely something sophistical about this argument, which begins by acknowledging the reliance of 'emancipatory politics' on the assumption of the sameness of human beings, only to end by translating the notion of sameness into that of absolute difference. For is this not to evade the key problem of how we could begin to discriminate between what is and what is not 'emancipatory' without invoking those ways in which human beings are similar not in being different but in something more shared: in the comparable nature of the pain or humiliation they will suffer, for example, when subjected to similar kinds of maltreatment? Remaining alert to the political and philosophical assumptions of speaking on behalf of the other, being sensitive to the risk of 'cultural imperialist' or ethnocentric perspectives that attend on all acts of representation, involves respecting the humanist presumptions which make sense of the charge of ethnocentrism in the first place.

Of course, in any given instance of cultural representation of the 'other', even when it is explicitly directed against the legacy of Western imperialism, there is always the risk of insensitivity. But as with feminism so with post-colonial theory: a distinction needs to be drawn between the form of critique that exposes the ethnocentric presuppositions of a particular use of humanist discourse, and the critique which damns any appeal to what is common in human beings as the product of a Western and ethnocentric perspective. Indeed, if what Marc Redfield calls 'the multiplication of cultures' is bound to founder on the humanism of its very project, then there is no way forward. It is towards this impasse that Redfield appears to be moving when he suggests that the opening of the academy and other cultural institutions to these developments must almost inevitably tend to a new form of oppressive containment. We are now in a position, he writes,

> to understand the relative ease with which a certain multiculturalism is accommodated and promoted by scholarly, pedagogical and other cultural institutions. As long as the multiplication of cultures remains integrated under the sign of the human (or, since the institutionalisation of feminism is obviously also at stake here, that of 'man'), and even as long as the noncanonical cultural objects studied are taken as examples of ethnic or national identity, an aesthetic logic controls the field of dispute, organising ethnic identity upon the neutrally white background of 'culture' itself, as the (Western, male, etc.) institution has defined it.[32]

Tautology or analytic statement here substitutes for empirical investigation and argument ('as long as' cultural institutions remain committed to a 'white, male, Western' conception of the subject, they will remain committed to that conception . . .). What is more, the claim is paradoxically reliant on an essentialising view of the Western (white, male, etc.) aesthetic logic as always in a position to control what counts as 'human'. It thus appears altogether too ready to rule out aforehand the possibility that the voice of the (female or ethnic) other could be 'integrated' in a way that allowed them to begin to call the tune on the definition of the 'human'. There is not a problem for cultural theory in the invocation of the concept of the human subject as a universally embracing category – and without it, it will be difficult, as we have argued, to explain the political offence of ethnocentric forms of reading or integration. But there is a problem with any critical position that has got so accustomed to denouncing this human subject as 'white, male, etc.' that it has no conceptual will to consider who, other than the white males, might even now be reconstructing its concept and on what other criteria of inclusivity.

There is a problem, too, in the normative idea that appears to underlie the post-structuralist attacks on the 'tyrannical' subject, the idea, namely, that there *should* be (even if, alas, there never can be) a politics without power, a space where entirely unpreconstituted 'selves' engaged in multiple, anarchic performative expression and interaction in the absence of any institutional mediation, moral norms, or formal political process. It is this which is the fantasy, and this which opens itself to the charge of invoking a certain desituated sense of theoretical capacity: that of thinking that one can defend one's own politics, or critique that of others, without any commitments at all on the nature of human need and desire; that one can criticise in the name of democracy without specifying what differences between selves will be discounted in the interests of equal treatment, or without having to specify what expressive constitutions of the self might not in the end be tolerable or compatible with the free expression of all.

To the extent, then, that post-structuralism can be defined by its emancipatory or 'democratic' urge to avoid any totalisation or trumping of other perspectives on truth or value, it is hoist by its own petard. For if every totalising form of critique is discounted as suspiciously 'imperialising', so too must be those which give meaning to the notion of cultural dominance or imperialism themselves. Thus even those like Lyotard and Foucault who spoke most intransigently in such terms have, in the face of the internal inconsistency of their arguments, reverted to a revisionist position.[33] What creates these inconsistencies, and prompts the revisions, is the impoverished understanding of subjectivity with which they are working. Post-structuralism is rightly sceptical of the extent of the autonomy of the autonomous subject of Enlightenment thought, but it too readily accepts this conception of a wholly self-controlling subjectivity as definitional of subjectivity. In the post-structuralist paradigm there are therefore essentially only two possibilities: either the autonomous, self-controlling subject; or the collapse of identity, a 'subjectless subjectivism', the reversion to a kind of pre-subjective flux which has abolished the relation to otherness which is constitutive of subjectivity.[34] What is denied any register here is the subject who is able in some relatively autonomous sense to reflect on its possible delusions about the extent of its own autonomy; who feels called upon to act as a rational and morally responsible agent of self-change from a position of unfreedom and uncontrolled formation. This is the subject, one might say, that opposes the totality from within it and under the influence of its conditioning. This idea is clearly problematic, yet without some such conceptualisation there is little point in moving any critique against manipulative cultural forces (or conversely, in recommending educative or cultural strategies designed to encourage personal autonomy). If subjects are never anything but the constructs of discourse, what sense is there in directing them towards that which is inauthentic, distorting or stereotypical in their representation? How can texts be exposed as a vehicle (say) of colonial or patriarchal perceptions, or alternatively explored as a site of contestation around such partial constructions, unless it is assumed that human beings are in a position to negotiate their identity by reference to discursive formations rather than being exhaustively constituted by them? It might of course be objected that if readers (or viewers) do indeed find themselves gratifyingly represented or confirmed in the identifications permitted by this or that text, it hardly much matters if the cultural theorist who is defending the value of such works precisely for those reasons is arguing from a Nietzschean perpectivism that strictly speaking denies the coherence of any such subjective self-discovery or identification. As we have already indicated, however, the liberating and self-realising power of cultural texts cannot be reduced to such affirming identifications, but depends on the work creating a context in which reader or viewer is able to stand in some critical relationship to its representations. Representation, in this politically accented sense, is not simply a matter of giving expression to the experience or aesthetic style of marginalised and victimised identities, but also about opening up perspectives from which these may be renegotiated, transcended, even directly disowned. Excluded groups, notes Terry Eagleton, 'urgently demand free expression; but the more fundamental political question is that of demanding an equal right with others to discover what one might become, not of assuming some already fully-fashioned identity which is merely repressed.'[35]

Identification, narrative, expression

We have focused here, as we shall in Chapter 3, on defending the coherence of the idea of cultural self-realisation with particular reference to the role of narrative forms in allowing readers to do more than 'identify'. Such forms, which afford the reader a perspective of critical transcendence in relation to any given representation, thus also afford some objective insight into the historical situation conditioning the production of the fiction itself. We are not claiming that such narrative potentialities exhaust the possibilities of cultural self-realisation: there are many other genres and media. There is, moreover, something limited (even philistine) in judging the qualities of a literary work solely on the basis of the self-narratives it may allow the reader, rather than in terms of what it exacts and demands in itself.[36] We can agree that part of the value of literature lies in what it allows us to do by way of becoming, in Paul Ricoeur's phrase, the 'narrator of our own story',[37] but only if we can construe the notion of 'our' story so that it becomes dependent on the forms of self-transcendence that we have here indicated; and only if it is allowed also to encompass within it many forms of detachment or distraction from the 'story', such as are often afforded in confrontation with works of art. Aesthetic shock, disturbance, and defamiliarisation can be just as important as what is overtly offered to the subject in the way of critical engagement and understanding; or rather, the former must always be allowed to figure in the latter. To the extent that self-realisation involves the distancing associated with the writerly imagination it veers away from narcissistic self-absorption and subjectivism. Nor should it be conceived in overly active and cognitive terms. It is not only a matter of learning, monitoring, reflecting and transcending, but also a matter of a more passive reception and disengagement, a by-passing from the life quest itself where that is too unswervingly set on the high road of Socratic self-knowing.

Given these limitations of viewing the cultural work simply in terms of its confirmation of identity, we would dissent from the comparable tendency to construe its expressive power solely in terms of its representation of recognisable experience. Much that is expressed in cultural work has not been directly experienced by either its creator or its consumer: the work may speak primarily to some yearning for experience. This seems above all true of the works of Romanticism, the movement which marks the shift from a neo-classical mimetic to expressionism, for it is impossible to listen to Schubert or to read the great works of the English Romantic poets, perhaps especially Coleridge and Keats, without an overwhelming sense that what is being expressed, and summoned forth for listener or reader too, is a desire for what has not been and perhaps cannot be experienced. This is still subjective expression in the sense of giving voice to a felt desire or yearning: but the desire is for an imaginary (or as we say 'unimaginable') experience, rather than for one actually felt or actualisable, and thus far remains in the objective mode. Citing the many works of the Victorian era in which the force of sexuality and the sensuality related to it become more palpable through concealment; or the passages of Brahms' music 'of such overwhelming tenderness that they could only be expressed by one deprived of it', Adorno has claimed:

> It is a gross simplification to equate expression and subjectivity. What is subjectively expressed does not need to resemble the expressing subject. In many instances what is expressed will be precisely what the expressing subject is not; subjectively, all expression is mediated by longing.[38]

In similar mode he argues elsewhere that the social energy of artworks must be directly related to their envisaging of a world that has not yet been experienced because it is yet to be made. In the case of *Romeo and Juliet*, for example, 'without the longing for a situation in which love would no longer be mutilated and condemned by patriarchal or any other powers, the presence of the two lost in one another would not have the sweetness – the wordless, imageless utopia – over which, to this day, the centuries have been powerless.'[39]

Expression is plainly not mimesis, but nor is it the articulation of the already felt. It comes from the space or difference between things as they are and how they might be, being rooted in the former through the voice it gives to its desire, and linked to the latter through the imaginative vision of fulfilment it holds out.

Democracy, cultural self-realisation and the 'good life'

Even if our defence of aesthetic and cultural value is granted, the overall idea of cultural self-realisation might still be charged with élitism insofar as it reproduces the idea of personal fulfilment as attained primarily by way of the life of the mind and through the forms of insight and pleasure afforded by imaginative production. A critic might object that even though we view the social potential for cultural self-realisation as itself fully realisable only in altered socio-economic conditions, we are nonetheless offering a presumptuous anthropology of human need which unduly privileges cultural-aesthetic forms of satisfaction and thus promotes the intellectual's or academic's version of the 'good life' rather than speaking for any more collective sense of value. Can such a version still claim any special ranking in a postmodernity whose defining feature, as Zygmunt Bauman puts it, is that 'the idea of the good life is the lack of all definition of the good life', and where cultural favouritism of any kind goes against the grain of market philosophy and practice?[40] It might also be objected that we too readily assume the potentially reciprocal and democratic character of cultural self-realisation as communal 'rich development of individuality', when in truth it is an altogether more emulative and factitious affair: to privilege culture as a resource for personal development is to encourage a striving for distinctions of a kind that cannot be granted to all and must result in acrimonious forms of social division.

These objections are not all on a par. Some bear more on the ontological presuppositions of our claims for cultural self-realisation; others on the concept of self-realisation itself, the interpretation placed on it, and the paradoxes inherent in attempts to reconcile the self-realisation of all with the encouragement of individual uniqueness, autonomy and self-esteem. In the former case, what is at issue is the legitimacy of our defence of a distinctively cultural and intellectual dimension to self-realisation, transcendent and irreducible to material and non-intellectual definitions of well-being. In the latter, it is the coherence of promoting cultural self-realisation as a collective aim, given the extent to which it will depend on individual self-distinction, a distancing of the 'realised' self from the self formed in a common culture. This objection focuses on the extent to which even those forms of self-realisation belonging to a cultural and spiritual flourishing are caught up in what Rousseau called the *fureur de se distinguer* ('passion to be distinguished'). As we noted in Chapter 1, Rousseau associated this with the peculiarly human form of vanity or self-love he termed *amour propre*, which he saw as both ineliminable and deeply troublesome. *Amour propre*, Rousseau tells us, is 'a purely relative and factitious feeling, which arises in the state of society, leads each individual to make more of himself than any other, causes all mutual damage men inflict on one another, and is the real source of the "sense of honour".'[41]

In reply to the first line of objection, let us make clear that we are not presenting the forms of self-realisation to be gained through cultural engagement as the only ones worth having. We have abstracted for purposes of developing our case from other aspects of need and fulfilment, but we are very far from denying them their role. Even if we distinguish, as we surely must, between needs and conditions of flourishing, or between the instrumental goods required as a condition of personal fulfilment and those which are valued intrinsically as constitutive of self-realisation (a distinction that admittedly could have a book to itself), it is clearly the case that the range of intrinsically valuable goods is enormous and that different individuals desire very different goods and will find (or at any rate seek) self-realisation through multiple and differing channels. Our defence of cultural self-realisation is not intended to discount all those forms of pleasure and fulfilment that are not found through cultural works.

In response to the second objection, we would suggest that while it may be neither possible nor desirable to eliminate the interest in self-esteem and the urge to distinction, we can curb those forms of commercial and entrepreneurial expression of *amour propre* which most distrain on the possibilities of reciprocal fulfilment. Culture has acted as a support system for some of these insofar as the acquisition of 'cultural capital' has been instrumental in reproducing social stratification. In our post-modern times, as Bauman and others point out, the prestige of culture is not what it was, and competes now in the market for fame and honour with many other types of distinction (not least that of wealth itself): the purely instrumental value of cultural education may perhaps be on the wane – though the democratic potentialities of cultural education remain damaged and circumscribed so long as the educational system as a whole has the effect, if not the prime purpose, of classifying most pupils as failures. What we understand by cultural self-realisation is the fulfilment which comes through the critical study of cultural work pursued for its own sake, and in higher education, at least, there is little doubt that – cynically realistic as they are about its prestige in the work world – many humanities students view their studies in terms of their intrinsic rather than instrumental value. So, too, do many who come back to study, often from within successful careers, and who value it as anti-utilitarian complement or contrast to their engagements in the work world. Culture and cultural education remain a counter-systemic influence and source of spiritual meaning despite the relative decline in their instrumental value.

Part of our answer, then, is that cultural capital no longer gives the same access to privilege as it once did, and has become less implicated in invidious self-distinction. Rather than aiming to restore its function in that respect, those involved in teaching culture can defend the democratic potential of the pleasures and forms of critical awareness it affords by linking these on the one hand to yearnings (or deprivations) intimated in the continued commitment of contemporary society to the values of the 'symbolic' domain, and on the other to what they can offer as a socially and ecologically benign source of creativity and transcendence. Not that culture alone affords such a source: but it has the advantage in these respects over many forms of consumption and self-fulfilment. It has democratic and ecological credentials denied to many other forms of activity and engagement precisely because it is essentially a matter of the spirit, and few intrinsic material and resource limits stand in the way of its extension. Unlike material forms of self-realising consumption, cultural democracy is, given the desire and the political will, indefinitely extendible. Cultural self-realisation conceived in terms of the transcendence of naive identification can also be said to be democratically oriented in its encouragement of reflexivity. The capacity to place oneself imaginatively in the position of the other, or to understand the dialogic relations of self and others in a constellation of social subjects, is plainly of critical importance to the development of a moral sensibility and adequate understanding of the concepts of justice and democracy themselves.[42] It is also quite helpful for thinking about the good life, and what social relations of production and forms of consumption might best promote the conditions of a more reciprocal development of individuality. In a formal democratic sense, these would be conditions in which there would be no de-differentiation of persons other than that required to render the self-realisation of any given person consistent with that of all others. In practice, we suggest, they would be conditions in which there would be smaller disparities at the level of material consumption (the instrumental goods of self-preservation), but a diversification of and wider participation in the intrinsically valued fulfilments of the aesthetic or cultural–spiritual sphere, on the basis of a growth in free time. In this sense, the reflexivity encouraged through cultural self-realisation reaffirms the rationale and possibility of its future democratic extension. But this – to revert to our chapter's main theme – is only one aspect of the dialectic: the marginal place of cultural self-realisation in the present constitution of society, and in most people's lives, leaves it all too vulnerable to its systemic, instrumental 'other'.

Fictional Representations

3

'A tendency to set the mind in motion': novel-reading and self-realisation

In this chapter we explore, in close readings of two novels, some terms in which one might claim that the engagement with cultural texts is a means to self-realisation. Readers can engage with novels by identifying with their characters; and this can be the basis not just of immediate pleasure in the text, but also of critical approaches which foreground 'identity'. When Mary Hays' *The Memoirs of Emma Courtney* was republished in 1986, Sally Cline wrote in her Introduction: 'Emma is a woman after my own heart. Indeed her heart could be mine. Or yours.'[1] To focus on this aspect, to compare the construction of (say) 'the feminine' in fictional representations with what we find in other discourses, can help us to reconstruct the relation between novel, context and experience. For such a criticism, fiction is just one more strand in the discursive web. Rather than seeking to apprehend some specifically cultural 'sublime', this approach suggests that novels are most rewardingly read when we stop singling them out as 'literature', and see them as not dissimilar from other kinds of writing.

Critics who foreground readings for identity have restored to currency some interesting literary works, and reminded us of the dialogic aspect of novel-writing and novel-reading.[2] However, to treat novels simply as instances of discourse is to neglect the fact that fiction has its own ways of signifying. The most developed ways of critical reading proper to the novel (but more fully available in more complex texts) allow, and require, the reader to engage with a 'writerly' or authorial point of view: to engage, then, with the imaginary activity of representation. It is because their authors constitute themselves as makers of a 'symbolic act' which represents not just character, but the world, that novels offer a transcendent perspective on the society they depict.[3]

This is not to claim that the reader must accept such authorial perspectives (must assent to Jane Austen's somewhat conservative views on 'sensibility', for example): we are as likely to quarrel with the author-in-the-text as to accede to her authority. It is, however, to argue that novels and other cultural texts are best read as complex acts of representation rather than as expressions of already existing 'identities'. This is one basis for criteria of evaluation which can discriminate between texts. More generally, it is because cultural works aim at that kind of general representation that 'the idea of culture' involves, as Raymond Williams put it, an 'effort at total qualitative assessment'.[4] In what follows, we give a fuller statement of this general argument, and illustrate it by considering two novels from the period 1790–1815, one Jacobin and one anti-Jacobin.

'A familiar relation of things'?

Novels published from the eighteenth century onwards have become central to the repertoire of valued texts kept current, as part of learned culture, through literary education in many anglophone countries; but most of their original readers will not have read them in that way. Much like TV soap operas today, novels – 'a new and rather shapeless literary kind, with little discipline and no classical tradition'[5] – tended at least until the late nineteenth century to be taken seriously insofar as they were taken as reflections on and arguments about the society in which they were made. This can be confirmed if one consults contemporary reviews of the major Victorian novelists.[6]

Given this status, and given that many novels offer 'a familiar relation of such things, as pass every day before our eyes' (to quote Clara Reeve's eighteenth-century definition in *The Progress of Romance*),[7] they do not seem to require a developed practice of reading, or indeed of writing, sensitive to aesthetic and epistemological questions. In her Preface to *The Memoirs of Emma Courtney* (1796), Mary Hays claims that 'every writer who advances principles, whether true or false, that have a tendency to set the mind in motion, does good', so making plain her adherence to the prevalent conception of the novel as didactic, argumentative and improving.[8] Hays' novel breaches many of the boundaries which we think of as separating the novel-text from neighbouring genres and discourses: she uses the authorial voice to make polemical assertions, frequently cites and quotes other authors (including Godwin, Rousseau, Helvétius, Wollstonecraft), and transcribes her personal correspondence verbatim into her text.[9] Hers is in some ways a special case, but there was nothing unusual in the broad assumption that fiction, as a mode of making personal and social experience available for reflection and of debating 'principles', is contiguous and overlapping with journalism, memoir, philosophical speculation and polemical argument.

A friend and associate of Wollstonecraft and of Godwin, Hays became celebrated, and was parodied, as a leading Jacobin and feminist. The reconstruction of the intertextual and associative network that connects her novels with other fictional and non-fictional writing of the 'revolutionary decade' and its aftermath can be taken as a paradigm of the kind of recent critical and scholarly labour that allows us to read, and teach, cultural texts in historical contexts.[10] The discursive formation is conceived in political and social as well as literary terms, and this, rather than 'literature' understood as a limited number of canonical texts chosen on aesthetic grounds, provides the main basis for intertextual juxtapositions and readings. The context is made newly accessible through a project of restoration and republication, which brings works back to attention through summary, paraphrase and reference, and (as with both Hays' and

Wollstonecraft's novels) restores to print texts unavailable since their original publication. Critics urge us to situate our own reading, including our re-reading of canonical novels, within this frame: the originality of Marilyn Butler's pioneering study *Jane Austen and the War of Ideas* lay in the way it situated *Sense and Sensibility* in a dialogue between Jacobin fictions, including those of Hays, and anti-Jacobin ripostes. 'Culture', though here restricted to written materials and thus to the communication of a literate minority, thus acquires something like the sociological and non-evaluative meaning that it has in contemporary cultural studies. Finally, the intellectual energy animating the scholarly endeavour is political: this is a feminist intervention, whose focus is set by a current sense of what needs to be interrogated, rethought and rediscovered rather than by an aesthetically inflected definition of cultural quality. If there is a teleology, its reference is to social and political history rather than to the constitution of anything like a literary 'great tradition'.

All this is premised on a more or less Foucauldian assumption about the social power of discourse in forming subjectivity, and on the related assumption that fictions signify and may be effective in much the same kinds of ways as other written interventions. We have seen that this was Hays' own belief and it remains among the governing beliefs of novelists through most of the nineteenth century. In the case of Enlightenment feminism, at least, there is every reason, a priori, to accept the presumption that novels, within what was an explicitly politicised discursive formation, contributed to a collective project with direct though very long-term social consequences. As Sartre puts it: 'If society sees itself and, in particular, sees itself as *seen* there is, by virtue of this very fact, a contesting of the established values of the regime.'[11] The writing of Hays and Wollstonecraft now seems a moment in the 'seeing' of the social construction of gender whose implications have continued to develop, unevenly enough (and pretty much *un*seen by the author of *What is Literature?*), ever since.

However, the fact that novels may be effective in ways that

invite us to read them alongside legal, medical, journalistic or political texts should not obscure the fact that they work in a distinctive mode. Fictions offer imaginary actions, resolutions, pleasures, and closures even as they represent 'familiar things'. Wollstonecraft, in her Preface to *Mary*, declares that she has written the novel to display 'the mind of a woman, who has thinking powers'; she notes that some have doubted whether women have strength for 'this arduous employment' (intellectual activity), but concludes, presumably with some irony, that 'without arguing physically about *possibilities* – in a fiction, such a being may be allowed to exist'.[12] That is, 'in a fiction' a desired state of things can be represented as actual, precisely in order that its possibility may be affirmed. At the same time, the persuasiveness of the affirmation depends on our being convinced of the work's having effectively grasped some truth of the social-historical moment: the novel's implicit realism tends (and even explicitly non-realist genres constitute only a partial exception) to make readers judge its 'fictions' by criteria which refer back to the 'physical possibilities' of experience.

Here we are touching on the largest questions about the kinds of truth and desire that mimesis and poiesis mobilise and represent, questions canvassed from Aristotle through Sidney to Shelley and beyond; and also, in our specific context of bourgeois more-or-less-realist novels, on the relations between fiction, ideology and social-historical being. As Fredric Jameson puts it:

> The symbolic act therefore begins by generating and producing its own context in the same moment of emergence in which it steps back from it . . . The literary work or cultural object, as though for the very first time, brings into being that very situation to which it is also, at one and the same time, a reaction.[13]

Realist novels, as a condition of their rhetorical effectiveness, have to produce a rendition of the social and historical 'situation to which they are a reaction': they must render things as they are in order to present things as they are not. Even where fictions have a didactic, critical or utopian dimension, realism is its grounding condition. 'Things as they are', 'man as he is', and 'man as he is not', 'the wrongs of woman' and 'the victim of prejudice' – titles and subtitles of five important Jacobin fictions of the revolutionary decade – all in different ways imply that the reader is to compare what is found in the novel with what is found in social experience.[14] The comparison is necessary to validate the authenticity of the fiction, as well as to enforce the conclusion that things might be otherwise.

This brings novels into close discursive relation with other kinds of writing, but in ways that require a dialectical understanding of fiction as both continuous with and distinct from 'textual production' in general. The self-realisation that fiction offers depends on the way it lets us participate in its meanings as simultaneously real and imaginary subjects; and the forms of identification which make us invest novels' outcomes with our own desire depend on a simultaneous indulgence of and resistance to their purely imagined status. As Wayne C. Booth puts it, 'the reader-in-the-text, at least when the text is what we call fictional, is *always* a double figure . . . both a credulous or "pretending" person, and a doubter.'[15]

This makes the novel, like other narrative modes, a powerful means for the expression of the desires, fantasies, frustrations or anger of readers who simply identify with the social subjects represented in the text. However, as we have noted, the novel represents not only particular embodied subjectivities but the intersubjective 'context' or 'situation'. The reader who only apprehends the text by way of his or her identification with characters has only a very limited means of grasping it as the imaginary representation of a historical moment. A more developed critical awareness explicitly interrogates a novel – formally, and in its relation to discourse and experience – as a representation. We can call this kind of awareness 'writerly' not because it should lead us to identify with the authorial figure created and implied in the text, but because it seeks to grasp as far as possible both the determining conditions of the writer's act and the nature of her or his imaginative and critical work.

The full development of that kind of reading, and its inculcation within the teaching of literature, comes only in the twentieth century, as literary modernism affects recently-inaugurated academic studies in modern languages and genres. (Modernism and the critical study of the novel can both be seen as reflecting and contributing to the metacultural self-awareness that develops as cultural mediation plays an ever larger part in making us who we are.) However, 'writerly' self-awareness, in the form of metafictional wit and explicit generic reflection, is of course found in fictions written long before modernism. Chaucer in *The Canterbury Tales* draws his own self-portrait as that of an incompetent poetaster whose 'drasty rhyming is nat worth a toord'.[16] We find metafictional reflection nearer Hays' day in Henry Fielding's preambles on novel-writing which open each Book of *Tom Jones* (1749): although most novelists of the later century approached fiction more pragmatically, as a capacious form into which heterogeneous elements could be crammed, Fielding's 'wit and learning' were singled out for praise – though his morals were deplored – in Clara Reeve's *The Progress of Romance* (1785). Reeve's book is itself further evidence of a critical awareness of genre and convention.[17] Sterne's inexorably metafictional *Tristram Shandy* (1760–1767) was very widely read in England, France and Germany.

A text more closely related to the novels we focus on here is Charlotte Lennox's *The Female Quixote*, published in 1752, and a favourite of Jane Austen's: 'The "Female Quixote" . . . now makes our evening amusement; to me a very high one, as I find the work quite equal to what I remembered it.'[18] Lennox's heroine, Arabella, devotes her time to the consumption of the 'great Store of Romances' in her father's library and to 'ranging like a Nymph through . . . the Woods and Lawns in which she was inclosed'. In consequence, 'her Ideas, from the Manner of her Life, and the Objects around her, had taken a romantic Turn; and, supposing Romances were real Pictures of Life, from them she drew all her Notions and Expectations.'[19] Lennox seeks to enforce the greater realism of her own imaginary text by contrasting it with the evident fantasies of romance (part of the interest of her novel lies, however, in how it shows why Arabella might find fantasy and romance attractive). Austen herself was, we judge from her work, at least as subtle as any of her predecessors in her sense of fictional form and convention, although her metafictional interventions (such as 'Let other pens dwell on guilt and misery')[20] are always succinct.

We must bring this discussion back to the question of culture and self-realisation. The novel-text in its dialogue with other discourses (including those of other novelists) is a form of pseudo-evidence, an argument, a claim: what we would now call an ideological intervention – transitive, socially purposive, tendentially didactic. Few of high realism's masterpieces, from *Sense and Sensibility* to *Anna Karenin* to *Middlemarch*, are without an ideological dynamic of some kind. The uses of culture in this mode, the self-realisation which it can enable, lie in the ways that the content of representation (say, the character of Wollstonecraft's Mary as 'a woman, who has thinking powers') can directly engage, challenge, support and extend the social consciousness of readers, in terms which are effective because they generate meanings that can be transposed from the imagined text into the social world. *The Memoirs of Emma Courtney* has been made readable in this way for new audiences today through the scholarly and critical restoration of historical and ideological contexts, and the related turn towards an understanding of fictional writing as social discourse rather than 'literature'. In these terms, identification of the reader with Hays' proto-feminist (and autobiographical) heroine offers the most obvious way into *Emma Courtney*.

However, a distinct form of self-realisation can come from the reader's critical participation in the moment of representation. We shall argue that Austen's *Sense and Sensibility* (1811) offers more than *Emma Courtney* to this second kind of reading, even though it is likely to be less sympathetic to many readers in that its characterisation was a conservative ideological riposte to

Jacobin ideals of 'progressives, sentimentalists [and] revolutionaries, with their optimism about man, and their preference for spontaneous personal impulse against rules imposed from without'.[21] At the apex of the hierarchy of voices that Austen orchestrates, we find the voice of an 'author' – the author-in-the-text – who has no counterpart in Hays' less complex fiction. It is not with any represented consciousness, but with this author, and with the authority of the closed text, that we enjoy our most productive and contentious engagements.

These two kinds of readerly engagement are coexistent rather than mutually exclusive, despite the tension between them. However, they are registered and fostered differentially by distinct forms of critical and pedagogical practice, which lead readers to relish different forms of pleasure and knowledge. The abstraction of texts from immediate contexts and the use of a critical terminology that foregrounds formal rather than ideological qualities was central to the post-Arnoldian construction of literary and cultural canons: 'culture' and 'literature', in this understanding, were intrinsically qualitative terms, and the purpose of education was to develop the cultured person as one who makes the right selections and discriminations. This approach to texts was in many ways reductive; but in its insistence on aesthetic, expressive and formal qualities, it acknowledged the importance of the writer's act of representation. The substantial work of representation tends by contrast to be ignored in readings-for-identity and sociological conceptions of authorless 'cultural production'; it is lost sight of in the emphasis on intertextuality and on discourse as an anonymous form or medium of power which is characteristic of cultural studies. In refusing claims of cultural transcendence as some special quality of the literary text, in seeing 'literature' as an illusory category ('"Literature" is, in effect, being recognised as the construct of a criticism which . . . has so constituted Literature as to reproduce and naturalise bourgeois ideology as "literary value"'),[22] radical criticism also risks ignoring the image of transcendence which is present in the writer's act.

Art and culture are not ultimately transcendent of their moment or context, any more than are the discourses of criticism or of politics. But what is specific to cultural self-realisation (we are arguing) is its relation to some totalising act or art. Beyond any element of identification with character, novel-readers participate in the making of textual meaning in their engagement with the moment of representation. Our discussion of Austen and Hays in the rest of this chapter is intended as a detailed exemplification of this point about readerly engagements.

'Emma Courtney' and 'Jane Austen'

Since Mary Hays' novel *The Memoirs of Emma Courtney* (1796) is unlikely to be familiar to most of our readers, we must begin with a brief summary. We will also summarise recent scholarship which indicates the extent to which Hays and Austen are working within common fictional and ideological parameters.

Emma Courtney is a first-person narrative consisting mostly of the reflections, self-analyses and correspondence of the heroine. Brought up by her aunt after the death of her mother, Emma acquires some literary culture through her visits to her father's library. Here, disappointed in her search for more of the 'adventurous tales' and 'romances' which she has devoured since childhood, she begins to acquaint herself with historical and theological learning. Her father has advised her (in what looks like an intertextual reference to Lennox's *Female Quixote*, whose heroine is another romance-reader comically prone to such 'mistakes'): 'Your fancy requires a *rein* rather than a *spur*. Your studies, for the future, must be of a soberer nature, or I shall have you mistake my valet for a prince in disguise, and my rational care for your future for barbarous tyranny.'[23] However, Emma finds Rousseau:

> In the course of my researches, the Heloise of Rousseau fell into my hands. – Ah! with what transport, with what enthusiasm, did

> I peruse this dangerous, enchanting work! – How shall I paint the sensations that were excited in my mind . . . Mr Courtney, one day, surprised me weeping over the sorrows of the tender St Preux [Heloise's tutor]. He hastily snatched the book from my hand, and, carefully collecting the remaining volumes, carried them in silence to his chamber: but the impression made upon my mind was never to be effaced – it was even productive of a long chain of consequences, that will continue to operate till the day of my death.[24]

When some time later Emma stays with Mrs Harley, an idealised mother-figure, she falls in love with the portrait of Mrs Harley's son Augustus:

> All the strong affections of my soul seemed concentrated to a single point . . . He was the St Preux, the Emilius, of my sleeping and waking reveries . . . I was compelled to acknowledge . . . that . . . I loved an ideal object (for such was Augustus Harley to me) with a tender and fervent excess; an excess, perhaps, involving all my future usefulness and welfare.[25]

The narrative then traces the progress, or rather the thwarting, of Emma's 'excessive' love, as she meets, and later sends numerous letters to, the largely unresponsive Augustus. Scholars believe that these letters are based on Hays' own letters to William Frend, of Jesus College, Cambridge, with whom she fell in love: we know that Emma's correspondence with the fictional Mr Franklin, from whom she seeks emotional and philosophical advice, is a transcription of that between Hays and Franklin's model, William Godwin.[26] In her letters and in her reflections, Emma vacillates between condemning and approving her own emotional unrestraint. Hays conceded later that although it had been intended 'not as an *example*, but as a *warning*', the character of Emma had been taken by many readers as 'recommending those excesses, of which I laboured to present the disastrous effects'.[27]

Augustus Harley eventually reveals that he is already secretly married. The novel concludes with a series of improbable, rapidly narrated and melodramatic actions. Emma, now the wife of her long-time suitor Mr Montague, whom she can esteem but does not love passionately, is alone with her baby and domestic servants when Augustus, whose wife (it transpires) has died, is desperately injured in a coach accident as he happens to be passing through the town. He is brought to Emma's door. She nurses him tenderly but at length he dies in her arms, confessing he has always loved her. Montague, consumed with jealousy at her tenderness to his old rival, seduces the servant in revenge, and later murders their illegitimate infant before shooting himself in his room – not before writing a thousand-word valediction to Emma in which he acknowledges how ill he has requited her 'heavenly goodness' and ends by hailing her as 'first, and last, and only beloved of women'.[28] Emma adopts Augustus's young son, also called Augustus, and brings him up as her own: the framing device in which the novel is enclosed presents Emma's narrative as the account given to the now adult Augustus of his hitherto unknown parentage.

This summary perhaps explains why even sympathetic literary historians have until recently been content to pass *Emma Courtney* over with a brief reference: 'an odd, pathetic, ludicrous and, for moments, noble book'.[29] At the same time, it may have begun to suggest how Hays and Austen can be seen as interlocutors in a common moral and ideological discourse. 'Sensibility', the key term in this, is referred to directly in the title of *Sense and Sensibility* (1811), and implicitly in the surname of Hays' Augustus Harley: Harley was the name of the hero of Henry MacKenzie's *The Man of Feeling* (1771), which along with Rousseau's *Nouvelle Héloïse* and Goethe's *Sorrows of Young Werther* was among the most important texts of the literary sentimentalism fashionable in the later eighteenth century.[30] Sentimental excess had been the target of conservative novelists before Austen. In particular, Jane West's *A Gossip's Story* (1796), whose characters include a self-indulgently emotional younger sister named Marianne, appeared about the time Austen was working on the unpublished first draft of *Sense and Sensibility* and has been seen as a direct influence on its conception.[31] Although in the published version Austen probably softened the schematic contrast between 'sense' and 'sensibility', the novel still reflects an engagement, not indeed with Hays or Wollstonecraft directly – there is no evidence that Austen read either[32] – but with the spontaneist ethos of romantic radicalism. Wollstonecraft's Mary, writing a 'rhapsody on sensibility' as 'the most exquisite feeling of which the human soul is susceptible', as that which 'expands the soul, and gives an enthusiastic greatness', is obviously akin both to Emma Courtney ('Rousseau was right, when he asserted that ". . . Energy of sentiment is the characteristic of a noble soul"') and to Marianne Dashwood: 'eager in every thing . . . generous, amiable, interesting . . . anything but prudent'.[33]

Hays' Emma and Austen's Marianne are both enthusiastic readers who form their conduct on the basis of a literary and cultural ideal of spontaneous feeling; both regard themselves as entitled, by their greater sensibility, to some exemption from conventional expectations, while being aware that (to quote one of Emma's letters) 'the deviation of a solitary individual from *rules* sanctioned by usage, by prejudice, by expediency, would be regarded as romantic';[34] both suffer because their commitment to spontaneity leads to emotional and sexual self-exposure. Both novels are metacultural in that the authors (and their heroines) recognise 'sensibility' as a cultural discourse; both appear to have in view a similar intention, namely to warn of its perils, but both produce equivocal texts in which the reader's identification with the character embodying sensibility works against this didactic aim.[35] It is only by resolving this equivocation in opposite directions that we can read Hays as a radical Enlightenment optimist, committed to 'fervent excess' despite the damage this can do, and Austen as a Christian conservative, sceptical about the virtues of spontaneous feeling even though she registers the irksome constraints of social propriety.

These opposed resolutions are authorised by the most fundamental structural distinction between the novels. Emma's voice wholly dominates the *Memoirs* because the other characters exist only in relation to her, and the complete identity of protagonist and narrator leaves no space for any separate authorial presence: as a result, Emma's own 'excessive' emotion mediates even her self-reproaches. By contrast, Marianne's position in *Sense and Sensibility*, although many readers will be drawn towards it in sympathy, is subordinate both to the rhetorically more privileged – and closely aligned – positions of Elinor and the narrator, and to an overall complexity of tone and perspective which forces the reader to assess all positions relative to others. It is with the creation of this complex perspectival effect, and not just of the narrative voice, that we must credit the author whom this more writerly reading must acknowledge: 'the subtlest technician among English novelists', she has been called.[36] We might say that whereas Mary Hays creates 'Emma Courtney', Jane Austen creates 'Jane Austen'. There is evidently a connection between the excellence and consequent canonical status of Austen's novel, its complex internal voicing, and its tendentially conservative relativising of all subjective claims based on 'identity'.

We can see Hays and Austen as ideological antagonists in a debate between Jacobin radicals and anti-Jacobin conservatives. Neither of them, however, is able to resolve their ambivalence about the meanings of sensibility for women. Both Marianne and Emma believe they will realise themselves only if they trust the authenticity of their 'excessive' feelings, and reading either novel requires a degree of sympathetic identification with this belief. Yet these feelings are diagnosed as the construction of dangerous discourses, and their effect is to imprison the heroines rather than to emancipate them: Marianne most resembles Emma when she is most abjectly in love, sending desperate notes to the unresponsive Willoughby. Irrespective of whether they offer an explicit or coherent analysis, both novels, in this unresolved ambivalence, reflect the social conditions which made 'sensibility' important for women and tended to make it a central preoccupation of their writing. Feeling was not coded as exclusively feminine: MacKenzie's Harley and Goethe's Werther were important male exemplars,[37] and while within the middle class men obviously enjoyed far more social autonomy than women, it does not follow that they might not feel powerless in relation to their feelings and desires. However, as a term connoting sexual desire, 'sensibility' carried especially contradictory meanings for women. For a woman 'sexual relations both inside and outside marriage [were] likely to involve denigration and degradation',[38] but women were likely to dwell on feeling because they had few opportunities for action or decision, and – if they were 'respectable' – none of the opportunities for premarital and casual sex that respectable men enjoyed. The only issue in which genteel young women were likely to exercise much power over their social fates was the right to refuse, and exceptionally to choose, a marriage-partner;[39] and the centrality of marriage-choices to the plots of women's novels reflects this. Such women made use of fiction, as both readers and writers, on a scale unprecedented for any other cultural form partly because its intimate, domestic and sentimental preoccupations made it answerable to their needs.[40] However, these limitations of scope were just what made the novel a 'feminine' genre, one which did not transgress gendered literary and intellectual hierarchies. 'Inquiry into abstract and speculative truths, into the principles and axioms of sciences' was not the province of women, Rousseau had declared. But fiction-writing might be seen as an exercise of feminine capacities – 'not the argumentative but the sentimental talents, which give [women] . . . insight . . . into the human heart', to quote the Reverend James Fordyce.[41] The feminisation of the novel runs in tandem with the domestication of middle-class women, ideologically and economically, from the last decades of the eighteenth century onwards: literate women might become novelists, though few would earn much by doing so, but other occupations they might once have followed were being taken over by men (Wollstonecraft's and Hays' middle-class heroines lament the difficulty of finding suitable employment in London).[42] The bourgeois domestic ideal of high Victorianism, with its rigorous allocation of gentlewomen to the private sphere, is foreshadowed here.[43]

The connection between women, sensibility and fiction has therefore an ambiguous and contradictory import, summed up in Jane Spencer's remark: 'If eighteenth-century English fiction is arguably gynocentric, eighteenth- and early nineteenth-century English society was emphatically not'.[44] The underlying social contradiction – the intimate, affective domain which is cultivated as the woman's social and cultural sphere is also the territory of her restriction – explains why romance and the celebration of sensibility were and remain important in genres used by women, even as their attractions are exposed as equivocal or delusive. This long historical perspective, in which both our texts can be seen to exemplify at a deeper level some of the contradictions which their narratives explore, was by definition not fully available to their time-bound authors. In that sense, there is no transcendence, and vision is necessarily limited: both Hays and Austen can be seen as the immediate producers of cultural texts whose determining conditions exceeded authorial awareness and intention. The two novels provide comparable kinds of cultural-historical evidence about social consciousness: Hays' ideological perspective as a contributor to metropolitan intellectual debate can be compared with Austen's as a dependent member of a rural gentry family.

Reading, identification, and the symbolic act

How might we distinguish the kinds of self-realisation which reading these two novels might afford? We have already suggested that while on one level this is a matter of the identifications the texts allow us to make within a common ideological matrix, at another level we have also to think about the respective authors' engagement with the act of representation.

Hays has been seen to offer a feminist point of identification in the character of Emma. *Emma Courtney* was first republished by Pandora, in 1986, and in her Introduction Sally Cline wrote: 'This novel speaks to me across [the] timespan [of 190 years], and it will speak to most women I know. Emma is a woman after my own heart.'[45] Emma's diagnosis of the highly contradictory relation to her own 'fervent and tender excess' in which she is caught up is intransigent and far-reaching. It includes the perception that enforced inactivity in 'the great, though often absurd and tragical drama of life', and confinement to 'the insipid *routine* of heartless, mindless intercourse', tends to leave spirited and energetic women little scope for self-realisation: 'hence the eccentricities of conduct, with which women of superior minds have been accused.'[46] *Sense and Sensibility* similarly implies – indeed, shows – that the routines of genteel sociability may be stifling, but suggests that this is a fate which must be negotiated rather than eccentrically refused: for every Marianne who thinks herself exempted from the demands of tedious courtesy, there must be an Elinor, no less intelligent but more sensitive, on whom 'the whole task of telling lies when politeness requires it' will always fall.[47] Crucially, Austen does not see the domestic and marital sphere within which her heroines remain as necessarily inadequate: it is a matter of choosing the right marriage, and thus the right framework for being a wife. Within this, time can be divided between charitable works, domestic supervision, familial and social intercourse, and the reading in which all Austen's heroines delight. Marianne's error was to trust Willoughby too ingenuously and choose wrongly. Emma Courtney pushes her self-analysis beyond these limits when she asks herself – disconnectedly and inconclusively, but keenly – whether she is not trying to 'preserve [herself] from . . . *languor and inanity*' by pursuing romantic sexual love:

> The mind must have an object: – should I desist from my present pursuit [i.e., her love for Harley], after all it has cost me, for what

> can I change it? I feel, that I am neither a philosopher, nor a heroine – but a *woman, to whom education has given a sexual character*. It is true, I have risen superior to the generality of my *oppressed* sex; yet, I have neither the talents for a legislator, nor for a reformer, of the world . . . Ambition cannot stimulate me, and to accumulate wealth, I am still less fitted. Should I, then, do violence to my heart, and compel it to resign its hopes and expectations, what can preserve me from sinking into, the most abhorred of all states, *languor and inanity*? Alas, that tender and faithful heart refuses to change its object – it can never love another.[48]

'Affections like these' (she reflects later) 'are not so much weakness, as strength perhaps badly exerted.'[49]

The historical and political perspective we have been taking offers a reading for identity, based on a feminist intertextual and conceptual supplementation of the terms in which Emma's proto-feminist consciousness expresses itself. In such a perspective Hays is as interesting a novelist as Austen, perhaps more interesting, given her close connection with Wollstonecraft and Godwin and the ways in which her work can be seen as integral to the radical moment of the revolutionary decade. She *sees* more, politically; does more to make us see ourselves as seen. The phrase 'a woman, to whom education has given a sexual character' invokes the feminist arguments appearing in the same decade as *Emma Courtney*, which included an *Appeal to the Men of Great Britain in Behalf of Women* now often attributed to Hays.[50] Following Wollstonecraft, Hays invokes Enlightenment ideas about the influence of education and environment on character in a narrative which forces us to consider gender as a social rather than a natural fact. By doing so in a sentimental fiction she confronts and dramatises the subjective contradictions between feminist insight and feminine susceptibility. That Emma hardly gets the better of these contradictions, even in thought, is part of the text's meaning, as in the similar case of Wollstonecraft's *The Wrongs of Woman, or Maria*, where (as Mary Poovey puts it) 'the narrator – and, by implication, Wollstonecraft herself – [falls]

victim to the very delusion it is the object of the novel to criticize': that is, the delusion that romantic love of a man will bring happiness.[51]

The unmanaged contradictions of Hays' novel, like its explicit and lavish intertextuality, its expostulatory and polemical style, its free use of directly autobiographical materials and its metonymic continuity with private discourses and their occasions, take us at every point from the text to other texts, to the biographical author, to ourselves and to the world. By the same token, they compromise its self-sufficiency, and thus its status in terms of classical literary standards. Hays' editor Eleanor Ty suggests we might read *Emma Courtney* as an instance of 'autonarration', a genre which sets out explicitly to raise the question of the relations between fictional narrative and lived experience.[52]

Sense and Sensibility, like the rest of Austen's fiction, exemplifies an antithetical conception of the novel, in which the text's closure and coherence (as well as its observance of criteria of probability which the wish-fulfilling elements in Hays' 'autonarration' merely flout)[53] are central to the aesthetic pleasures it affords and also to its project of representation. Recall the remark of Jameson:

> The symbolic act therefore begins by generating and producing its own context in the same moment of emergence in which it steps back from it . . . The literary work or cultural object, as though for the very first time, brings into being that very situation to which it is also, at one and the same time, a reaction.

Relative to Hays, Austen works much harder at constituting, within her novel, a convincing and objectified image of the historical 'situation'. One important measure of this has already been mentioned: the diversity of characters, the fact that they can be seen from diverse perspectives, and the constitution of an authorial position clearly distinct from that of any protagonist. (This can be described in technical or generic terms, but we should be clear that it is an intellectual achievement dependent on the exercise of exceptional intelligence, judgement and – to use the Joycean word – cunning.) Austen's novels are symbolic acts which themselves produce meaning of a kind which those of Hays cannot. This is because they offer the possibility of complex and dialectical readings within the space of the text, and because they require and reward a practice of reading attentive to this perspectival quality. Wolfgang Iser's is perhaps the best-known account of the phenomenology of reading. In *Prospecting*, he describes the reader's creation of meaning thus:

> As the reader's wandering viewpoint travels between all these segments [of the text], its constant switching during the time flow of reading intertwines them, thus bringing forth a network of perspectives, within which each perspective opens a view not only of others but also of the intended imaginary object. Hence no single textual perspective can be equated with this imaginary object, of which it forms only one aspect. The object itself is a product of interconnection, the structuring of which is to a great extent regulated and controlled by blanks.[54]

Iser's description is of a practice of reading that works much better for certain kinds of text: complex, writerly, canonical. It is not necessarily the practice of all actual readers. Norman Holland, one of Iser's interlocutors, objects that while 'many readings, particularly by critics' answer to Iser's description, according to which reading 'consists of building some consistent, explanatory reality', plenty of readers don't attend to texts in that way.[55] However, those who stop short of that effort only engage with part of what the text means. We may well want to dissent from the terms in which the 'consistent reality' of the writerly novel is authorised – to note, for instance (as Raymond Williams noted), the ways in which the 'knowable community' of Austen's novels is created by systematically excluding from view those who lack wealth; or more generally to deplore the limited socio-geographical scope of this whole novelistic formation[56] – but we need to establish them first. To criticise as well as to appreciate literature requires that we engage with texts not simply as places where identities are registered, but as acts of representation whose complex imaginary transcendence involves offering among other 'imaginary objects' an objectified image of their own historical situation. It is in these terms that we can defend some idea of the cultural 'sublime', and resist the reduction of novels to discourse.

4

Culture and self-realisation: realist engagements

In this chapter, we consider a group of novels representing characters who seek self-realisation in culture. In many of them, the pursuit of culture – whether or not it is successful – changes the protagonist's relation to the world: to acquire culture means to place oneself beyond, above or outside the everyday life of society. If in its classic form the English *Bildungsroman* (novel of formation) 'linked the individual's moral, spiritual, and psychological maturation with his economic and social advancement',[1] these later novels, whose heroes mostly seek cultural transcendence rather than worldly advance, stress the incompatibility of that desire with the existing social order: neither 'maturation' nor 'advancement', but isolation – and in several cases (Jude Fawley, Martin Eden, Leonard Bast), destruction or self-destruction.

Writing and culture may be defined in terms of the intrinsic value of what they offer us, and also in terms of their social co-ordinates and functions. When learned culture is pursued by those whom it has excluded, its social meaning insistently registers alongside its aesthetic and spiritual claims. Jack London's autobiographical hero Martin Eden is a proletarian autodidact who discovers Swinburne and oil-painting at the price of being 'overwhelmed with consciousness of the awkward figure he was cutting' in a genteel drawing-room.[2] Jude Fawley, told to 'remain in his sphere and stick to his trade', can only reply in Biblical graffiti: 'I have understanding as well as you', he chalks on the

College wall, but he cannot get in.[3] The culture sought by Jude, Martin and others has for them an intrinsic value and offers a self-realisation that is prized above worldly advancement, but its pursuit leads to social isolation and unhappiness. Even those whose quest for culture is motivated by social as well as intellectual or spiritual aspirations may find that it brings little practical advantage. Walking the south London streets in search of work, Nancy Lord (in George Gissing's *In the Year of Jubilee*) reflects:

> In the battle of life every girl who could work a sewing-machine was of more account than she. If she entered a shop to make purchases, the young women at the counter seemed to smile superiority. Of what avail her 'education', her 'culture'? The roar of myriad industries made mocking laughter at such futile pretensions. She shrank back into her suburban home.[4]

Matthew Arnold's claim that culture 'seeks to do away with classes' and offers an ideal that is above class – 'the best that has been thought and known' – is doubly tested.[5] The culture these characters seek may be fenced off to prevent their access; if they manage to break in, it may prove disorienting and destructive as well as enlightening. It is this complex relationship between cultural aspiration, social mobility and personal fulfilment which we trace here. No simple diagram of their mutual bearings emerges – partly because the novelists have different perspectives, and partly because the relationship is revealed as inherently contradictory: individuals can indeed value cultural ideals for their own sake, but they exist socially only within the hierarchies in which they are embedded.

The fact that these themes become central in a number of novels published in the late nineteenth and early twentieth centuries reflects the opening up during these decades of educational opportunities to people outside the established cultural élite. We concentrate on works by Thomas Hardy, George Gissing, Jack London and H.G. Wells, who all came from relatively obscure backgrounds.[6] Some have autobiographical elements and give a version of the author's literary apprenticeship and social ascent.

All address general questions about the relationship between culture, social mobility, commerce and democracy. In discussing them, our first aim is illustrative and historical. This was the period when the gradual introduction of universal adult suffrage made citizens formally equal, and widening (though still very restricted) educational opportunity began to make the idea of a democratic culture thinkable. But of course economic inequalities have remained, as has the division of labour, whose forms have become more complex but which offers most citizens little or no chance to develop or use their intellectual and aesthetic faculties at work. These novels, in which cultural aspiration is the dynamic of social self-making, test the viability of the abstract cultural ideal by setting it in that material and psychological context.

They also deploy a developing idea of culture as the basis for autonomous critical judgement. Culture is not just the inspiration of their protagonists, but also the basis of the author's critical authority. As readers, we may identify with the protagonist and also with the author-in-the-text who represents and judges their search. The sometimes problematic relationship between these two positions is a further theme of this chapter.

Cultural opportunity: 'continual aspiration'?

In the decades following the publication of *Culture and Anarchy* (1869), educational developments might seem to have been preparing the ground for the realisation of Arnold's ideal of a culture beyond class. The 1870 Education Act pointed the way towards free and universal elementary education, which was secured by subsequent legislation in 1876, 1880 and 1891. From the mid-century, provincial colleges of the University of London (itself founded in 1832) were gradually widening access to formal higher education, though this remained restricted to a small minority, by gender as well as by class: only in 1878 did women become eligible to take London degrees, and they remained excluded from graduation at Oxford and Cambridge for many years after the foundation in the 1870s of the first women's colleges there. Complementing the older-established Mechanics' Institutes (now increasingly devoted to accredited technical and scientific preparation), University adult education was bringing travelling lecturers to locally-based voluntary organisations from the 1850s onwards. This was placed on a formal footing with the setting up of extra-mural Syndicates and Delegacies at Cambridge, London and Oxford in the 1870s. University extension, declared one of the first Cambridge lecturers, R.G. Moulton, would become 'a sort of stream that runs from the mountain tops of the University . . . over the whole land, and everybody helps himself as he can'. Late in the nineteenth century, the various branches of the new socialist movement placed great emphasis on education, organising Socialist Sunday Schools and Adult Schools and putting out widely-circulated 'Fabian tracts, Fabian book-boxes, and I.L.P., S.D.F., and Secularist pamphlets'.[7]

The State played the central role, responding to social and political demands. After the franchise was extended in the Second Reform Bill (1867), the ruling class decided 'we must educate our masters', in the phrase attributed to Robert Lowe, vice-president of the Committee of Council on Education.[8] Educational measures from the 1870s onwards complemented successive extensions of the franchise under organised pressure from working-class, feminist and socialist campaigns. The Trades Union Congress was founded in 1871, the Social Democratic Federation in 1891, the Independent Labour Party in 1893, the Women's Social and Political Union in 1903.[9] As well as playing their part in gaining new educational entitlements, working-class organisations pressed for reductions in working hours and better holidays. The 1870 Bank Holidays Act was one milestone (and covered even employees in non-unionised occupations). By the last decade of the nineteenth century, an increasing number of firms offered annual paid holidays, though legislation to require this was not implemented until the 1940s.[10] J. Walvin sums these developments up as follows:

> The . . . emergence of the shorter working week and Saturday free from work was slow, fragmentary and uneven and did not reach the unskilled until the later years of the [nineteenth] century. But it is revealing that when in 1897 the Webbs debated working hours in their book *Industrial Democracy*, they accepted eight hours as 'the Natural Day'.[11]

These legislative and political developments were not, of course, sufficient to give the majority the educational and cultural opportunities enjoyed by the leisured and professional classes. Nor was that their intention. Novels by Hardy, Gissing and Wells point to the inadequate scale of educational provision and its defective nature and quality, at times anticipating the view of a subsequent radical historian that 'educational reforms were carefully managed by the new ruling class coalition in order to maintain class distinctions and to preserve privilege'.[12] Gissing and Wells have some memorable school scenes, illustrating the limitations of elementary classrooms and the empty pretensions of more genteel establishments (though Gissing's hostility towards elementary education after 1870 can seem sometimes to imply that no education at all should have been provided for the masses).[13] Jude's rebuff at the hands of Christminster emphasised that higher education was still a very exclusive business. Lack of time and the stress of tedious or exhausting work are shown as drastically curtailing adults' opportunity to study, formally or informally. Martin Eden sets his alarm to keep his nightly sleep down to five hours, and we see him 'batting his head savagely' as he struggles in vain to keep awake and read at the end of a fifteen-hour day in the steam laundry where he works.[14] Kipps, like Hoopdriver in *The Wheels of Chance* and like Wells himself, is apprenticed to a retail draper: he starts work at six-thirty in the morning and is kept busy until beyond nine in the evening, after which (the narrator ironically comments) 'the rest of the day was entirely at his disposal for reading, recreation and the improvement of his mind . . .'[15] Jude Fawley's work as a stonemason is quite congenial, and he finds time to read and think; but when Forster rewrote the character as Leonard Bast and transformed the footloose Arabella into the all-too-constant Jacky, he presented the combination of confined domestic space and mechanical clerkly labour as overwhelming Leonard's rather feeble spirit: 'Oh, it was no good, this continual aspiration . . . To see life steadily and to see it whole was not for the likes of him.'[16]

The Arnoldian phrase about 'seeing life steadily'[17] reminds us that *Howards End*, like *Jude*, can be read as a quasi-documentary exploration of the viability of Arnoldian cultural ideals: imagining a protagonist who lives for culture, but lacks leisure and opportunity, the novelist exposes the ill fit between ideal and actuality. The 'tragedy of unfulfilled aims'[18] which results can be seen as indicting society for its failure to provide educational openings. Even where their tone (as in Forster's case) is equivocal or sceptical, and although they mostly lack detailed accounts of educational practices and institutions, all our texts contribute to a critical, realist portrait of the opportunities and difficulties met with by those seeking cultural self-improvement around the end of the nineteenth century. In such a reading, the culture-seeking protagonists are representative figures: pioneers, rather than typical members of their class, but forerunners in a track where others will follow. 'It was my poverty and not my will that consented to be beaten. It takes two or three generations to do what I tried to do in one,' says Jude.[19] Social-democratic progress since the early twentieth century has made education more widely and less unequally accessible, so these fictions have been prophetic as well as critical. However, a reading that stops there, at their implications for social policy and educational opportunity, fails to take the measure of what they represent, which is something more intransigent but also more contradictory. Our own discussion will take their progressive social-policy implications for granted (recognising how fortunate we are to be able to so do), and focus instead on the less explicit, more problematic dynamic of 'culture' as transcendence.

Before we turn to the texts, we need to remind ourselves that while state education was evolving towards a broadly Arnoldian model of 'cultural diffusionism',[20] where good culture as defined by educationists would be made much more widely available than ever before, culture itself was becoming more diverse and commercial. Educational legislation in the decades after 1870, which laid some long-term foundations for the building of a cultural democracy, had the immediate effect of enlarging the occupational group of non-manual workers. By the end of the century, this included the clerks, secretaries, journalistic entrepreneurs, and advertising salesmen and copy-writers who figure in *In the Year of Jubilee*. Richard Altick writes that 'the amorphous stratum between the old-established middle class . . . and the working class proper' grew rapidly during the nineteenth century, and this had 'special significance in the history of the reading public' since it was from this 'amorphous stratum' that many new readers came.[21] Beyond the margins of the middle class, literacy and book-buying were spreading among poorer people who lacked the cultural capital that had formerly tended to accompany the desire to read. The final decades of the century saw a cheapening of books and a commercialisation of literary marketing which encouraged the diversification of the reading public.[22]

Increasing free time did not just give a studiously inclined worker a little more opportunity to read and think; it opened new markets for commercially organised leisure. The nature of free time was in any case being transformed by technological changes, though their full effects would be felt only in the next century. The years between Gissing's twentieth and fortieth birthdays (1878 and 1898) saw the opening of the London telephone exchange, the first practical applications of electric power, the perfection of the 'ordinary' bicycle and the introduction of the pneumatic-tired 'safety', the first internal combustion engine, the inauguration of the London underground and the first aeroplane flight.[23] Cultural activity of whatever kind would from now on take its place in lives whose pace and variousness had no precedent. Many new forms of culture were not presented or experienced as means to intellectual self-development, and were associated neither with the abundant leisure and extended education of the well-to-do nor with specialised preparation for the learned professions. They met the need for entertainment and relaxation, on the margins of a life dominated by the rhythms of work. Culture-as-leisure included new kinds of reading matter, such as the weekly papers Gissing parodied in the 'Chit-Chat' of *New Grub Street* (based on Newnes' *Tit-Bits*, founded in 1880 and soon followed by similar publications from Harmsworth and Pearson).[24] It also included quite new activities – watching professional sport, taking seaside holidays, visiting the music hall or the shopping arcade – which, even before the rise of film, radio and television, were competing with older forms of popular and learned culture.[25]

His engagement with these changes gives Gissing's work much of its special interest. *New Grub Street* is a comprehensive picture of the new cultural market-place from the literary producer's point of view, and *In the Year of Jubilee* has much to say about the audience. Gissing's habitual disdain for those who enjoyed new cultural forms is unattractive, but he was prescient in grasping how these innovations would call into question the pertinence of traditional (or perhaps we should say, newly reified), Arnoldian ideas of culture – and would challenge the currency of literary practices, including his own, premised on careful and reflective reading.

The other writers we have mentioned, with the exception of Wells, have less to say about commercial culture, and tend to accept as axiomatic the assumption that cultural self-realisation comes from the pursuit of established excellence. *Martin Eden*, for instance, defers to British and European literature despite its Californian provenance and setting: when he names the British Ambassador 'Sir John Value', and has him pronounce that there are 'no poets in America', London may seem to be parodying establishment attitudes, but the poem that is to prove Sir John wrong, Brissenden's 'Ephemera', complies (so far as one can judge) with traditional canons of poetical 'value'.[26] However, even when they take 'culture' to mean learned culture many of these works register the split between 'high' and 'popular' that was reflected in the self-constitution of literary modernism, and was to become central in twentieth-century cultural policy and academic criticism.

The diversification and commercialisation of culture is of crucial importance for the ways these novels represent cultural self-realisation. To claim that everyone should realise themselves in an engagement with learned culture is to defend educational democracy, insofar as it is to insist that 'the best that has been known and thought' should be universally available. It is also to assert that some cultural forms and texts are more deserving than others of our serious attention. When they proclaim culture's emancipatory potential, literary writers can be seen as upholding the educational rights of previously excluded citizens. They can be seen also as policing popular pleasures and enjoining deference to the kinds of culture that writers and educated people have found congenial – so epitomising the 'paternalistic' aspect of social democracy, the belief that a benevolent élite should guide the development of popular needs, including especially cultural needs, which cannot safely be left to the marketplace.

The narratives we are considering expose cultural ideals to the test of social difference and subjective experience, rather than assuming that their appeal and meaning are unproblematically universal. Nonetheless they tend to figure authentic cultural self-realisation (as opposed to the socially-instrumental show of 'culture' which Gissing, especially, depicts) in ways reflective of their authors' 'writerly' understanding of selfhood. The authorial position created in the text is always important in articulating or implying cultural norms and standards, especially in novels sceptical or ironic about their characters' aspirations. The absolute nature of protagonists' cultural desires and the positions some of them come to occupy – self-marginalised, outside but also in some sense above the everyday – reflect the transcendence associated with the authorial imagination. Authorial positions in the novels are as important as their narrative and characterisation (and are sometimes in tension with these) in registering and contesting the wider cultural politics of this period, in which the currency of minority or élite genres and performances is challenged by new demotic forms. In the case of other cultural media (music, painting), and even of other literary genres (poetry), the specialised skills and formation of artists are taken for granted, but the novel's public everyday concerns and its discursive closeness to other kinds of writing makes overt artistic self-differentiation there more problematic. As the novelist's voice becomes more audibly identified with 'culture', it might seem to remove itself further from readers in their actual social positions.

Some of these texts, deconstructed, might even be held to make 'culture' a token in the relation between the growing popular readership and the literary intellectuals, who (from Arnold on) deploy cultural discourse to shore up their own threatened prestige.[27] This is a reductive view: these novels explore the cultural ideal in the spirit of Arnold's dictum that 'the idea of culture is the *social* idea', and test as well as affirm notions of cultural value.[28] There is no doubt, however, that taken together they must be read both as representing (and often defending) democratic claims to culture and education, and as expressing – consciously or otherwise – the grounds on which literary intellectuals were coming to identify themselves as what Bourdieu has called 'the dominated fraction within the dominant class'.[29] The 'dominated fraction' sought to distinguish itself, often by invoking aesthetic and cultural norms, both from the ruling-class entrepreneurial bourgeoisie and from the petty-bourgeois suburban crowd. We can see this kind of authorial self-positioning in novels as different as *New Grub Street*, *Martin Eden* and *Howards End*. *Vis-à-vis* the crowd, writers may well deploy anti-democratic cultural discourses: which is not to say that their critique of popular or mass culture, then or now, reduces to this aspect of self-vindication. Cultural discrimination and self-positioning have to be understood and evaluated dialectically as responses to a historical situation which was new, rapidly changing, and visible only in its emergent outline; and any account of these novels has to deal much in contradictions; as indeed do the novels themselves.

In the Year of Jubilee and *Martin Eden*

We shall be drawing on a dozen novels published between 1876 and 1910 (all but two of them between 1891 and 1910).[30] The best-known of these – *New Grub Street* (1891), *Jude the Obscure* (1896), and *Howards End* (1910) – will be familiar to many of our readers; and to several of the others we shall refer only in passing. Here we offer a critical commentary on two less well-known novels, *In the Year of Jubilee* and *Martin Eden*, indicating their leading themes and questions and so initiating our more general historical exploration.

In the Year of Jubilee (1894) deals with a number of topics already noted: the education of women, the uses of inherited culture in contemporary conditions, writing in its commercial and aesthetic aspects, the development of the 'suburban' way of life. These are broached through a carefully differentiated group of characters who represent distinct social types and variations within these. While the text mediates some stridently held prejudices, its overall effect is ambiguous and contradictory. The narrative voice, not associated with any one character but tending to adopt a perspective more or less close at various times to each of the main protagonists (Nancy Lord and Lionel Tarrant), is at once assertive and unstable. Their relationship at first seems a predictable representation of established, male, literary culture confronted with – and seduced by – its female, petty-bourgeois, inauthentic other. But uncertainties of tone make it impossible to interpret character and event unequivocally. As often with Gissing, it is precisely in his inability to secure a stable perspective that he becomes most interesting. The ambiguities of *In the Year of Jubilee* illuminate both the pressures of emerging mass culture upon literary authorship, and wider uncertainties about the social meaning of established forms of cultural education and self-fulfilment.

Tarrant, an Oxford graduate, is initially shown as a not unlikeable but rather complacent snob: 'His face signified contentment with the scheme of things as it concerned himself; . . . he had come to regard his own judgement as the criterion of all matters in heaven and earth'.[31] He becomes Nancy's lover, marries her, disappears to America leaving her to fend for herself and their child, but returns towards the end of the novel to restore her to sequestered domesticity – not in the suburbs of Camberwell where she comes from, but in leafier Harrow, 'beyond the great smoke-area'.[32] When he first meets Nancy, Tarrant '[regards] her as in every respect his inferior', '[amuses] himself with her affectation of intellectual superiority', and decides 'to study her as a sample of the pretentious half-educated class . . . This sort of girl was turned out in thousands every year, from so-called High Schools; if they managed to pass some examination or other, their conceit grew boundless.'[33] Nancy, educated (she still attends evening classes), female and lower-middle-class, represents a new and important group of cultural aspirants, and challenges Tarrant's – and the narrator's – literary authority. The characterisation of most of the other women is misogynistic and anti-feminist (one of them, Jessica Morgan, is studying for a BA at London University but breaks down under the strain of cramming for exams). However, the narrative voice takes some distance from Tarrant's initially detached and sadistic attitudes towards Nancy: the verbs 'regard', 'amuse', 'study' can all imply criticism of the person who sees other people in that way. Tarrant is soon obliged to acknowledge the persistence of his desire for Nancy and the inadequacy of his original view of her, and in the central section of the novel the narrative voice is positioned close to Nancy. In the concluding phase, however, it swings back behind Tarrant and his assertion of protective patriarchal authority.

Tarrant represents culture, but of an over-comfortable, selfish kind. If we hope to locate any principle of cultural transcendence in him we shall be disappointed. The cultural capital he starts out with was bought by money: his father owns a blacklead firm, though the son is careful not to advertise the fact (Nancy at their second meeting, in revenge for his exposure of her ignorance of geography, discomfits him by showing she knows this secret). He becomes a writer of sorts; but his satirical journalism, turned out in a frankly commercial spirit, is hardly literature – Nancy's painfully authentic, all too personal novel, which she writes while he is in America and which he advises her on his return to store away in a cupboard so they can sentimentalise over it in their old age, has a more plausible claim. What is more, the contrast between Tarrant and his rival for Nancy, the advertising agent and entrepreneur Luckworth Crewe (among his projects is the development of a new seaside resort, Whitsand), never works through in the terms we might expect. Crewe – who personifies the commercialisation of culture, leisure and language – is a witty and not unattractive character, as several of the first reviewers agreed. He makes a good case for the role of his profession in developing new needs (are these cultural needs?): 'Till advertising sprang up, the world was barbarous. Do you suppose people kept themselves clean before they were reminded at every corner of the benefits of soap?'[34]

Crewe helps Beatrice French, another young woman from Camberwell, to set up the South London Fashionable Dress Supply Association. This prospers, and the jobless Nancy ('of what avail her "education", her "culture"?') is reduced to seeking work there. She visits Beatrice in her bachelor flat in Brixton, and is entertained to an acceptable dinner – 'very sound Stilton cheese . . . two wines, sherry and claret' – followed by the offer of cigarettes: '"I buy these in the Haymarket, special brand for women".' Stereotypical though it is, this contrasts interestingly with the equally stereotypical scenes in *Howards End* where in another Brixton flat Leonard Bast endures joyless domesticity and nasty food.[35] Forster's novel (though published almost two decades later) never convincingly shows, as Gissing does here, the new kinds of pleasure available to those who were doing well in the ever-growing imperial metropolis and did not bother themselves unduly about 'culture': people who were, as one reviewer of *In the Year of Jubilee* put it, 'vaguely outlined' in terms of established class distinctions, having '"got on" pecuniarily but hardly "gone up" socially'.[36]

Gissing's reviewers seized on the novel's suburban locations and on the fact that many of its characters belonged to 'a social class for which our tongue lacks a term of accurate definition – that of "la petite bourgeoisie" having no exact equivalent in English'.[37] Suburbia was to become the emblem of a life whose mundane pleasures evinced no spirit of transcendence. The Liberal Cabinet Minister C.F.G. Masterman declared the year before *Howards End* came out that suburb-dwellers' preferred reading matter was 'mean and tawdry and debased, representing a tawdry and dusty world'.[38] This topos prefigures how (assumed) cultural tastes would be central in the ways lower-middle-class people were represented by both left-wing and conservative critics after modernism. But Gissing, who helps to inaugurate that topos here, paints suburbia in less drab colours than we find in *Howards End* or in Orwell's *Coming up for Air* (1939): Luckworth Crewe and Beatrice French are energetic and hedonistic, and their indifference to learned culture is all the more disquieting for that. *In the Year of Jubilee* sketches a world where the fate of high culture may be determined by the fact that most people will not care much about it because they have other pleasures. In this it differs from *Jude* and *Martin Eden* and from one emphasis of Wells' early fiction, where culture is seen as threatened not by popular indifference but by the barriers of class and money which still exclude worthy aspirants.

The plot-device which has Nancy poised between Tarrant and Crewe is crude, but at least switches the gender roles usually found in this motif, which binds the choice of a cultural destiny to the choice of a sexual partner. As a rule the male protagonist chooses between two women: Arabella and Sue, Jacky Bast and Helen Schlegel, the homely haberdasher's daughter Ann Pornick and the pretentiously arty Miss Walsingham in *Kipps*, and in *Martin Eden* 'wild, defiant' working-class Lizzie Connolly and 'ethereal', bourgeois Ruth Morse. This formula projects refined culture as the opposite of sexual nature. The woman who represents cultural aspiration must be sexually reluctant, if not virginal. We can read this figure two ways: as betraying unavowed male desire for something less demanding and respectable than the cultural ideal men are meant to favour, but also as bespeaking men's wish for new and less carnally reductive ways of loving women.

Nancy Lord is a pursuant (of sorts) rather than a muse-like embodiment, and she is sexual without being an 'incarnation of turpitude', which is how John Savage in *Brave New World* (1932) describes Lenina, representative – for Huxley is drawing on the familiar schema – of mass culture and too-easy pleasure.[39] Nonetheless, Gissing's generally misogynistic characterisation might be thought to confirm Andreas Huyssens' thesis that at the turn of the nineteenth and twentieth centuries 'high culture', as 'the privileged domain of male activities', is represented as beleaguered by feminised 'masses'.[40] Gissing's 'half-educated' females, all the more threatening because they have a veneer of the real cultural thing, are from the lower middle classes rather than the proletarian masses. One must be careful not to conflate different processes: new demands of middle-class women for educational and cultural opportunity and parity, the growth of petty-bourgeois audiences for novels and journalism, the development of mostly non-written mass culture aimed at the populace (primarily the working classes), and the conservative disquiet about any or all of these which was sometimes expressed in anti-feminist terms. Nonetheless Gissing's misogyny, intermittently but repellently succumbed to (or summoned up), clearly does offer – like the wider discourse Huyssens identifies – a means of handling large cultural anxieties.

However, and even though Tarrant, abetted by the narrator, tries to tidy her away, it is Nancy who remains the most sympathetic and fully realised character. Early on, pursuing a diverse cultural education that includes scientific as well as classical topics (a development traced further in Wells' fiction), she is already uncertain about its value. Her impatience here, and her later recognition that cultural education is not worth much in the marketplace, stay in the mind: its scepticism about culture is the most distinctly memorable aspect of this novel. We might see

Nancy, Beatrice French and Luckworth Crewe as revealing their inferior natures through this scepticism or indifference. However, we doubt the credentials of the alternative represented by Tarrant: the (strongly male) culture he stands for is neither fully distinct from nor obviously preferable to its frankly commercial opposite. These are the terms of choice as Nancy sees them once she has got to know both Crewe and Tarrant:

> Nancy was no longer inclined to study, and cared little for reading of any sort. That new book on Evolution, which she had brought from the Library just before Jubilee Day, was still lying about . . . Evolution! She already knew all about Darwinism, all she needed to know. If necessary she could talk about it – oh, with an air. But who wanted to talk about such things? After all, only priggish people – the kind of people who lived at Champion Hill [where she first met Tarrant] . . . She wanted to live in the present, to enjoy her youth. An evening like that she had spent in the huge crowd [in the London streets on Jubilee night], with a man like Crewe to amuse her with his talk, was worth whole oceans of 'culture'.
>
> 'Culture' she already possessed, abundance of it. The heap of books she had read! Last winter she had attended a course of lectures, delivered by a young University gentleman with a tone of bland omniscience, on 'The History of Hellenic Civilisation'; her written answers to the little 'test papers' had been marked 'very satisfactory'. Was it not a proof of culture achieved?[41]

So much for the 'stream that runs from the mountain tops of the University . . . over the whole land'.

In the Year of Jubilee is confused as well as complex; it represents contradiction, but is flawed by unmanaged contradictions of its own. Its particular interest within the group of texts we have selected is threefold. First of all, it voices a radical scepticism about the idea that self-realisation through learned culture is universally desired, and suggests that new life-styles will revolve around new kinds of pleasure. Secondly, it shows how in the Darwinian, urban struggle between cultural styles and forms, high-cultural positions may be at once called in question (everything is in flux) and reified (because they are invoked to support claims of authority and to mark social boundaries). In this setting, it becomes hard to isolate purely cultural motives in the choices people make. Finally, like much of Gissing's fiction (especially, of course, *New Grub Street*), *In the Year of Jubilee* makes us think about how writing itself is implicated in the representation of cultural value: the commercial practice of literature and its ideal image of itself are both present, and we have to judge how the author-in-the-text secures his position in relation to these alternatives. In all these ways Gissing anticipates the anxiety, relativism and self-consciousness that characterise later critical and theoretical approaches to culture. We shall see below that although he tries, out of this, to find some way of projecting culture as transcendent still, he is not entirely convincing when he does so.

One mark of the involuted map of culture we find in *In the Year of Jubilee* is its lack of a single, dominant narrative line: no obvious track can be struck out across this terrain. Jack London's *Martin Eden* (1909) seems an opposite case. From the moment that Martin, returned from the sea where he works as a sailor, strides awkwardly into the drawing-room of the middle-class Morse family (he has been invited to dinner after rescuing the son from a group of roughs in a brawl), he sets himself to acquire learning, to become a writer, and to win Ruth Morse as his bride. His feats of reading and writing, the persistence with which he ignores rejection and goes on sending out his manuscripts, his defiance of poverty, his friendship with the consumptive poet Brissenden who scorns his infatuation with Ruth and writes one 'fantastic, amazing' masterpiece before dying: these episodes, many having a directly autobiographical basis, are told with the headlong energy of the hero's own quest.[42] The rejection-slips mount up, but at last Martin (like London himself) wins sudden fame and wealth. Even his courtship of Ruth ends in a kind of triumph. During his poverty-stricken apprenticeship, she eventually rejects him at her parents' bidding, because he insists on following his literary star rather than getting an office job. Ruth is outraged when Martin defends his ideas with unseemly vigour at the Morses' dinner-table, telling their guest, Judge Blount, who has spoken sarcastically of Herbert Spencer: '"To hear that great and noble man's name upon your lips is like finding a dew-drop in a cesspool. You are disgusting."'[43] Almost at the end of the novel, however, she makes her way to Martin's room at the Hotel Metropole and offers to '"come to [him] in free love"': '"All that is dearest to the bourgeoisie I will flout. I am no longer afraid of life."' Now, it is his turn to reject her.[44]

Wish-fulfilment fantasies are present here, but the wealth he got from writing did indeed allow London to fulfil many of his wishes. *Martin Eden* was written, a few years after the great international success of London's first published work, on board the *Snark*, the ketch made to his own design on which he had set off to sail round the world. Amidst escalating nautical disaster, London doggedly wrote his thousand words a day because he had to earn money to keep pace with his extravagant financial commitments.[45] Victorian novelists had made money too, of course: Dickens did well, Bulwer Lytton and others did better, and complaints about hacks' willingness to satisfy sensational tastes were often heard.[46] *New Grub Street* shows how a smart writer might weigh up market opportunities, and Whelpdale's sketch of American journalism in that novel suggests that transatlantic conditions favoured literary enterprise. Tarrant, we recall, spends some time in the United States too.[47] London's fortune was a portent, indicating what success in the mass market would mean in the twentieth century: the ten fastest-selling English-language paperbacks of the year 2000 all grossed over £3.5 million.[48] All this emphasises that *Martin Eden*, despite the hero's deference to ideas and art as goods in themselves, might be read as a guide to literary self-advancement. Martin, one could say, pursues ideas and culture to acquire technique and information, and to make himself socially acceptable to his potential customers in the same spirit in which he adopts bourgeois table manners and gives up swearing, strong drink and tobacco. 'Culture', in short, is an appurtenance of the middle-class lifestyle, and this gives an opportunity to whoever can supply it: from either point of view, cultural value is inextricably bound up with the monetary value to which it is conventionally opposed.

This indeed is what London's novel shows. However, Martin sustains his faith in culture's intrinsic value all through his penniless apprenticeship. (We might note that so long as his writings are being returned as unpublishable, the only value they *can* have is non-monetary.) His need to believe that poetry and art are not just properties of the middle class is confirmed by his friendship with the bohemian Brissenden; London's own need for that belief determines how the character is deployed, and perhaps partly accounted for the intensity of his friendship with the poet George Sterling on whom Brissenden was based.[49] Brissenden, as a true literary artist, mocks the cultural pretensions of the bourgeoisie, insisting that the Morses and their circle are 'animated stomachs guided by the high intellectual and artistic pretensions of clams'. As an antidote, he takes Martin to meet the radical self-taught working-class philosophers of the Market Street ghetto.[50] However, this opposition between high art and respectable money, which holds apart the twin terms in the phrase 'bourgeois culture' against so much in Martin's experience that tells him they belong together, collapses when it turns out that his writing is marketable after all:

> It was the bourgeoisie that bought his books . . . and from what little he knew of the bourgeoisie it was not clear to him how it could possibly appreciate or comprehend what he had written. His intrinsic beauty and power meant nothing to the hundreds of thousands who were acclaiming him and buying his books. He was the fad of the hour . . . The hundreds of thousands read him and acclaimed him with the same brute non-understanding with which they had flung themselves on Brissenden's 'Ephemera' and torn it to pieces – a wolf-rabble that fawned on

> him instead of fanging him. Fawn or fang, it was all a matter of chance.[51]

Despair follows almost immediately on fame. Martin makes a plan to escape: he will buy land in the Marquesas and live a simple life in a grass palace. But he slips at night from a porthole on the boat taking him south, and drives himself by a last effort of will down into the sea's depths where he drowns. That London was writing the novel while at sea suggests how closely he imagined this moment of liberating self-destruction. London died at forty, seven years after *Martin Eden* was published, from an overdose, which may have been deliberate, of the drugs he used as pain-killers.[52] The causes of the self-destructive behaviour that undermined London's health included, as *Martin Eden* illustrates, the collapse of his belief in the intrinsic worth of literary work and in the power of cultural creation to endow life with meaning.

Martin's ambivalent relation to his own success can be linked to wider tensions within the idea of 'culture', seen also in *In the Year of Jubilee*. The connection between bourgeois wealth and high culture by no means disappears as new kinds of social subject are culturally and politically enfranchised: on the contrary, socio-cultural mobility foregrounds culture's social meanings and determinations. Yet the aesthetic and intellectual attractions of culture's high texts may be experienced as real and powerful, and as quite independent of the bourgeois setting in which they are encountered. To aspire culturally need not be the same as to seek social advancement. Martin, like Jude Fawley and like the writer Harold Biffen in *New Grub Street*, refuses to accept that 'culture' is just a commodity. All three live for the autonomy of culture and all three perish. Leonard Bast, even though by the end he has given up seeking after culture, dies under a cascade of books in the entrance hall of Howards End. Such dénouements do not resolve the ambiguity of their narratives: they leave us still asking whether the belief in cultural self-realisation is a faith to die for or a fatal illusion.

Representing 'politics'

'Culture' and 'politics', in the tradition of critical discussion in Britain, denote rival but in some ways coterminous discourses, each offering a vantage-point on the social-historical seen as an intelligible totality. We can contrast culture, as the making and enjoyment of texts that interpret the world, with politics as collective activity intended to conserve or change it; but we can also liken them, as related forms of critical discourse and sensibility. 'Culture', beyond its reference to particular works, implies a subjective, usually critical relation towards society which arises from knowledge of culture (especially literature). Cultural engagement in these novels often leads as much to the gaining of a new consciousness of the social self as critical outsider as it does to the development of a specifically aesthetic sensibility.

In this respect the texts anticipate the cultural–political critique later expressed in more abstract or theoretical terms in post-World War II social-democratic Britain. The 'basic element' in 'the idea of culture', Raymond Williams wrote, is 'its effort at total qualitative assessment'.[53] Despite Williams' cautions in *Culture and Society* (1958) against the Romantic investment in culture as 'something superior to the actual course of events',[54] the 'Culture and Society' tradition resists the conclusion that 'politics' can provide an exhaustive explanatory metalanguage for 'culture'. Rather, politically inflected criticism interprets and deploys what is comprised in culture as a 'separate body of moral and intellectual activities'.[55] Critique is premised on an understanding of material history, and expressed in a broadly focused discourse of social analysis and projection, especially from a more or less Marxist perspective. But it is neither the specialised technical discourse of economists, sociologists and political scientists, nor the practice and experience of collective activity in a party or social movement, though it may draw on both of these. Political critique in this sense – talking and writing at large about social-historical questions, and the 'political imaginary' which such discourse sustains – is itself a form of culture even if it also figures as culture's opposite or 'other'.

This intertwining runs both ways: even in the founding text of *Culture and Anarchy* (1869), which seems intent on asserting the independent, higher status of culture *vis-à-vis* politics, Arnold had ended up showing the ineluctably political dimensions of culture. As we suggest in our Introduction and Conclusion, the historically developing ideas of cultural self-realisation and the cultural 'sublime' derive from this imbrication of learned culture, political democracy and critical discourse. Both cultural and political life were opening up, during the period 1870–1930, to new interests, pressures and participants. Although politics as a discrete theme figures only marginally in the novels we are considering, several of their authors interested themselves in political questions. When protagonists encounter political ideas and movements in the course of their cultural self-making, this reflects the tension between related but alternative ways of regarding society and positioning the self in relation to it. In *Jude* and *Howards End*, however, politics is a theme only by implication. Culture is central to how the arty middle-class Schlegels understand their difference from the business-minded middle-class Wilcoxes, but the specifically political differences (presumably the Schlegels vote Liberal and the Wilcoxes vote Conservative) are left unstated. The Schlegels try, but fail, to make culture the principle also on which the petty-bourgeois Leonard can win inclusion into the liberal collectivity and self-realisation as an individual.[56] The inference is that the cultural principle works effectively to distinguish quasi-antagonistic sections of the middle class – we are back with Bourdieu's 'dominated fraction' – but has little immediate meaning to those from subaltern classes. Like *Jude*, on which it draws but whose central dynamic it revises (Leonard's cultural aspirations, unlike Jude's, are presented externally, *de haut en bas*), *Howards End* has political implications, since in both cases the protagonist's cultural exclusion is the consequence of social conditions. But neither novel makes much direct reference to contemporary political events and arguments, or deploys political terms in the narration or commentary. It is left to the reader to draw what may well be political conclusions.

Direct references to political activities and commitments are to be found in *Martin Eden*, *Kipps*, and many of Gissing's novels. They often function to define the political as a form of sensibility or perception which the central figure takes cognisance of but leaves behind – as Stephen Dedalus a few years later, in the definitive *Portrait* of cultural self-making, listens patiently to the Irish nationalist Davin but tells him: 'You talk to me of nationality, language, religion. I shall try to fly by those nets.'[57] The protagonist keeps clear of the political engagements which may engross minor characters; he does not come to see his own relation to society in political terms. The transcendence towards which the narrative points subsumes the moment of politics as an element in its own making.

By the time he wrote *Martin Eden* London was well known as a speech-maker on behalf of socialism (and he became a favourite author of Lenin and Trotsky), but he presents the radical Market Street ghetto, where socialists and anarchists drink cheap wine and debate theosophy and philosophy, in just two isolated chapters. His first evening there gives Martin what he calls 'a glimpse of fairyland', and he later returns with Brissenden, to a hall 'packed by the Oakland socialists, chiefly members of the working class'. In reply to the speech of a 'clever Jew . . . [whose] stooped and narrow shoulders and weazened chest proclaimed him the true child of the crowded ghetto', he delivers a Nietzschean–Malthusian attack on socialism as a slave morality. When this is subsequently misreported in the press, making Martin seem to have spoken in favour of revolution, he and Brissenden administer a 'spanking' to the journalist.[58] The novel disavows the imputation of socialism to the hero in this bizarre homoerotic scene, where Brissenden and Martin, joint representatives of literature, punish the 'young cub' who here embodies both politics and commercial publishing. Although for the most part closely based on London's life, *Martin Eden* offers no equivalent for his decision to become active in left politics – temporarily and rather unreliably, as it turned out. It remains a portrait of the artist as artist; and Martin mostly asserts his difference from the 'bourgeoisie that bought his books' not politically but in intellectual and aesthetic terms. London claimed his novel was intended to represent Martin's Nietzschean individualism critically, as the cause of his despair and suicide, but he conceded that 'not a single reviewer' had seen this and 'even the socialists missed the point'.[59] What the novel shows, at all events, is the difficulty, even for a professed socialist, of representing the dynamic of the writer's development as tending towards a collectivist politics: if there is a politics of writing, London implies, it is most logically the politics of the will-to-power. His own 'socialism', blemished from the start by white-supremacist and eugenicist traits, evolved this way.[60]

Wells too was for awhile personally involved in politics, as a Fabian. Like London, he nourished 'Nietzschean', pseudo-Darwinian fantasies; and his grandiose political ideas are set forth in futurist parables and in numerous tracts and prophecies.[61] In his earlier and less immodest days, he produced in *Tono-Bungay* (1909) a condition-of-England novel of wider scope and in some ways sharper political focus than *Howards End*. *Kipps* (1905), by contrast, more narrowly (though not fully) autobiographical, tends to retreat from its own political implications. The sympathetic representation of socialist principle in the character of Sid Pornick, owner of a bicycle shop at the time when the link between cycling and progressive politics was being forged,[62] is undercut by the would-be Dostoevskyan characterisation of Sid's tenant, Masterman. Masterman is a caricature: a chain-smoking, consumptive stage revolutionary. However, his intemperate denunciations of the world make a number of points borne out by Kipps' own early experience.[63] If Kipps had not come into money, he would never have escaped the 'monotony and toil and contempt' Masterman describes as the lot of the wage-slave. Masterman's bitterness because he is too old to qualify for any University scholarship, having had to prepare himself in his own time ('I worked all day and studied all the night'), recalls Kipps' indifferent schooling and lack of later educational opportunities. It may also put us in mind of the struggles of Martin Eden, of

Jude and of Wells' own Hoopdriver, another apprentice draper who works a twelve-hour day but resolves, at the end of *The Wheels of Chance* (1896), to spend years studying so he can make himself worthy of the middle-class girl he has met on his cycling holiday.

These details remind us that Wells, himself born into the suburban lower middle classes, well knew the barriers that impeded their aspirations. As Patricia Alden observes, in the actual conditions of late nineteenth-century Britain, '[Matthew Arnold's] spiritualized version of bourgeois individualism – the freedom to cultivate the self without respect to material or social estate – was in fact an unattainable ideal for those who might find it most appealing: the aspiring men from the culturally disenfranchised lower-middle and working classes'.[64] Only political change would alter this. But Wells is trying to dismiss politics in Masterman's overheated rhetoric: '"I've been crushed, trampled and defiled by a drove of hogs"'. His manner of speech itself functions rhetorically, implying authorial disavowal of the opinions he asserts; it expresses intemperately what is made to seem the crude political anger of the dispossessed. Wells is trying to place externally, and neutralise, that anger.

Cultural dispossession and yearning and their traumatic meaning for an intelligent, thwarted boy are important in several of Wells' novels, but even when shown sympathetically they are often represented in a somewhat knowing, comic retrospect. At the close of *Kipps*, we are taken to Folkestone for a last look at the hero, returned to obscurity and contentment as a bookseller after the loss of his inheritance. The narrator asks us not to 'tell Kipps that he is "Kipps", or that I have put him in this book'.[65] The authorial perspective seeks not just to transcend but to erase that of the represented character (the novel is subtitled *The Story of a Simple Soul*). For the author-in-the-text, cultural self-realisation brings distance and allows irony to erase pain. For Kipps, it is vouchsafed only in the parodic form of bookshop-owning. He will never be a writer, nor even a displaced intellectual like Jude or Nancy. Kipps, whose cultural aspirations collapse under the pressure of trying to sustain what he finds an alien social self, in this respect (and some others) anticipates Mr Polly, who became, especially in his postwar filmic incarnation, 'perhaps the originating archetype of the suburban little man, the clerk with dreams . . . These are dreams of escaping from social realities.'[66]

Gissing, alone of our authors, offers not only a range of engagements with politics as a theme, but also a politicised and dialectical understanding of literary practice.[67] His essay on Dickens (1898) was perceptive in delineating new pressures on the authority of Victorian realism, in which formal and social aspects of representation had earlier been indissolubly linked.[68] As the social origins of writers grew more diverse, they became less ready to identify with ruling-class values: Gissing himself, ambivalent and later hostile towards democratic and proletarian aspirations, was hostile also to bourgeois commerce (though it is an overstatement to claim that 'from first to last he loathed and feared it').[69] As well as growing less homogeneous, the ruling class was losing its monopoly of the franchise, and was subject to strong ideological challenges from socialist, feminist, and anti-imperial movements.[70] Novelists of the mid-century had represented social conflicts in the same confident discourse that analysed the motives and set forth the circumstances of characters, but now the old terms of authorship came under pressure as the 'cultural' and the 'political' grew more visibly distinct. The representational claims of fiction were also challenged by new kinds of explicitly socio-political writing in documentary, sociological, and anthropological forms.[71] This, together with the self-differentiation of novelists along dividing lines of aesthetic principle and audience, is part of the background to English fictional modernism discussed in our next chapter. It is important in terms of our overall theme because shifting conceptions of writerly identity affect how writers represent the culturally realised self.

Charles Dickens draws an implicit contrast between Gissing and his great precursor. Gissing feels, and expresses, a 'spirit of antagonism to his readers' that Dickens never showed.[72] But Dickens, he says, was restricted as well as enabled by his intimate (we might now say, 'organic')[73] relation to the rising middle class: he spoke as 'the mouthpiece of his kind, in all that relates to simple emotions and homely thought', and paid a price for this in a characteristic 'avoidance of the disagreeable'.[74] The metaphor of the 'mouthpiece' recurs. Gissing had once called himself the 'mouthpiece of the advanced radical party', and the novelist Osmond Waymark, in Gissing's early *The Unclassed*, declares: '"Art, nowadays, must be the mouthpiece of misery, for misery is the keynote of modern life."'[75] However, in the dialectical understanding which Gissing arrives at (reflected in *New Grub Street* in the fact that the author-in-the-text stands apart and must be distinguished from any of the authors whom the text represents), the writer must strive to be more than a mouthpiece: he must assert his uniqueness, even if the field within which he does so is determined for him. When his friend Julian Casti says the novel Waymark is working on is '"a kind of art only possible in an age when the social question is predominant"', Waymark replies: '"True, very likely. Every strong individuality is more or less the expression of its age. This direction may be imposed on me; for all that, I understand why I pursue it".'[76] This idea of an imposed 'direction' in relation to which the self must try to find authentic expression is evidently more complex than any notion of the cultured self as embodying a free transcendence.

In Gissing's version of this ideal of consciousness, society and politics impose the 'direction', externally: 'strong individuality', an inner power that mediates and resists, depends on literary and cultural understanding. Few characters in Gissing try to sustain that position (none in *Jubilee* or *New Grub Street*), but the author battles to achieve it in many of his most interesting novels. Gissing's naturalism, though its documentary qualities were praised by the social investigator Charles Booth,[77] involves an active, splenetic, literary mediation, rather than the 'objective, impersonal language' of the new social sciences or of more measured French writing.[78] Rachel Bowlby notes:

> For naturalist authors, the complex position occupied by the artist in contemporary society took on a particular interest which is demonstrated by the fact that Dreiser, Gissing and Zola all wrote novels about the literary and artistic world of their time. While the defenders of realism and naturalism were explicitly opposed to the idealist tendencies of the Romantic view of art, they still needed to seek ways of attributing distinctive if not subversive power to art and artists.[79]

The distinctiveness of art had for Gissing to be asserted not only against a purely commercial valuation of writing, but also against what is implied in the metaphor of the 'mouthpiece', with its suggestion that writing has no inner dynamic but is wholly determined and/or wholly ideological (as we would now say).

Gissing's work includes several novels centred on political questions and struggles, and several others where political positions are incidentally but strongly articulated.[80] No nineteenth-century English novelist had a sharper sense of the determinations that social conditions and political ideology brought to bear on subjectivity and culture. It was just this sense, however, that led Gissing to represent 'politics', often, as the negative pole against which the autonomy of the cultural and authorial sensibility must be affirmed. 'Culture' must subsume politics – otherwise it will be subsumed by it. It is with the author, with his developed cultural perspective and his too-voluble assertion of autonomy, that readers of Gissing are cajoled or instructed to identify themselves.

We can conclude these reflections on the differentiation of cultural and political consciousness by turning to the portrait of Samuel Bennett Barmby in *In the Year of Jubilee*. Barmby, the third of Nancy's suitors and thus the representative alongside Tarrant and Crewe of a third, rival version of 'culture', is a suburban clerk. The young men's debating society he belongs to sometimes discusses social questions, and Barmby plans to give a paper there on 'the Age of Progress . . . with special reference to one particular – the Press'.[81] Gissing expects us to smirk here, as he does later in the novel when Jessica Morgan goes to hear Barmby speaking on 'National Greatness: its Obligations and its Dangers' to a 'society of mutual improvement at Pentonville'.[82] This is presumably the kind of association described by Richard Altick in *The English Common Reader*:

> During the years [towards the end of the nineteenth century] when the [Mechanics'] institutes were proving inadequate as educational agencies for the working class . . . little mutual-improvement clubs . . . sprang up, many of them composed of members of institutes who had been alienated by the absence of democratic management and the rigid censorship of discussion and reading.
>
> . . . We know little about these mutual-improvement clubs . . . But from the many allusions found in the memoirs of working-class men, it appears that hardly a village was without at least one such group, and usually there were several; for they had various purposes. Some went in for theology, some for radical politics, some simply for general literature.[83]

It is this kind of club – 'an Artizans' Mutual Improvement Society' – that Jude Fawley, 'active in furthering "equality of opportunity" by any humble means open to him', attends while Sue and he are living at Aldbrickham (he is asked to resign when his irregular domestic situation becomes known).[84] In *Jubilee*, Gissing is drawing on the experiences of his now disowned radical past, when as a young man newly come to London he had given a lecture on 'Faith and Reason' in Paddington, 'before a workingmen's club of which his uncle was a member'; the following year he would publish two sympathetic articles on socialism – and would describe himself as a 'mouthpiece'.[85]

Neither Hardy nor Gissing gives much detail, but we can imagine Jude and Barmby attending meetings where the cultural self-improvement of better-off artisans and clerks had a political dimension that became explicit when social questions were discussed. (The Californian Market Street anarchists and socialists, in *Martin Eden*, are a more radical, bohemian parallel, and

Barmby's favourite authors, like Martin's, include Herbert Spencer.)[86] The cultural politics of Gissing's sardonic representation then seem straightforwardly negative: he wants us to mock at Barmby's pretensions – Barmby is 'quite uneducated', we are assured, 'in any legitimate sense of the word'[87] – because they represent an autonomous alternative to the academic culture which Gissing, the son of a retail chemist, had set out to acquire as a brilliant, impoverished classics student at Owens College in Manchester.[88] (Owens College was marginal compared to Oxbridge, and Gissing never completed his degree: the consequent insecurity helps explain the scorn expressed for the mere autodidact Barmby.) Barmby, who wields what the narrator calls 'the cleric pen', represents the suburban 'amorphous stratum' of non-professional intellectual workers who were complicating 'legitimate' cultural stratifications and status patterns and whose cultural tastes would increasingly dominate the literary market. The radical and working-class associations of 'mutual improvement' meanwhile made it a doubly tempting target for the satire of a writer asserting his 'strong individuality' in and against the medium of politics. Mockery of lower-class cultural aspirations is the nastiest kind of class prejudice, here and in Gissing's gibes against the vulgarity of Beatrice French and her sisters; but mockery secures the author's cultural authority. Or rather, at this distance, it displays the need to seek authority which drives Gissing into reactionary élitism. The 'culture' that dissociates itself from lower-class 'politics' turns out to have a politics of its own.

As ever with Gissing, there is another twist. We have taken Barmby in Pentonville as a hostile representation of a progressive social movement. However, the implied content of his speeches associates him less with radical politics than with bland faith in 'progress' and complacent social imperialism. When he evokes 'the Age of Progress with special reference to the Press', the mention of 'the Press' should remind us of Gissing's keen eye for cultural and ideological forms that exploited popular ignorance – as, Arnold argued in *Culture and Anarchy*, the dissenting preacher the Revd. W. Cattle had exploited it in his anti-Catholic speeches in the Midlands ('When all the praties were black in Ireland,' Cattle would ask his audience, 'why didn't the priests say the hocus-pocus over them?'). It is sometimes forgotten by Arnold's critics that ignorance does exist and that not all expressions of popular political sentiment are admirable.[89] In *The Nether World*, Gissing describes Bank Holiday sideshows at the Crystal Palace where crowds tested their strength by throwing coconuts or raining blows on figures representing the Empire's enemies: Russians, 'treacherous Afghans', 'base Africans'.[90] In *The Whirlpool* (1897), Harvey Rolfe is discovered enthusing over Kipling's *Barrack-Room Ballads*, then newly published. He pulls himself up short: he enjoys Kipling's 'great artistry', but deplores poems that make popular 'savagery' respectable. '"The bully of the music-hall shouting "Jingo!" had his special audience. Now comes a man of genius, and decent folk don't feel ashamed to listen this time."'[91] Here Gissing foresees the ascendancy of reactionary texts that work both culturally and politically, and for 'decent folk' as well as for the music-hall audience. The engagement with this politics, and this culture, will not lead to forms of self-realisation we approve. Of course, that is itself at once a political and a cultural judgement.

How do writers and critics distance themselves, situate themselves, in order to undertake an 'effort at total qualitative assessment'? What founds the possibility of a transcendent critical perspective? Gissing, London and Wells were acutely aware of how, arriving from the margins, they had had to construct a workable authority. Representations of 'politics' in their texts suggest its significance as a disavowed alternative to the literary culture which as authors they were joining. Given the individualism of their production and consumption, and the nature of their audience, one can always identify literary texts with 'bourgeois culture' (hard though many writers resist that linkage), and arraign their élitism from the standpoint of a 'politics' understood as popular–democratic and collectivist. To do so suits the populist orientation of much recent academic criticism. However, other twentieth-century critical traditions, and not only conservative ones, have insisted that 'culture' may sometimes be a basis on which to assess 'politics'. In their contradictory search for a cultural position that would distinguish itself from that of 'the bourgeoisie that read their books', the novelists we have been discussing help us to reconsider the uses and viability of such a self-positioning as a goal of cultural, or cultural–political, development.

'Reading steadily, his face glowing': cultural object and cultural distance

Our novels represent culture in that they are themselves cultural works whose forms of understanding the reader can partake of and assess. At this level, the protagonists' search for self-realisation is subsumed into the novels' overall representation: the cultural ideal is defined, modified, or called in question in the metacultural fiction. The novels also represent 'culture' in a more specific, localised sense, as the initial object of the heroes' desire – the passages from Ruskin that Leonard Bast struggles to follow in his 'semi-basement', the Greek that Jude cons as he drives his aunt's old horse around the lanes delivering bread, the Latin that the narrator in *Tono-Bungay* looks forward eagerly to learning, the 'Hellenic Civilisation' that rather bores Nancy, or the volume of Swinburne that Martin Eden picks up in the Morses' 'spacious hall' on his first visit and which he begins 'reading steadily, forgetful of where he was, his face glowing'.[92] In most cases the cultural object is conventionally prestigious, as these references to art and architecture, classical learning and poetry confirm. In the instances just cited, Forster and Gissing may intend a certain irony, but elsewhere – in relation to the music of Beethoven in *Howards End*, and the poetry of Keats which Tarrant reads to Nancy – they assume readers will share established cultural values.

However, attempts to represent cultural pleasure often fall

flat. When Forster describes Leonard reading Ruskin, the target of his irony is uncertain, and he seems to mock either the reader or the text – if not both.[93] Gissing in some of his novels gives what we are enjoined to read as a positive image of a 'cultured' life, devoted to reclusive study, especially of the Greek and Latin classics. The best-known example is the late, quasi-autobiographical *The Private Papers of Henry Ryecroft* (1903), a meditation on the pains of commercial modernity and the pleasures of rural, bookish, masculine seclusion. Some critics have seen *Ryecroft* as deliberately showing the limitations of its protagonist's conservative ideal of culture.[94] Inadvertently or otherwise, the book reveals the marginal relevance of classical and literary learning to the practice of a writer working in the modern city: only when a legacy enables him to stop plying the literary pen and retire to Devon can Ryecroft devote himself to 'culture' – and then, he soon dies. In *The Unclassed*, the friendship of Waymark and Casti is founded on a shared love of Keats and the classics. Casti pursues his dream of writing a blank-verse drama and then an epic poem about Rome (both unpublished), and dies young of consumption: Waymark publishes a novel, and survives. Waymark's, we recall, is the text whose 'direction is imposed', but which will nonetheless express the author's 'strong individuality'.

Gissing's schema – effectual writing as a this-worldly practice partly 'imposed' by society, versus a classical ideal associated with evasion and escape – subverts as well as reproduces the reified idea of literary culture found in *Culture and Anarchy*. (Arnold's essay leaves us uncertain whether he truly regards contemporary writing, or indeed any prose writing in English, as capable of offering 'sublime' pleasure.) However, we have seen that cultural discrimination and the assertion of cultural authority remain indispensable to the framework, or voice, through which Gissing creates critical perspective. As well as references to the classical and poetic canon, he offers us one admirable cultural object whose genre, prose fiction, is the same as his own: Harold Biffen's novel, *Mr Bailey, Grocer*, in *New Grub Street*. This is worth not just more than money but more than life. Biffen risks dying in a house-fire to save the manuscript, and as he rushes up to rescue it he leaves the drunkard who started the fire to perish on the stairs. Biffen's novel is a premonition of the writerly text of fictional modernism, and we return to it in Chapter 5. Unfortunately, it is feebly described: 'Each sentence was as good as he could make it, harmonious to the ear, with words of precious meaning skilfully set.'[95]

London presses hard to achieve a resonant image of literary pleasure, but fails notably, in *Martin Eden*. The record of Martin's intellectual endeavour is moving, but the representations of its objects (like the descriptions of Ruth Morse) evoke the naivety of the aspirant rather than the sublimity after which he aspires. Brissenden is brought in to reinforce our faith in the authenticity of culture; however, the longer it goes on the less convincing Martin's description of Brissenden's masterpiece, 'Ephemera', becomes:

> Martin's face, flushed at first, paled as he read on. It was perfect art. Form triumphed over substance . . . in so perfect construction as to make Martin's head swim with delight, to put passionate tears into his eyes, and to send chills creeping up and down his back . . . It was terrific, impossible; and yet there it was, scrawled in black ink across the sheets of paper. It dealt with man and his soul-gropings in their ultimate terms . . .[96]

Technical difficulties aside, there is perhaps a substantial reason why these texts struggle to represent the cultural delight so important to their narratives and characters. The theme that animates them is not after all 'culture' as a sublime object, representable as such, but rather the self-realisation that its pursuit may bring, the pursuit itself, and the obstacles it meets. The distance between the unrealised and the realised life, though presented in individual terms, has a general implication in an unequal society beginning to imagine itself as a political and cultural democracy. Images which figure that distance as closed, showing the attained cultural object rather than the thwarted energy which seeks it, no longer capture the aspiration of the outsider. Walter Besant in his novel *All Sorts and Conditions of Men* (1882) represents the Palace of Delight, built by charity (from the profits of brewing) in the East End, as magically assuaging the deprivation East Enders suffer from, but this cultural centre, equipped with gymnasium, library, concert-room and theatre, fails to convince us as the object of anyone's needs or wishes.[97] Analogously in some ways, the cultural world of William Morris' *News from Nowhere* (1891), with its keynote of contradiction resolved and harmony achieved, can seem tedious rather than inspiring. In his lectures published in 1882 as *Hopes and Fears for Art*, Morris had insisted that most people had no opportunity to appreciate artistic excellence ('How can you really educate men who lead the life of machines?'), while defending a view of genuine art as what gives pleasure to all. Art thus seemed impossible in contemporary conditions, where only a minority could enjoy it: 'Art has such sympathy with cheerful freedom, open-heartedness and reality, so much she sickens under selfishness and luxury, that she will not live thus isolated and exclusive.'[98] Yet if there was to be an 'art' at all in late nineteenth-century Britain – or, we might add, anywhere at any time before or since – it would have to survive amidst 'selfishness and luxury'. In fictions of cultural aspiration, novelists addressed this tension in writing that showed culture both as desirable and as excluding the majority. So the distance, the tension, is kept open between desire and its object.

Paradoxically, the very ineptitude of London's writing keeps that distance present to us, by reminding us that the author is culturally naive despite the would-be sophistication of his language – though (in another paradox) London's ineptitude will perhaps be registered as such only by culturally educated readers, usually members of the 'bourgeoisie that bought his books'. When the authorial consciousness is successfully pitched at a level of cultural literacy or sophistication to which the protagonist can only aspire, and addresses an implicitly cultured audience, the distance between author and protagonist may express itself in a tone (deliberate or otherwise) of patronage, facetiousness or even contempt. In *Jude the Obscure*, the narrative voice resists this splitting of voices and sensibilities. The novel entertains from the start a complex ambiguity about Jude's cultural aspirations: Christminster when the young Jude first sets his face towards it is 'either directly seen, or miraged in the peculiar atmosphere'.[99] But this never shades into superciliousness or mockery. Hardy is concerned not so much to judge whether Jude's cultural aspiration pursues a mistaken goal (or a correct one) as to show Jude as caught up in a historical process that is socially determined as well as individually chosen. '"I was, perhaps, after all, a paltry victim to the spirit of mental and social restlessness, that makes so many unhappy in these days!"', says Jude: and to raise the thought that Jude is a 'victim' is to suggest that his fate should be read as typical, in the Lukácsian sense – not everyone is like Jude, but the meaning of his story is a meaning 'immanent in the world or the life of man'.[100]

Hardy does not question the worthiness of Jude's cultural desire, but the novel shows the inadequacy of Christminster's kind of culture. Gissing, in a more sardonic spirit, suggests that the borders between cultural self-development and social ambition, literature and commerce, are hard to police. However, neither Gissing nor Hardy ultimately dismisses the idea that engagement with cultural works can lead to self-development. Wells, by contrast, in the tone he adopts, often casts doubt on the notion that established literary and cultural values offer any means of self-realisation. In *Tono-Bungay*, the narrator's uncle uses the money he has made from the patent medicine that gives the book its name to buy up an old-established literary journal, *The Sacred Grove: A Weekly Magazine of Art, Philosophy, Science and Belles Lettres*.[101] We are shown a wrapper listing the articles for one number: 'A Hitherto Unpublished Letter from Walter Pater', 'Charlotte Bronte's Maternal Aunt', 'The Genius of Shakespeare' – and so on. All around the contents list are advertisements for the 'Twenty-Three Liver Pill, Not a Drug but a Live American Remedy'. The narrator half-mocks himself for his old-fashioned sensibility which is affronted by the 'incongruous combination'; but the text seems to be mocking the sedateness, the inertia, of a merely heterogeneous and antiquarian 'belles lettres'. Wells implies that in the unstable, money-driven world which his novel depicts, the objects of literary culture are turning into a collection of bric-à-brac.

'Fragments I have shored against my ruin', says the speaker of *The Waste Land*.[102] Eliot, like Joyce in *Ulysses* (though in a more mandarin, less democratic spirit), can be seen as trying to reassemble some cultural monument by registering, in the very texture of writing, the simultaneous presence of the demotic and the élite, the rarefied and the everyday: the traces of myth and learned culture that structure the text are at once remote from and akin to the experience of the modern city-dweller. Wells prefers more dismissive gestures. When Kipps comes into his unexpected fortune he seeks cultural guidance from Chester Coote, a pompous self-taught house-agent. Coote instructs him in deportment and also advises him to 'read one Serious Book a week':

> Of course we can learn even from Novels, Nace Novels that is, but it isn't the same as serious reading. I made a rule, One Serious Book and One Novel – no more. There are some of the Serious Books I've been reading lately – on that table: *Sartor Resartus*, Mrs. Twaddletome's *Pond Life*, *The Scottish Chiefs*, *Life and Letters of Dean Farrar* . . .[103]

The target is uncertain. Are we laughing at Coote's defective cultural equipment (the preceding description of his room and desk have established him as a Barmby, a Bast – an interloper, or aspirant unsympathetically seen)? At the absurdity of all attempts to choose the best books, when there is so much diverse knowledge to be had? At the fact that someone coming into money is not able to carry it off, socially, until they get 'culture' to go with it? At the very idea of self-realisation in culture? The ever cruder irony with which cultural objects are represented in Wells' fiction between *The Wheels of Chance* (1896) and *Tono-Bungay* (1909) suggests that he came, over these dozen years, to the conclusion that the pursuit of culture was little more than an adjunct to or cover for the pursuit of wealth. Like Arnold Bennett, Wells was to become a prolific writer and journalist and to make a lot of money from his work: the two of them would epitomise the middlebrow writing against which modernism was to define itself.[104]

'The more exceptional couple'

Wells' facetious and sentimental authorial tone sets him apart from his protagonists and allows him to evade the question his narratives keep raising: What is the inner meaning of the transformation of the subject brought about by education and cultural self-differentiation? Nonetheless, though he chooses to present this evasively, for Wells as for Gissing, and for London in *Martin Eden*, cultural self-realisation culminates in the developed sensibility of the writer. The distance travelled is at once personal (autobiographical) and social: the author has become someone who speaks a different language from the one spoken by the youthful self.

This different, literary language is, we have suggested, one that Hardy is reluctant to speak. Of all the great Victorian realists, he has the least sophisticated style, sophistication being in this context an equivocal accomplishment. The narrative voice in *Jude* is often ballad-like and impersonal, sometimes clumsy, never knowing and sophisticated.[105] This refusal, or denial, of cultural distance between protagonist and author is one factor accounting for the simultaneously democratic and unworldly quality of *Jude*. Of all our novels, it most clearly asserts the cultural and educational rights of outsiders, and most clearly expresses the utopian belief that cultural self-realisation is an intrinsically valuable goal, separable from the social advance that it often accompanies. Even in failing to enter Christminster, and certainly in failing to win worldly success (which indeed he upbraids himself for briefly desiring), Jude embodies the ideal imagined by Clym Yeobright, the principled middle-class ascetic who sets up a night school for the heath-dwellers in *The Return of the Native*. In Jude's story, as in Clym's ideal, we see 'bucolic placidity quickening to intellectual aims without [the pursuit of] social aims as the transitional phase'.[106] Nor is there any suggestion that Jude will become a writer. Here perhaps Hardy evades what many authors, drawing on comparable, broadly autobiographical materials, have acknowledged: that it is precisely in becoming a writer or artist that one may achieve, simultaneously, a position in the social and economic world and some realisation of one's 'purely' cultural desires. (Hardy had much earlier produced a concealed, bizarre account of his self-making as an author, in *The Hand of Ethelberta* (1876), where writing is not so much masterly transcendence as a blend of self-advancement and servitude, self-exposure and self-concealment.)[107] Hardy's reluctance to cast his *Bildungsroman* in the form of a *Künstlerroman*, a novel of specifically artistic self-making, is a reluctance to represent the full distance his travels had taken him from Dorset and from what Dorset meant. But as we have argued, this refusal to deploy a culturally specialised and socially distanced narrative voice – as, in their different ways, Gissing or Wells or, later, Lawrence all do – plays a part in ensuring that Jude's sensibility is not seen as naive. The ordinary working rural world from which he originates, attenuated though its presence has become in this late novel, is never held up to mockery. In Hardy, less educated speakers are not patronised, as they often are in Gissing and Wells. When in an early scene a carter whom Jude meets on the road says of Christminster 'They raise pa'sons there like radishes in a bed', and tells him the college fellows can 'earn hundreds by thinking out loud',[108] a dialogue is initiated which runs across the novel. Finding employment in a workshop that restores Christminster stonework, Jude recognises that 'here in the stone yard was a centre of effort as worthy as that dignified by the name of scholarly study within the noblest of the colleges'. ('But he lost [this true illumination]', the narrator continues 'under stress of his old idea', the idea that only 'scholarly study' is noble.)[109] At the culminating moment of his self-doubt and self-vindication, in the speech he makes outside the theatre where the rich undergraduates are getting their degrees, Jude's interlocutors and encouragers are not the students or fellows, who have no idea of his existence ('I'm an outsider to the end of my days'), but Sue and the working-class acquaintances he has made in the city.[110]

Hardy in this way sets Christminster's, and Jude's, cultural ideal in the context of a popular life which is a little sceptical about its claims, though not – so far as the question comes up – about Jude's merits in deserving what it refuses him. This anonymous collective setting also provides, in the largest historical reading of the novel, the meaning of Jude's comment that 'it takes two or three generations to do what I tried to do in one': it is not so much that his and Sue's children are imagined as succeeding where he has failed, as that his attempt will have struck out a path that all those others in the background can follow later. As a mason Jude eschews the specialisation which was coming to mean that 'in London the man who carves the boss or knot of leafage declines to cut the fragment of moulding which merges in that leafage';[111] more generally, though his studies make him very different from his peers, specialised distinction and difference never seem his aim.

The texture of the novel deepens these democratic intimations in Jude's love affair with Sue Bridehead. The contrast between Sue and Arabella is predictable in itself and in figuring Jude's 'cultural' and 'natural' selves, and Sue's sexuality mostly continues to be represented along those schematic lines, but the fact that she is Jude's intellectual partner – brighter indeed and more educated than he ever becomes – means that every step Jude takes after he has met her is taken not in egoistic competition but as part of a shared journey. This is why the collapse of Jude's educational plans and objectives, which happens quite early in the text (Christminster tells him to 'stick to his trade' in the second Book and his ideas of ordination become impossible once he begins to live with Sue), does not end the story or lead to the disavowals and negative ironies we have found in some other texts. Jude, Sue and their children go on living, for a time. In their obscure life in the margins, the novel implies a condition we would as soon call emancipation as alienation. This is a cultural self-realisation, a development towards critical 'qualitative assessment', which functions not as specialisation within the social division of labour but as the basis for a new level of consciousness. Its utopian aspect is figured literally, problematically, but not for the moment in denial, by the fact that there is nowhere Jude and Sue fit in: 'a shifting, almost nomadic, life, which was not without its pleasantness for a time'.[112]

We are hardly allowed to glimpse this: partly, perhaps, because its full representation was beyond the limits of Hardy's self-restricting language – the real theme of the later books, the thoughts and passions of the lovers, is never adequately realised in dialogue or in the representation of consciousness. Just one chapter (Book V, vii) covers two and a half years of the novel's timespan, during which Sue bears two children and conceives a third: this if ever is the time of their sexual happiness. Then comes the destructive dénouement, in which Hardy destroys the image of hope he has created. The reasons for destruction seem rooted in a complex of temperamental and professional disaffection, even despair: Hardy cited the novel's hostile critical reception as the reason he lost 'further interest in novel-writing' after its publication,[113] but the whole trajectory of his oeuvre, drawing on ever more recent experience and confronting him ever more insistently with the distance he had crossed, makes *Jude* its destined point of conclusion.

The tragic dénouement is a verdict on Jude's cultural aspirations. Soon after he arrives in Christminster, the narrator comments that 'the deadly animosity of contemporary logic and vision towards so much of what [Jude] held in reverence was not yet revealed to him',[114] and the ensuing narrative is the gradual revelation of that animosity. The project of cultural self-making, with no 'transitional social aims' and against the odds which only educational and political reform would shorten, is a too wilful defiance of practical possibility. A utopian – placeless – form of critical consciousness, marginal and nomadic, leaves those who bear it too exposed: integration and acceptance may be imperative for survival, even if that means compromise and worldliness, as in the decision of the hymn-composer whose music moves Jude but who turns out when Jude takes a day's journey to visit him to have abandoned composing (which does not pay) and set himself up in the wine-trade.[115]

This moment of irony serves to underline the relative purity of Jude's aspirations, rather than to question them. But what is not called in question morally may be doomed in practice as quixotic. This is the implication of another episode, which sets off Jude and Sue against the pragmatism represented by Arabella and her husband Cartlett, with whom she runs a 'little corner public in Lambeth'.[116] This 'excellent, densely populated, gin-drinking neighbourhood'[117] is Gissing territory, brought for a moment closer than is usual in Hardy's rural and provincial world, for the shilling popular excursion train on which the Cartletts travel is one of many bringing visitors from London and other towns to the agricultural fair where the two couples meet by chance. Arabella and Cartlett, leaving the station in the crowd of trippers, are described as 'a short, rather bloated man . . . [and] a woman of rather fine figure and rather red face'; Jude and Sue, watched narrowly by the jealous Arabella, are contrasted with them, and with the crowd, as 'the more exceptional couple'. Even though this scene in the flower pavilion is the strongest image of their happy sexual relation, they are doomed, like the flowers that will be 'withered within a few days'.[118] Hardy can call his couple 'exceptional' freely here because he does not see the urban mass with the democratic fellow-feeling he extends to rural people: Arabella is, from the start, a country girl sophisticated by town ways, made less pure and tougher. And Arabella, and behind her Lambeth, are the future. Whatever 'exceptional' consciousness Jude and Sue have won only makes them vulnerable, in this urban future figured according to the usual theorems of cultural pessimism. Their kind of attempt at self-realisation will have no place in the world to come. The novel which has offered the purest and most generous image of cultural aspiration (and the one best-known today, when most of our other texts are little read) also offers the gloomiest and most absolute premonition of its redundancy.

5

Culture and self-realisation: modernist distances

In the realist and naturalist novels we discussed in Chapter 4, culture is an element in society – 'Christminster', 'Swinburne', 'Beethoven'; and it is a dynamic of self-development, determining the social fates of characters. In the modernist novel, 'culture' in the sense of specialised aesthetic intelligence has become prominent in the texture of the work, its distinctive language and mode of representation. 'The content of the work of art, its "statement", recedes ever more as compared with the formal aspect, which defines itself as the aesthetic in the narrower sense.'[1] Self-fulfilment in culture is now what the work offers in itself – but only as the reward for whoever can successfully read it. For in modernism, the novel, historically the most accessible and least 'aesthetic' of literary genres, becomes difficult. Compared to its realist precursors (and to the thousands of realist novels published during the period of modernism), this text presents itself as recalcitrant and obscure. In societies beginning to pay some service to the idea that education should make culture more widely available, it sets out apparently to repel readers. Confronted, for example, with the opening of the third chapter of *Ulysses* ('Ineluctable modality of the visible . . . *Maestro di color che sanno* . . . Diaphane, adiaphane . . . *Nacheinander* . . . *Los Demiurgos* . . .'),[2] someone unversed in the relevant languages and traditions might (it seems) reasonably decide that modernism indeed represented 'a determined effort, on the part of the

European intelligentsia, to exclude the masses from culture'.[3]

Modernist difficulty is not always or only of that learnedly rebarbative kind. Moreover, Joyce is here difficult (it might be said) partly because he is rendering Stephen's thoughts. The textual difficulties of *Ulysses*, at which we glance again at the end of this chapter, are mostly of another sort. But even in less demanding instances, as in the unannounced shifts of perspective and initially unattributable pronouns that we may encounter as we start a new section of *To the Lighthouse*, modernist fiction makes reading problematic. The characteristics that tend to daunt or repel inexperienced readers – the work's 'highly conscious artifice', the prominence of formal aspects in our apprehension of it, its self-referentiality, its difficulty which 'signifies in and by the very act of offering resistance' and is 'inseparable from its mode of signification' – served as a means of marking it out from everyday records and representations in the burgeoning print culture amidst which it appeared.[4] Even when not manifestly difficult, such work assumes a familiarity with the norms against which it defines itself, and requires the reader to engage in an interpretation of style and form: the apparently unmarked prose of Flaubert's *Sentimental Education* (1869), for instance, challenges us in its very blankness to discern the perspective from which the well-concealed author-in-the-text expects us to construct meaning, irony and depth. To do so requires conceptual and empirical knowledge of other texts and conventions – cultural capital of a kind that only experienced readers will have. Something analogous is true of modernist poetry, painting and music. But in the case of the novel, whose language historically had for the most part been close to that of everyday prose, the resort to unfamiliar and problematic expression makes an intervention in the linguistic currency of the everyday.

This intervention can be regarded as both radical and élitist. The modernist text establishes new kinds of cultural distance in two senses. Its formal and linguistic originality, in its challenge to the taken-for-granted of representation, can make us re-read the social: Adorno has modernism above all in mind when he insists that only insofar as 'art has set itself apart in qualitative terms from . . . immediate reality' can it give us knowledge, a knowledge not of 'existence' but of the latter's 'essence and image'.[5] Since diverse, often reactionary, political positions can be read or inferred in the manifest content of modernist writing,[6] any progressive general politics of modernism must be located in the works' language and form, despite the fact that modernism's textual practice is 'objectively élitist'[7] in excluding less-educated readers. Because it will not yield to unreflective practices of reading, the work draws attention to language as mediation and as social construction not only in its own case (in the supposed 'detachment of art from practical contexts')[8] but in general. 'The textual openness of *Ulysses* encourages awareness of the social power of language.'[9] No-one has written like Joyce; but even more linguistically and socially conservative novels of modernism (such as Flaubert's) oblige the reader to construct meaning actively.

However, just this aspect, which challenges the 'bourgeois' ideal of a representation that would naturalise ideology as transparent language, reproduces (from another point of view) the familiar bourgeois equation of the valuable with the exclusive. Modernist distance in this second sense involves a deliberately created fracture within cultural audiences, between avant-garde minority and suburban mass.

Modernism is a paradigm case, in its difficulty, for critics who hold an allegiance both to an exacting high art and to left-wing democratic politics. As the editors of *Aesthetics and Politics* put it, the tensions between the 'progressive' and 'objectively élitist' aspects of the artwork that we find in modernism have been 'a central focus of aesthetic controversy on the left' because they mark a 'contradiction . . . which has never been durably overcome'.[10] This contradiction energises and plagues (to take two otherwise contrasting instances) the aesthetic theory of Adorno and much of the cultural criticism of Williams.[11] It informs and parallels the ways culture since modernism has been taught and critically discussed, within institutions that have both disseminated learning and reproduced élites. It shapes the project of this book, which questions whether self-realisation in culture can be understood not just as the individual acquisition of cultural capital or the individual enjoyment of refined cultural pleasures, but as the form or ideal of a general, democratic social development. We shall explore some of its dimensions here, bearing in mind that the most durable contradictions cannot be overcome in thought.

Modernist specialisation

Modernism in anglophone fiction follows on the struggle of literary novelists in the late nineteenth century to establish their difference from fellow practitioners. In and against the situation discussed in Chapter 4, where education was enlarging the readership for writing of all kinds, the literary audience became increasingly sub-divided. From the late 1880s, argues Allon White in *The Uses of Obscurity*, 'the market for the "respectable" novel seems to have split internally into an "élite" or reviewers' public and the more traditional Victorian public', with the formally and syntactically demanding work of George Meredith, Henry James and Joseph Conrad favoured by the élite audience.[12] This internal differentiation of novel-writing is reflected in debates on 'the art of fiction' taking place at the time, in which some argued in new terms for 'the high aesthetic integrity necessary to the novelist'.[13] Gissing ruefully commented that Scott and Dickens had known nothing of 'our grave Art of Fiction, a bitter task-mistress'.[14] Nonetheless, as we have seen, Gissing's own textual authority is premised on the author's cultural self-differentiation, and this can be seen as anticipating the 'objectification of the other' that Peter Nicholls sees as typical of modernism.[15] Gissing is a formally undemanding writer, using familiar devices of narrative and characterisation. However, we noted in Chapter 4 that Biffen's novel *Mr Bailey, Grocer* (in *New Grub Street*, 1891) can be seen as Gissing's sketch of a proto-modernist fiction. Its positive qualities are feebly indicated, but Gissing describes it negatively – and praises it implicitly – by telling us how reviewers castigate it because it is not 'amusing', 'does not tell a story', and is too close to life to suit established conventions.[16] This registers the element of recalcitrance that literary authorship was coming to involve, a resistance aimed against one's own reviewers, readers and fellow-writers; ultimately indeed against one's own second nature as a writer.

Biffen's novel fails miserably to win an audience. The real-life literary novelists were a small minority, and once we reach the moment of high modernism their audience was small too. The circulation of Dora Marsden's periodical *The Egoist* certainly never came anywhere near that of Dickens' *Household Words*, whose early numbers sold 100,000 copies. (*The Egoist*, named in honour of the philosophical solipsist Max Stirner, first published chapters from Joyce's *Portrait* and *Ulysses* and Wyndham Lewis's *Tarr*, as well as poems by H.D. and Pound.)[17] This is not a matter only of numbers. The readers of those many Victorian novelists whose works came out in more or less miscellaneous periodicals like *Household Words* would encounter fiction alongside other commentary and reporting on social matters. The positioning of novel-episodes cheek by jowl with heterogeneous workaday prose epitomised what literary writers opposed when they redefined the novel as 'the art of fiction': by distinguishing itself as a more clearly specialised kind of writing, it would become indisputably part of 'culture'. By the same token, however, it would sever some of its links to everyday rhythms and interests, and forfeit the broader influence enjoyed by less austere forms. Reflecting on this in a much later context, Andreas Huyssens notes the great public impact in Germany of the showing there in 1979 of the American TV series 'Holocaust', compares this with the relatively limited impact of modernist dramas dealing with the same theme, and concludes that modernist textuality, while it does have a 'truth content' of its own, forfeits the possibility of 'emotional audience identification'.[18] Huyssens is certainly right to emphasise the complexities involved in any judgement on the relative use and value of high and popular forms, and to question the assumption that the cultural politics of avant-garde work are necessarily or simply progressive. His discussion respects (as too many others do not) the need to discuss both cognitive–aesthetic and cultural–sociological aspects of the text, while refusing to collapse the former into the latter.

The self-differentiation of literary novelists can be seen as a 'Darwinian' evolution of literary production, in response to social and cultural change. However, we must be wary of functionalist accounts which obscure questions of agency and principle.[19] While from one point of view modernists sustained their project by creating a new élite audience and securing a degree of cultural influence disproportionate to the size of this readership, from another they were prepared to risk, and suffer, obscurity and marginality. Their position can be characterised in negative terms, as the rejection of a popular audience. But the rejection of an audience, even where it involves social snobbery,[20] may also be an assertion of aesthetic and cultural discrimination. Ford Madox Ford meant exactly what he said when he judged that 'with each cheapening of the mode of production the public has seemed to read rottener and rottener books':[21] the rottenness of the books was what distressed him.

To characterise the split that modernism reflected and helped to bring about in terms solely of the micro-sociology and competing identity-choices of literary production would be to ignore the aesthetic arguments and practices of modernists. This is to reduce all texts to their undifferentiated commodity status, except insofar as they can be read as vectors marking the supposed direction of cultural authority. In one widely used recent volume on *Cultural Politics*, the authors assert near the start:

> In this book we make a scandalous claim: *everything* in social and cultural life is fundamentally to do with *power*. Power is at the centre of cultural politics. It is integral to culture. *All signifying practices – that is, all practices that have meaning – involve relations of power.*[22]

The last sentence has an element of truth as regards published texts – though the 'signifying practices' of recipe books and gardening manuals (for instance) can normally be said to 'involve relations of power' only if one's concept of power is so diffuse as to lack much analytic use.[23] But it is a completely false inference from the premise to treat cultural texts (as these authors mostly do) as if their meanings could be *reduced* to the 'relations of power' they embody and reflect. To refuse such a reduced language is not to endorse all the tenets of a particular, modernist aesthetics, or to assert that cultural value can be described in purely aesthetic terms or settled beyond disagreement: disagreement is its essence. It is, however, to insist that there are cultural values.

There are questions here that we return to in our Conclusion. We do not, in any case, claim that cultural value is self-defining. Culture can only ever be the development and variation of languages already current, and the 'essence and image' it creates is not transcendence but a particular kind of mediation: mediation, we might say, through imaginary transcendence. Literary and artistic works are answerable to human communities; it is these which determine their value. This is not denied in the Romantic idea of poetry's higher truth. Shelley's figure of the poet as 'unacknowledged legislator' implies accountability to other people, as well as to the demands of art. As critics have noted, modernist practice both draws on and challenges post-Romantic ideas of art's autonomy.[24] Joyce is at once ironically distant from and intimately close to the Stephen Dedalus of the *Portrait* who invokes Shelley's *Defence of Poetry* and is immodest enough to call himself, as an artist, 'a priest of eternal imagination, transmuting the daily bread of experience into the radiant body of everliving life'. At the end of the *Portrait*, he notoriously sets himself the task of forging 'the uncreated conscience of [his] race'.[25] There is no doubting Stephen's arrogance, but nor is there any denying that this phrase invites, insists on, the judgement of its readers. (And it is Joyce/Stephen who begins the paragraph with another problematic reminder of the limits and social basis of artistic freedom: 'Mother is putting my new secondhand clothes in order.')

Nonetheless, both writer and reader of the modernist text may imagine that they are distinguishing themselves socially, not so much perhaps from the 'mass' or the proletariat as from something called the 'bourgeoisie': 'all these movements . . . claimed to be anti-bourgeois'.[26] In practice, modernist art and writing in most of their now canonical forms were built on, and helped deepen, divisions of reading and viewing practices and audiences *within* the literate, book-buying, gallery-frequenting public.[27] In Woolf's polemical pamphlet 'Mr Bennett and Mrs Brown', the writers whose example she eschews (Galsworthy, Wells, Bennett) are middlebrow literary novelists. The history of Woolf's own paper, delivered as a talk at Cambridge and then printed in T.S. Eliot's *Criterion*, indicates the nature of the alternative audience she sought.[28] If French and anglophone literary modernism strove to pull apart the phrase 'bourgeois culture', it did so by taking 'culture' too far, too seriously, beyond the point where the average bourgeois wanted to read on. Even the most textually defiant gesture was nonetheless by its nature aimed at the 'very class to which [most modernist practitioners] belonged' and which 'provided the only real audience [they] could expect to have'.[29]

The emphasis on culture as self-differentiation is found in several of the novels we discussed in Chapter 4, but they also show (ruefully or gleefully) the difficulty of claiming or sustaining a position of autonomy on a cultural basis. The blacklead factory pays for Tarrant's Oxford education, the Schlegels depend on Wilcox-driven entrepreneurial capitalism, *The Sacred Grove* sells liver pills, it is the bourgeoisie who buy Martin Eden's and Jack London's books – and Biffen lives on bread and dripping. When he wrote a variation on *New Grub Street* (1891) in *Keep the Aspidistra Flying* (1936), George Orwell suggested that not much had changed in the intervening decades, modernism notwithstanding. Commerce, and the petty-bourgeois audience, still exert their pressure against the aesthetic discourses that artists prefer. Money, if nothing else, reminds the writer of the social limits within which imaginary transcendence moves.

Limits can constrain without immobilising. Neither Gissing nor Orwell opted for the extremes of isolation or incorporation which they represented in their work, and some spirit of eventual compromise can be detected even in *Ulysses*, where Joyce counterposes the superb isolation of Stephen with Bloom's more creaturely sense of life. Bloom, we might say (despite John Carey's contention that he 'would never and could never have read *Ulysses*':[30] we return to this), is a figure of the petty-bourgeois reader, fallen and this-worldly, as against the aristocratic, writerly Stephen. But there is not much compromise in the way the book is written. If Joyce – like Bloom, like Gissing's Luckworth Crewe, like Orwell's defeated and happily-incorporated Gordon Comstock – had spent his days selling advertisement space or dreaming of advertising slogans, there would have been no *Ulysses*. As in novels of cultural aspiration, but now by way of textual difficulty and resistance as well as in plot and characterisation, Joyce's registering of contemporary experience depends on the creation of a perspective in which 'culture', acknowledged as part of society, still provides a distinctive point of vantage upon it. That vantage is attainable, for the present, only by a minority. If modernist literary culture offers self-realisation by way of distance, the reader addressed is one who has chosen to distance himself or herself from a 'bourgeoisie' to which he or she almost certainly belongs in the first place.

Modernist specialisation has had implications which go beyond the reading of modernist works, for it has provided influential paradigms for criticism and pedagogy in general. Allon White shows that in response to more difficult fiction, newly sophisticated kinds of 'critical attention' and 'symptomatic reading' were being brought to bear in the late nineteenth century.[31] These tended to scrutinise the text for evidence of the author's psychology, but this model of hermeneutic reading applied to modern, vernacular works would prove adaptable to other kinds of enquiry. Textual difficulty both generates and requires critical interpretation: insofar as 'the success of Modernist fiction depended . . . on a new kind of reader being created', then the critic and the educator were in a new kind of symbiosis with the author.[32] In the long run, moreover, the self-problematising nature of modernist fiction would impel critics to develop more sophisticated ideas about fictional form as such, drawing on work that had already begun to appear around the turn of the nineteenth and twentieth centuries. Because modernist texts pushed their readers to engage with representation, readings that focused only on manifest content were plainly inadequate to their interpretation. If we argue today (as we argued here in Chapter 3) that the fullest critical apprehension of any novel must engage with – though of course it need not endorse – the writerly perspective implicit in the text as a whole, this reflects the enduring influence of modernism. Whether or not one regards modernist aesthetics as offering models relevant to cultural work today, critical evaluation must acknowledge the distinctive quality of the 'writerly' work, as incorporating a self-reflexive relation to its own means of representation: the limitations of many popular forms such as soap operas and broadly realist historical novels are bound up with their refusal of self-reflexivity, which has cognitive as well as aesthetic implications.

Methods devised for the explication of difficult texts are now routinely brought to bear on diverse cultural works, including many which pose few overt problems of interpretation. Semiotics and semiology are tools for popular-cultural analysis as much as for literary criticism, and the structural linguistics in which they are rooted makes an integrally modernist move in analysing the doubleness of the sign. In a period which has seen the inauguration and subsequent rapid growth of English literary studies in the academic humanities,[33] and in which criticism and pedagogy have needed technique and legitimation, modernist ideas have played their part in the eventual constitution of a critical practice which closely analyses the text as an act of representation, a mediation rather than any kind of mirroring (though academic study of English was of course not in its early phases 'modernist' in this way). In terms of audience, however, as with the original moment of modernism, specialised development of this kind inevitably tends to make critical language itself inaccessible to less educated readers.

Modernism has also played a crucial role in literary and artistic canon-formation. The anglophone literary canon for the period 1900–1930 is heavily biased towards the modernist writing which comprised only a tiny proportion of published work, and it would be difficult to conceive of critical selectivity as applied to twentieth-century writing in the absence of modernist criteria (not that these have been uncontested: but they have provided a major point of reference and orientation). The connection between modernism, the academy or museum, and the idea of the canon is foregrounded with subversive intent by a contributor to a 1984 anthology on *Postmodern Culture*, who declares that 'the criteria for determining the order of aesthetic objects throughout the era of modernism – the "self-evident" quality of masterpieces – has been broken, and as a result "anything goes".'[34] Sustaining some mutable but defensible 'order of aesthetic objects', and debating how any such order is arrived at, has been until recently a primary purpose of cultural critique and education, and postmodernism as academic theory is partly definable by its scepticism or hostility towards that purpose. Here again, the modernist text is paradigmatic of the texts of learned culture, whose continued currency has been inextricably bound up with institutional practices of selection, critical commentary, and teaching.

The culture preserved by these practices is intrinsically valuable (we believe). But it is preserved within a framework of socio-cultural difference and self-differentiation marked by the structures and contradictions we have been tracing in these last two chapters: these have evolved but their basis remains, in a division of labour which is also a hierarchy of status, education and wealth. While the incorporation of cultural study in universities and schools secures a position for learned culture and makes available to many people the kinds of fulfilment which it can offer, it does so at a price. The role of education in the reproduction of hierarchy tends to turn all taught culture into cultural capital (as it is, directly, for those who make a living by teaching it), and to mean that in school it is regarded with suspicion at best by those who think they are not going to make the cut. So long as the educational dissemination of texts and ways of reading is rooted in a division of labour which education depends on and reproduces, the separation of learned culture from the vernacular of everyday life tends also to be a separation between specialists and others. Subcultures (one subcultural critic writes, from within the university) 'have elaborate ramifications in the lives of individuals . . . whereas the humanities, almost by definition in their current meritocratic mode, have to be specially inculcated. The attenuated social location and allegiance of a profession is not sufficient to keep . . . literary culture relevant and persuasive to the rest of society.'[35] Mass civilisation, minority culture, as in the title of Leavis's 1930 pamphlet.[36]

Its minority status has been a principal reason why critics from the 1930s to the 1990s have criticised modernism. Lukács' views are a classic point of reference. As Zygmunt Bauman has noted, the 'venom and malice' of the response to John Carey's book *The Intellectuals and the Masses* (1992) suggest that this too was in its own way an important intervention.[37] Both Lukács and Carey tend to offer sociological demonstration or assertion about the artwork's audience as if this could substitute for substantive critical evaluation. Lukács recurs to a somewhat reified 'realism' as the positive pole against which to counterpose his cursory dismissals of modernism as deranged, chaotic, narrowly personal and subjectivist; and Carey avoids substantive critical discussion of texts.[38] Conversely, Marshall Berman's generous and optimistic account of modernism in *All that is Solid Melts into Air* (1982), whose textual analyses show how modernist works engage with the 'complex and comprehensive ideal of *development*'[39] that Berman regards as the core of modernism, is evasive and unconvincing on the question of their audience. When he implies that the ordinary dweller in the modern city uses those texts to enrich or interpret everyday life – and still more when he identifies popular resistance to autocratic governments in developing countries as a manifestation of 'the modernist spirit', and suggests that the 'modernist vocabulary of opposition' forged by Kierkegaard, Baudelaire, Marx, Engels, Nietzsche, Eliot, and others might be deployed against the 'expressway modernism' that has destructively remodelled post-war cities – Berman is surely transposing his own response onto imaginary readers.[40] As we know, in truth 'Modernism and the avant-garde, in any of their forms, have never involved, as producers or publics, more than minorities; often very small minorities.'[41]

Those who would defend in democratic terms the value in contemporary societies of exacting cultural works like those of modernism would do better to accept rather than evade the contradiction which arises from their limited audience (we can also, of course, welcome any evidence that the audience is getting larger). Maybe neither modernism's textual strategies nor its creation of a self-differentiating readership provide a model for cultural work today; but it is still the case that textual difficulty restricts the circulation of books and makes them unintelligible to the uneducated. So long as we believe that some ideas and arguments are inherently complex but also illuminating, we must live with the same underlying contradiction. Insofar as this arises from social and educational circumstances, only changes in society and education could dispel or mitigate it.

Can Bloom read *Ulysses*?

Bloom, declares John Carey, 'would never and could never have read *Ulysses*'. Bloom is an appropriate focus for a last review of the tensions we have been tracing, because in some respects he epitomises, and was surely meant to epitomise, petty-bourgeois 'mass man'.[42] (The question of 'mass woman' and of the specific ways gender is involved in the Joycean world and in the writing and readability of modernism will take us too far if we pursue it here.)[43] He is a city-dweller rather than a suburban, but he has suburban aspirations: when he rejects the vision of a semi-detached villa called *Rus in Urbe* ('The country in the town'), preferring to daydream of a grander residence 'upon a gentle eminence with agreeable prospect from balcony with stone pillar parapet over unoccupied and unoccupyable interjacent pastures and standing in 5 or 6 acres of its own ground', these are very suburban daydreams.[44] We have seen that suburban life was a common theme for disdain among cultural intellectuals.[45] Although Bloom is not in our view held up for that kind of hostile scrutiny,[46] the gap between himself and Stephen is emblematic of the gap between suburbia and bohemia, commerce and culture, or (as Joyce puts it) between 'dietary and civic self-help' and 'the eternal affirmation of the spirit of man in literature'.

We might answer our question quasi-empirically, by asking whether some contemporary equivalent of Joyce's character might enjoy his book. *Ulysses* has got a bit easier to read: some of the once recherché techniques of modernism pose fewer problems than they did, being more familiar in advertising and other cultural forms, and their self-referential, parodic, always-already-mediated quality echoes the proliferation of voices and the discursive mediations of identity that characterise our social experience. If 'Bloom' came across *Ulysses* today, it would probably be in an educational setting, where modernist canons and paradigms are unfashionable but postcolonial fictions and representations of diasporic identity are much studied. There is a fair chance he would be asked to read the novel, or bits of it, if he chose and got admitted to the appropriate kind of course, and could pay for it. In short, the currency of modernist texts largely depends on the internal and social politics of cultural education: the case it can make for itself, as offering valuable kinds of self-realisation, the ways it conceives this and the textual means it uses.

A second answer is internal to the text. How does *Ulysses* represent Bloom as a possible reader? 'Art does not provide knowledge of reality by reflecting it photographically' (says Adorno, defending modernism, *contra* Lukács), 'but by revealing whatever is veiled by the empirical form assumed by reality.'[47] 'Photographically', and in the 'empirical form' of a society divided in the ways we know, the gap between Bloom and Stephen follows the material and cultural divide between writerly specialism and everyday consciousness: Bloom is primarily interested in 'dietary and civic self-help', Stephen in 'the eternal affirmation of the spirit of man in literature'. But when this form is 'unveiled', when the linguistic and social medium in which it exists is subjected to Joyce's utopian humanist alchemy, these fixed positions loosen, approach one another, and momentarily dissolve.

In the penultimate chapter of *Ulysses*, narrated in strikingly impersonal and catechistic style, Bloom has taken Stephen – drunk, but getting soberer – back to Eccles Street where he will give him some cocoa and the two will talk. We never hear the speakers directly but are given a rendering of their speech and thoughts that is at once distant and exhaustive. At the outset, we read:

> Were their views on some points divergent?
>
> Stephen dissented openly from Bloom's views on the importance of dietary and civic selfhelp while Bloom dissented tacitly from Stephen's views on the eternal affirmation of the spirit of man in literature.[48]

The quotation illustrates how, all through this chapter, apparently cut-and-dried affirmations draw attention, in paradigmatic modernist manner, to representation itself. (The linguistic devices are specific to the chapter, but in their effect they are characteristic of how the novel as a whole works.) Representation, once foregrounded like this, in turn draws attention to language; and then to what lies beyond language, which in *Ulysses* is nothing if not social. The characters 'Bloom' and 'Stephen', while continuing to exist for us – here towards the end of a long fiction – as eminently known, distinct beings, also approach one another, and lose their distinctness, because we apprehend them both in a medium which they partly share and which also partly creates them: a language, and ultimately a society. At the same time we see how social being, although individual being depends on it, creates difference and division as the very texture of the individual self – nowhere more so than in education, the learning of language and culture, whose ideal principle is universality:

> Did they find their educational careers similar?
>
> Substituting Stephen for Bloom Stoom would have passed successively through a dame's school and the high school. Substituting Bloom for Stephen Blephen would have passed successively through the preparatory, junior, middle and senior grades of the intermediate and through the matriculation, first arts, second arts and arts degree course of the royal university. [49]

'Can Bloom read *Ulysses*?' *Ulysses* invites us to question the idea of 'Bloom' as the petty-bourgeois who, by virtue of his status, 'would never and could never' read. It makes us aware of the mutually defining and interdependent nature of identity, and restores us to culture's utopian realm where we recognise ourselves in each other, and recognise the diverse and universal potentiality that is masked, but not erased, in the fixities of occupation and status. We cannot conceive of 'the eternal affirmation of the spirit of man in literature' without bringing it into contact with 'dietary and civic self-help': the terms used, at once lapidary and inadequate, contribute to that peculiarly Joycean tone which acknowledges irony and relativity without foregoing affirmation.

In this there are similarities (but also differences: Joyce sustains language as common medium across wider distances of class and status, and his vocabulary is much richer) with how Woolf, especially in *To the Lighthouse*, represents the collective experience of people sharing a life in ways that both transcend and confirm individual memory and feeling. Cultural transcendence is identified not with an author constituted (in the manner of realism) within social hierarchy, but rather, through the deliberate self-cancelling of any stable authorial position, with language itself.[50] Language in *Ulysses* is abundant, diverse, and resistant to many normative and hierarchical taxonomies. To refer back to a phrase of Jameson's quoted in Chapter 3, when this work 'brings into being that very situation to which it is also, at one and the same time, a reaction',[51] part of what it brings into being are those other, more familiar kinds of representation, against which it invites us to weigh its own inventiveness: not just in a battle between ancient and modern styles, but in a questioning of the kind of cultural work the old styles did. This utopian gesture could only be made in the sphere of culture, and any determination of its social meanings and effects must refer to the vexed question with which we began, the question of literary modernism's readability and of the indissoluble link we find in many of its works, including *Ulysses*, between difficulty and critique. We leave our readers to consider whether this link should still be made, and to reflect on the relation today between easiness (the first principle of mass culture) on the one hand and difficulty, critique, specialisation and arrogance on the other.

Conclusion: Culture and self-realisation in postmodern times

Both in the longer philosophical tradition and in the literary works from the post-Arnoldian decades that we have reviewed, a tension insistently makes itself felt between the implicit or proclaimed universality of the cultural ideal and the limits of its actual application. We can see now that this tension is there from the start within the very discourses of cultural self-realisation, but only in the historically recent (and geographically limited) conditions of general education and universal political citizenship does it enter widely into experience and consciousness. From Arnold's time on, and still today, individual cultural aspiration and the social ideal of cultural democracy may run up against barriers of unequal wealth and leisure. The professed ideal of equal access to culture can serve (as it does, implicitly or explicitly, in some of the works we have discussed) as one basis for the immanent critique of the society which professes it.

Here, the critical force of the cultural idea depends on its universal normative claims. Only if the ideal of self-development through an appreciation of learned culture is accepted as a general good can we deplore the social circumstances which exclude some people from it and which may indeed mean that they do not perceive it as a good in the first place. Critiques of mass entertainment, projects to encourage and facilitate wider access to higher education, and – more ambitiously – criticisms of the de-skilled nature of most work and the new ideological hegemony of the work-ethic, all rely on a conviction that many people would enjoy and benefit from intellectual and cultural enrichment which the conditions of their lives deny them. In the broadest historical terms, this conviction both informs and depends upon the social-democratic 'grand narrative' and its project of making economic and cultural goods that have historically been the preserve of élites available to people in general.

Within education, learned culture has indeed been made much more widely accessible in the period since 1945 than it ever was before. At the same time, however, all grand narratives and projects, not least that of diffusing 'good culture', have been vulnerable to the ideological revisions of our postmodern times. In everyday life, the saturation of public and domestic space with mediated signifiers, narratives and representations, and the self-celebratory 'cultural' dimension which various forms of identity-style bring with them to every setting from the office and the stadium to the night-club and the bedroom, make it impossible to argue that most citizens of our over-developed societies suffer from cultural lack in any quantitative sense. The idea that there are cultural goods of which people are deprived and which education can make available to them thus more than ever depends on and implies qualitative cultural judgement. But (as Jim McGuigan laments) 'confused and helpless silence' has recently tended to reign where once teachers of culture spoke confidently of values and quality.[1] Cultural intellectuals are reluctant nowadays to present themselves as knowing what is best for others, and most of them recognise that the making and evaluation of learned culture has been socially implicated in hierarchies and exclusions: of status, class, gender/sexuality, centre/periphery, metropole/colony, 'race'. However, to say that culture is implicated in history and society is by no means to say that it has no specific forms or criteria of value. The difficulty – too easily evaded in love-affairs with the popular, retreats into incomprehensible 'theory', or pious invocations of old canons – is to sustain a critical discourse that respects these complexities.

We have discussed aspects of these questions at various points above: for example, in relation to postcolonial and other critiques of the subject of Enlightenment in Chapter 2, and in our commentary on Gissing's recognition of new cultural forms in Chapter 4. Here in conclusion we focus at greater length on some contemporary contexts within which the ideal of self-realisation through culture is challenged but which also (we shall argue) justify its continued defence. We end by engaging with some difficulties of evaluative argument in academic cultural studies. First, however, we discuss the relations between work, free time and culture, asking how far concepts of alienated and deskilled labour are still pertinent, before turning to 'cyberculture' and drawing up the balance between empowerment and narcissism within this contemporary cultural form.

Work, free time and cultural self-realisation

Even when it is promoted, as in the social-democratic context, as a desirable pursuit for everyone, cultural self-realisation involves activities that for most people remain separate and distinct from those carried out at work or in the servicing of everyday needs. In this sense, culture figures in the main as antithetical to work, and any gratification or self-realisation to be derived from it is a product of leisure and dependent on some measure of free time. There are those – writers, artists, teachers, for example – whose work itself offers cultural self-realisation; and skills acquired through cultural education may be called upon in other kinds of work, even if that work has little to do with culture and offers no distinctively cultural satisfaction. But for most people most of the time the domains of work and of cultural self-realisation are pretty much mutually exclusive.

This is not to say that there are no fulfilments attached to work itself whether or not this is intellectually demanding or culturally oriented: as we acknowledge below, work does, at least in principle, offer its own distinctive forms of satisfaction. Nor are we implying that people would necessarily be drawn into an engagement with learned culture if they had more free time. However, that work and culture are generally perceived as antithetical itself suggests that the social and technical division of labour denies individuals the opportunity for cultural self-development. Those who have discovered an interest at school or university will usually find it difficult to integrate it into their working lives. What stands in the way here is not a lack of educational commitment or provision, but the structuring of society.

The further realisation of cultural–democratic hopes and individual cultural aspiration – and any possibility of making demanding cultural work and complex cultural criticism available outside their current subcultural, academic domains – depends in this sense not on changes in access to education but on wider social changes. Schools and universities, so politicians frequently complain, are failing to fit their students to the job-descriptions of the commercially competitive and vocationally specialised work-world. But to school-leavers and university graduates this can feel like a looking-glass logic: it is the work-world that has let them down and sacrificed their talents and potential to narrow profit-driven imperatives and mechanical work routines, and often to the production of worthless and wasteful commodities. Who is failing whom when teenagers go from schools that claim and strive to foster self-reliance, and the all-round development of the individual child, into parcellised and de-skilled work which allows those who do it little or no initiative or control? Who is failing whom when graduates who have spent three years studying the Mediaeval lyric, Wittgenstein on mental concepts, environmental ethics, or the Scottish Enlightenment find themselves earning a subsistence wage in a cubicle in some hangar answering queries about mobile phone bills or car insurance renewal? (Now that companies are moving their call centres outside Europe in pursuit of even cheaper English-speaking labour – in India, where several have relocated, graduates get starting salaries of only £2,500 as opposed to £12,500 – even this source of employment may begin to dry up.)[2]

Jude Fawley's premature demands have in some sense finally

been met. Cultural education is more widely available than ever before in Western societies. However, the objective and subjective pressures of work and the market still mean that few people enjoy lives in which intellectual and cultural self-realisation figure as an integrated, lifelong pleasure. It is over seventy years since Weber characterised the ascetic dimension of capitalist industry in his image of the 'iron cage':

> When asceticism was carried out of monastic cells into everyday life, and began to dominate worldly morality, it did its part in building the tremendous cosmos of the economic order. This order is now bound to the technical and economic conditions of machine production which today determine with irresistible force the lives of all the individuals who are born into this mechanism, not only those directly concerned with economic acquisition. Perhaps it [*sic*] will do so until the last ton of fossilized coal is burnt.[3]

Weber's gloomy prophecy has come to look increasingly realistic. Technological mastery and enhanced productivity have served not to free people from the domination of work, but to confirm them in an essentially 'primitive' dedication to toil.[4] Not everyone finds work, of course: during recessions, many do not (and some predict an era of 'jobless growth' in which work will be chronically scarce). But even in the wealthiest societies, almost everyone's life is dominated by the combined impact of the capitalist mission to enhance profits by cutting jobs and of the puritan insistence that work is the condition of pleasure, a 'moral' insistence which in our kinds of society is an all too material fact: if you are deprived of the former then you have little entitlement to the latter. Wherever social democracy has yielded ground to neo-liberalism, and the value of state pensions and other social benefits has fallen, the grip of this economic–cultural dynamic has tightened. We see its effects in the demoralising penury of those without work, in the swelling ranks of marginal and part-time workers with no benefits or job security, and in the coercion – or seduction – of full-time workers into 'workaholic' routines. All are victims of an economic imperative which requires the hugely increased productivity of social labour to realise itself not in more free time, but in the production of more and more material commodities and commodified 'services'.

This imperative is realised by way of the 'objective' (socially and legally instituted) character of the capitalist economy. But there is a dialectic here: the imperative also requires social and political agreement or toleration. Unmet needs for more free time, greater autonomy, more space for self-chosen activity, constitute a counter-systemic potential, a pressure against the bars of the 'iron cage'. In rich societies, this is certainly a more subversive potential than the 'need' to consume more commodities (which is not to deny that there are many poor people in wealthy countries). The full scope of this question is very wide. As Lucio Magri put it in the early 1980s:

> It is not possible to confront the problem of underdevelopment seriously without putting into question our own ways of producing and consuming, our whole system of values. Any new relationship with the Third World presupposes a qualitative change in our own type of development. Such a change would have to involve a reorientation of the European economies away from the quantitative multiplication of goods for consumption and export, and the wastage of natural resources that goes with it, towards another style of development: one that was sober in its consumption, exported technology and knowledge rather than commodities, sought a reduction in labour-time performed, gave priority to improvements in the quality of living.[5]

This is an eco-socialist vision, very different from the 'Third Way'. But steps to reduce 'labour-time performed' can begin within social democracy, as has happened with the introduction of the thirty-five hour week in France. As André Gorz has long argued, a reduction in the amount of time spent on the heteronomous (other-determined) labour required by modern mass production would lead to the expansion of the sphere of creative, autonomous activity. This can include work as *poiesis* ('making'), in which individuals or groups choose to meet their own material needs by their own labour; it includes sport, games, leisure pursuits generally, and the enjoyment of culture.[6] The essential point is that cultural self-realisation, as one aspect of 'improvements in the quality of living', is doubly bound up with the enjoyment of free time. The future extension of cultural education depends on political and economic change. But if the need for cultural satisfactions is not sustained in the here and now – if education is comprehensively redesigned as preparation for work – then the prospects for any such change are lessened.

We are not arguing that the social division of labour can be abolished. In a non-capitalist society, it would be easier to resist the de-skilling of work and to introduce greater variety into the labour process. But no complex society could dispense with specialisation in knowledge, skill and function, nor is it obvious that this would bring any gain socially or individually.[7]

From the perspective we adopt here, the crux is the overall subordination of work to a system for which more free time is a threat to prosperity rather than a form in which that prosperity can be realised. From this standpoint, a substantial reduction in work time, especially if accompanied by greater security of income, would at once meet and encourage the need for greater autonomy.

We argue for such changes and for their intrinsic connection with cultural value and opportunity even though some would contest the idea that most work under present conditions is alienated and unsatisfying. Feminists have understandably rejected left-wing polemics against the systemic alienation of work in the public sphere which seemed ready to overlook the dreary and isolating nature of housework and to conspire with patriarchal culture at large in confining women to domesticity.[8] For many women who responded to Second Wave feminism, alienation consisted in being tied to the kitchen sink, and emancipation involved gaining access to the world of work. If experiences to be had at work now play a greater part in the lives of both women and men, that may indeed be partly accountable to the influx of women into new kinds of workplace and the consequent transformation of gender relations there. Culturally, the domestic space has receded in significance, losing its connotations of 'hearth and home' and becoming akin to a resting station or bivouac where the worker catches a few hours sleep between days devoted to the more engrossing occupations of the office. Even work's stressful aspects can be celebrated as contributing to its exciting atmospherics. But this picture, evoking the kind of light-and-airy open-plan office we see in TV commercials, hardly captures the variable reality of wage labour. Moreover, it is often the public sociability of the workplace that makes work 'culturally' attractive: not the tasks performed, but the camaraderie and social dynamics that give texture to the performance.

We do not in any case suggest that work as such, work considered in an abstract philosophical–anthropological sense, is dispensable to self-realisation. To argue that people would be better fulfilled if they did less work is not to argue that they would be more fulfilled if they did none. No utopia of 'play' and '*faire rien*' (as envisaged by Marcuse),[9] even if it were feasible, would provide the satisfaction that comes from hard graft and is associated with a republican interest in making one's own contribution to a collective matrix of goods and resources. Human beings derive satisfaction from the forms of objectification of themselves provided by work, the social orientation of their labours, the deployment of skills and expenditure of effort involved. This is a satisfaction associated with subordination of the self (to the needs of the community at large, to the demands of a collective practice or operation, to the sheer rhythm of physical exertion, and so on); it is distinct from the expressive and self-reflective forms of self-realisation that derive from culture. Hegel captures something of its quality in his Master–Slave dialectic, where the eventual triumph of the 'slave' relates to the necessity of working for the 'master', and the forms of activity, self-abnegation and objectification that this requires.[10] So, too, does Tolstoy in his depiction in *Anna Karenin* of the obscure craving that Levin finally (if temporarily) gratifies when he scythes in the fields alongside the peasants on his estate.[11]

Tolstoy's scene is a vivid reminder of how anonymous and mechanical work can provide fulfilments of its own. However, Levin's enjoyment of scything is the enjoyment of one who does it by choice and for a few hours. Much of his life provides opportunities for something more directly self-expressive; and his education and wealth mean that for him (unlike 'his' peasants, and unlike Hardy's Tess Durbeyfield), the division of labour can be temporarily transgressed. All the more reason, therefore, to suppose that those whose work does not provide such opportunities would benefit from the expansion of free time for interests that can compensate for the tedium of work and allow a more critical relationship to it. Cultural education figures doubly in this: as one kind of rewarding activity in a future less driven by work, and as contributing now to the sense of possible alternatives. The perspective on the 'totality' developed in the engagement with serious culture provides a source of individual self-realisation. It can also sustain collective intellectual dissent from instrumental conceptions of progress and the good life. Culture encourages just what most work must suppress, namely a reflection on ends and values.

Cyberculture?

We can distinguish between the forms of self-realisation made possible through the educated encounter with learned culture, and those gained from other autonomously undertaken free time activities. Where, in this, do we place the opportunities opened up by the information technology revolution and the rise of the 'Network Society'?[12] What is the nature and quality of the fulfilments available through virtual reality and cyberculture?

Computer technology allows an unprecedented range of texts

and information to be accessed and processed faster than ever before. It has offered corresponding benefits to scholarship and cultural activity and in that sense has played an instrumental role in furthering the engagement with learned culture itself. Beyond this, the incorporation of new information technologies into everyday gadgets and subcultural activities exposes people to an ever faster and denser flow of words and texts. It acts synergistically with the parallel proliferation in 'traditional' media such as TV and radio channels, but differs in offering opportunities for interactivity and dialogue. It seems beyond doubt that this expansion and diversification are inducing qualitative changes in the ways we relate to writing and information. However, the consequences for cultural education and for the currency of learned cultural texts are not easily predictable. The sheer flux of undifferentiated words tends in principle to make textual canons more useful, as well as more vulnerable. The expansion in opportunities for informal communication and networking may well engender growing interest in the more academic study of writing, culture or local history. In any case, cultural change is overdetermined by many social forces, and in our view social decisions about the nature and intensity of work, and the relations between work and education, are likely to be the single most important factor in shaping the cultural future, far outweighing the specific influence of new media and communications technologies.

Here, having acknowledged the larger questions involved, we focus primarily on the claims made for the intrinsic *sui generis* fulfilments of new media as a communicative and expressive cultural form, compared to those offered by learned culture as this has been taught and transmitted within traditions of selection, historical scholarship and critical commentary. We do not dispute that there are enjoyments and sources of self-expression to be found on the net. Nor do we question that for some people, these possess peculiarly compelling qualities thanks to the indefinite, anonymous nature of the communication involved and/or the virtuality of the reality it accesses. Here is a world of interaction, self-expression and self-experimentation which is in some respects without precedent – though its newness often has more to do with its technical dimension as a medium than with any radical departure in the forms of entertainment and self-staging for which it has proved a vehicle. It introduces a novel kind of dislocation between mind and body, but many of the styles and pleasures it draws on (for example, those of anonymity, gender disguise and masquerade) have their analogues in Homer, or at any rate in Plautus.

This new-found cerebral existence has been much hyped by advocates of hyperspace and cyberotics as revolutionary empowerment. Once freed from the 'chrysalis of matter', we will be able to 'rechoose reality', and may even be 'destined for a wholesale leap into the next dimension'; we can all (promises Timothy Leary) be 'linked in thrilling cyber exchanges with many others whom we may never meet in person . . . Face-to-face interactions will be reserved for special, intimate, precious, sacramentalized events.'[13] In 'the soft hail of electrons that is cyberspace', information is removed from all the corruptions attendant on its attachment to *things*;[14] through cyberism, we shall finally attain a position where we can throw off our 'bestial nature' and 'become pure in spirit'[15] – and so on. However, while these voices celebrate the cyborg 'escape from meat', others, more compellingly in our opinion, point to the ways in which such 'escape' desensitises and prosthetically encumbers the body, and to the reactionary puritanism of its revulsion with the flesh.[16] (Other cyberists, very loath to appear to advocate a prurient and hygienic world of cerebral sex, tie themselves in even more curious and comical rhetorical knots around 'hard' and 'wetwares', 'Dionysian castration' and SM dismemberment.)[17]

The cybernetic medium may be novel, but its conceptions of pleasure are neither incontrovertible nor necessarily progressive. We should also note the ontological confusions and paradoxes in the case made for cybercultural self-realisation.[18] To name but some: the enthusiasts and technicians of virtual reality seem obsessed with the exactest mimetic replication of the world of actual perception even as they revel in the licence it gives to redesign reality; freedom from identity and the opportunity for gender-swapping depend on the restrictions of text-only dialogue, now shortly to be transformed through the 'liberating' move into a simulated visual and tactile cyberspace; though always heralded as revolutionary, the emancipation on offer is made to sound banal and retrograde (we will enjoy a magical mystery tour, a spiritual voyage of discovery, a religious awakening, and so on).[19] To promote the net as a forum for an unprecedentedly candid and democratic interchange, a kind of 'ideal communication situation', is rather inconsistent with praising the opportunities it offers for deceptions about role and identity. And all this hyperbole ignores the fact that four out of five of the world's inhabitants are still without a telephone.[20]

Beyond these ironies and inconsistencies, there is a more fundamental contrast to be drawn between cultural self-realisation as we understand it and the conceptions of self-enhancement and self-fulfilment invoked by the cyberists. Cyber satisfaction is centred on self-narrative, self-mirroring, self-display: its cultural object is nothing other than the reflected self. Learned culture makes sometimes arduous intellectual demands, requires a certain detachment from questions of selfhood, and elicits forms of attention and engagement relatively indifferent to one's own role, identity, and sexuality. Cyberculture is easy, spontaneous, egocentric, and focused on personal identity and its self-pleasuring performative powers. Where cultural self-realisation might be said to be self-transcendent, self-realisation in cyberia is narcissistically immersed in the appearances, impressions, prompts and stimulations of the moment. If its immediacy is one feature of cyberculture which absorbs and rewards its fans, another is its potential to fulfil fantasies. Cyberia is hailed as the realm where we can indulge the tastes and enjoy the gratifications that are either impossible in reality or forbidden by the moral and legal restrictions of a still boringly 'humanist' culture.[21] But all these gratifications are not so obviously different from what we can get from watching television or videos or reading magazines: a form of consumption which offers no necessary connection to any world of values transcendent to those of consumerist enjoyment generally, and no counter to or critical mediation of privatised or work-directed or instrumental rationality and sensibility.

The actively expressive use of IT obviously has other kinds of cultural potential. It can extend and give a platform to personal, amateur forms of expression formerly carried out just for one's own pleasure and that of one's friends: the writing of diaries and letters and stories and poems, the making of videos or taking of photographs. The new media have also become a tool in collective making and performance: new kinds of oral and local history and collaborative publishing, new partnerships between community groups, museums and educational institutions. Along with 'history from below' we have 'culture from below', whose scope widens as the Internet provides contacts, networks and forms of publication.

It is too soon to predict the long-term effects of these new or revitalised forms, which compete with commercial popular culture as well as with high culture, and whose advent complicates previous boundaries between private and public, individual and collective, producer and receiver, artist and audience. They are obviously likely to strengthen subcultural networks and affiliations: whether of local historians or limerick collectors, football fans or foot fetishists, pigeon fanciers or paedophiles. For their members, such circles will offer welcome confirmation of an existing cultural identity. In contrast, the valued texts of learned culture (the poems of Dante or Elizabeth Bishop, the paintings of Goya or Jackson Pollock) neither assume nor depend on any a priori interest in their makers' personal interests and concerns. The forms of cultural self-realisation we have been affirming in this book are those whose reward is not a signature or image of the self nor an encounter between selves, but an opening to the new ideas and previously unrecognised perspectives of the author, artist or musician. The material distinction between private and public textual forms may be blurred by new communications media, but this distinction in principle remains.

Teaching culture: cultural value and the 'category of totality'

It is the specialised or unfamiliar conventions and languages of learned culture's texts, as well as the practices of critical and interpretative reading associated with them, that are responsible in part for their separation – for better and worse – from everyday forms. Any advocacy of the value of learned culture as offering a space for reflection and self-making therefore relies (as it has done since Arnold) on cultural education, which continues to occupy an important place in secondary schools and in the university. Cultural intellectuals have become more 'self-conscious about the implicit hierarchies of taste and value we live and teach by'; and they will certainly agree that 'the elevated rank of intellectuals as agents and arbiters of historical progress' can no longer be assumed or sustained.[22] But this need not be a cause for regret: to make values explicit and recognise their contestable nature, and to work accountably within accountable institutions, is not to forego the possibility of exercising influence. The saturation of everyday life by cultural signs has made it more obviously useful for people to develop analytical understandings of culture. The recent expansion of higher education is a good in itself[23] for anyone who believes in the long-term project of cultural studies, as a practice of democratic and interdisciplinary popular education.[24] The neo-vocationalism of recent policy discourse is chilling (though familiar), but as well as emphasising that studying culture imparts useful skills, teachers can encourage students to think critically and historically about the immanent contradictions we have just discussed between educational self-realisation and the nature of most work. In short, several viable projects can compete, and combine, within the field of teaching culture: helping readers understand difficult texts and make critical evaluations, the sociological analysis of cultural production and consumption, and the preparation of specialist cultural, intellectual and media workers.

Larger political claims tend to fade out in such a redefinition, but even some left-wing critics now see this as a realistic adjustment of vision. 'Cultural theorists *qua* cultural theorists' can contribute little to the resolution of political problems, Terry Eagleton has recently written. Francis Mulhern suggests that it is time to abandon the would-be regulative 'romance' of metacultural discourse: culture may denominate 'a mass of heterogeneous possibilities old and new', since the cultural 'field of interests, values and identities is always excessive', but in its interplay with politics 'culture' cannot be invoked as if it were a higher authority.[25] The implicit practical injunction – that critics should acknowledge the political inefficacy or impertinence of metacultural criticism, and pursue politics if they want to in better designated spheres – seems reasonable.[26] Tony Bennett, from a different perspective, questions the presumption that the politics of cultural study is essentially a matter of critique: there is a positive aspect to any work involving the intellectual formation of cultural makers, policy-makers, interpreters and administrators, and those who do it should abandon their self-ascribed status as critical outsiders.[27]

However, to proceed intellectually with too narrowly contextualised a sense of culture and its study, and to disavow all metapolitical reference, is to acquiesce in a foreclosure of historical perspective. 'Culture' has been in the broadest sense a political–critical term, referring not simply to individual pleasures of aesthetic and intellectual enjoyment but to an ideal of self-development whose implications are social. Increasingly recognised even by its own advocates as partial, specialised, determined, dependent, culture in this wider sense is nonetheless presented as normative, regulative and universal. It refers, then, to what Fredric Jameson – lamenting, twenty-five years ago, that it had been 'systematically undermined' – called the 'category of totality'.[28] Moreover, inasmuch as the cultural ideal invokes a 'total' development that has not yet come about, its claims to universality are not positivistic but critical and utopian. This is to say that they are tied symbiotically to its normative and evaluative claims, whose own 'universal' reach is therefore called to account.

Our explorations and discussions, throughout, have sought to acknowledge these tensions, and to suggest that it is precisely from their contradictory coexistence that the idea of culture derives its energy. Let us consider them as they are dramatised in one last scene that foregrounds the ambiguous relations between culture, class and democracy. The scene occurs in Satyajit Ray's film *The World of Apu (Apur Sansa).* The trilogy of which this forms the final part, made between 1955 and 1959, was based on two novels by Bibhutibhusan Banerjee that had been successfully serialised in a Calcutta journal in the late 1920s. Their story of a poor country boy who succeeds in winning scholarships and seeks to make himself a writer in the city was based on the author's life, but is clearly influenced (as no doubt that life also was) by European novels,[29] and can be placed alongside analogous fictions which we considered in Chapter 4.

Ray's own cultural formation is described by Andrew Robinson in his book *Satyajit Ray: The Inner Eye*. His well-to-do family was associated with the so-called 'Bengal Renaissance' (in which Hindu, Islamic and British and European cultural influences had run together from the 1830s). Ray himself had an unusual but impassioned interest in European classical music. Among his teachers at Presidency College in Calcutta was the left-wing literary critic Humphry House.[30] Fortuitously, during the shooting of the first film in the trilogy, *Pather Panchali*, Ray met Monroe Wheeler of the New York Museum of Modern Art, while Wheeler was in Calcutta: Wheeler arranged for the film to be premiered at MOMA. *Pather Panchali* received financial support from the Government of West Bengal, whose Chief Minister, Dr B.C. Roy, 'was sympathetic but, from the beginning, misunderstood the film's nature, seeing it as a documentary promoting rural uplift'.[31]

The trilogy's canonical status in world cinema may owe something to these European and American connections as well as to its exceptional artistic qualities. Undoubtedly the ideas of learning, culture and self-realisation deployed by Banerjee and Ray have a partly colonial provenance, and their specific form (Apu wants to write like Dostoevsky) reflects the dominance of European texts. Who, then, is such a film for? Who is to read this story of the poor, anonymous rural boy caught up, not unlike Hardy's *Jude*, in a culture to which he is marginal but which defines the nature of his aspirations, making him imagine himself as a successor to Dostoevsky? How will different viewers see it?

These are the questions raised by the scene we want to comment on. Apu, having finished his studies and come almost to the end of his funds (he has pawned his copy of the *Oxford English Dictionary*), is looking for work. He applies for a job in a back-room factory or sweatshop, unsure exactly what task he will be set to perform. The manager, sitting at his desk, asks if he has any experience of 'labelling'. No, says Apu; but he believes he will be able to do it. The manager jerks his thumb, pointing along a corridor, and Apu peers in at the door at the corridor's end. There in front of him, at workbenches piled high with glass bottles, five or six people sit in the gloom: their job, not so unlike Dickens' in the blacking factory (and, we suppose, not so unlike the jobs of those who make trainers for multinational firms today), is to take a bottle, glue a label onto it, take another bottle, glue a label onto it, take another bottle, glue a label onto it, and so on, all day. Apu looks for a moment at them; his look is returned; he moves away from the door without speaking, and when we see him next he is back out in the street.

'Cultural treasures' have an origin that we 'cannot contemplate without horror', for 'they owe their existence not only to the efforts of the great minds and talents that have created them, but also to the anonymous toil of their contemporaries'.[32] More directly than any scene in *Jude the Obscure*, the encounter in the bottle factory stages a confrontation between the urge to cultural transcendence, as it gives meaning to a life, and the world of anonymous toil which is its antithesis but also its continuing context. (A nearer literary analogy, perhaps, is in the momentary encounters in *The Portrait of the Artist* which remind Stephen Dedalus of the squalor and self-abnegation in which his sisters live.) The question which the scene poses is, precisely, how to read the distance between Apu and the labellers, who represent in this explicitly metacultural moment 'great mind' and 'anonymous toiler'. Is 'culture', the realm in which Apu seeks meaning, not just alien but meaningless to those who return his gaze? Or is the gap between them and him, in being made so visible, also in that moment given meaning, and so made less tolerable and perhaps less certain to endure? – a reading that implies that a labeller who went to the cinema and watched this scene might identify not with herself or himself, but with Apu.

We want to read the scene, and the film, positively: to see its invocation of the idea of alienation as part of an emancipatory critique, legible to the subaltern 'other' though encoded in a postcolonial form. Others, perhaps trying to find a closer identification with the anonymous labellers, might make a case that it is Ray who is alienated here, in privileging Apu's 'European' sensibility; and might locate the most important actual politics of the film there. (Apu, we should add, probably never becomes a writer. A compelling image shows the pages of his manuscript floating like leaves in the wind to which he has thrown them. He is a displaced, uncertain intellectual at the film's end, not unlike Jude, though younger. In today's world, as a graduate in India, perhaps he would qualify for a job in a call centre working for an American medical practice or London financial services company: not so vastly preferable to labelling.)

There is certainly an argument to be had about the film, the scene, and the problems of reading that they highlight. How do we weigh the progressive claims of normative, would-be 'total' cultural discourses in the balance against their always particular origins and settings? And how does criticism, in attempting to do this, understand its own (usually institutional) situation, and the relation to 'totality' which that situation implies? – for even critics who might argue against the offered identification with Apu and with authorial, literary consciousness could hardly deny that they for their part belonged to the world of ideas and culture rather than of anonymous toil.

Let us conclude by considering some ways these questions have been engaged with, and evaded, in recent cultural criticism. We noted in Chapter 2 that the ideal of self-realisation in culture invokes a certain conception of the subject as self-reflexive and self-directing, and relies on works of artistic and intellectual culture that address this 'inward' and complex self. Such a conception of the human subject, we argued (against its post-structuralist critics), properly has a universal dimension and this certainly need not involve the repression of difference: on the contrary, it is under the sign of the 'human' that a more inclusive concept of human subjectivity is best developed. We went on to discuss texts and textual canons and to make the case that the self-realisation offered in complex (often, canonical) literary and cultural works cannot be limited to the ways they may confirm a pre-given 'identity'. We return here to these themes, approaching them now from a somewhat different angle: whereas our primary focus in Chapter 2 was on underlying conceptions of subjectivity and self-development, here we attend mainly to the implications of these for our engagement with inherited texts.

We can begin with Raymond Williams' argument (in 1961) that an inherited textual canon should be made generally available because its 'meanings and values' were ultimately 'universal':

> Meanings and values, discovered in particular societies and by particular individuals, and kept alive by social inheritance and by embodiment in particular kinds of work, have proved to be universal in the sense that when they are learned, in any particular situation, they can contribute radically to the growth of man's powers to enrich his life, to regulate his society, and to control his environment.[33]

The claim met sceptical rejoinders in class terms when it was first made: was not Williams, even though he wrote from a working-class experience and perspective, too indulgent to the bourgeoisie who had made and preserved most of these 'meanings and values'?[34] Equally striking to us now is the absence, in *Culture and Society* and *The Long Revolution*, of any recognition of feminist culture and politics, despite the activity of women and feminists as writers and critics throughout the period surveyed.[35] Paul Gilroy, in *The Black Atlantic*, has charged Williams (and some other New Left cultural critics and historians) with a failure to register the imperial and post-imperial dimensions of British national culture and specifically with a reluctance to confront the implication of the Victorian literary élite in the history of Empire.[36]

These kinds of critique, like the political activity of the new social movements to which they are related, refer beyond Williams to the whole project of postwar British social democracy. The 'universal subject' of hoped-for progress allegedly turns out to look too much like 'Man' – white, European by origin, and heterosexual, and perhaps rather bourgeois, even if no longer axiomatically so; and the culture associated with his advance is marked by (although reluctant to acknowledge) the oppressions and exclusions which the concept of 'Man' has ratified. It can then be argued that the ground of humanist universals, including especially literary and aesthetic universals, had best be explicitly abandoned. Marc Redfield, whom we quoted in Chapter 2 as arguing that 'the sign of the human' must always actually designate subjectivities that are 'Western, male, etc.', sees 'aesthetic history' and its canons as the vehicle for this illicit operation by which 'the sheerly empirical qualities of being European, white, middle-class, male, and so on become either tacitly or overtly essentialized'.[37] Those who ally themselves with excluded or marginal groups and subcultures should contest universalist claims, Alan Sinfield urges, since these are paradigmatically made on behalf of the dominant culture: they should make sure their own first allegiance is to subcultural ties and loyalties rather than to an academic discipline, and should emphasise the grounded particularity of their own readings. 'A divided society should have a divided culture; anything else must be a mystifying pretense.'[38] In various versions, this strategy – which we shall call cultural particularism – has united those speaking for many different excluded constituencies in a general assault on universalism.

Universalist claims were certainly ripe for examination and could not be expected to survive in uninflected form. Whereas an abstract conception of the self-reflexive human subject as one capable of realising greater agency and autonomy through learning and self-development is (we have argued) properly universal, cultural works and traditions reflect and express particular, inherently limited experiences and conceptions. The period since Arnold has seen a great expansion in the means and processes by which learned culture has been opened up to – or foisted upon – those formerly excluded from it: canonical texts were bound to come under question as a result. Someone else's idea of 'the best that has been thought and known' may not be readily pleasurable at all:

> As many generations of painful and confusing experience now testify, to become 'literate', and still more – for a few – to come to acknowledge the value of 'literature', is, for a working-class child, to be caught up in a social and ideological process that is profoundly ambiguous and disorientating in its movement and destination.[39]

The textual strategies which George Eliot, Elizabeth Gaskell or even (perhaps especially) the working-class D.H. Lawrence use to represent working-class life, as well as the general tenor of their cultured discourse, might certainly force upon a working-class reader questions of identification like those we discussed above in relation to *The World of Apu*. Am I absent, misrepresented, disparaged, or am I somehow to find myself by transposing myself – this, we argued in Chapter 3, is a necessary moment even in a critical or antagonistic reading – into the imaginary position of authorship? Analogous (though not identical) ambiguities arise for all readers who identify themselves with excluded, silenced or marginal social constituencies and find themselves engaged with an author who speaks as if for a totality which excludes these.

But the positioning of the self as particular reader (say, 'queer' or 'English' or 'working-class' reader) in no way precludes the possibility of engaging, perhaps ambiguously and painfully, with the wider field of meanings and values, aesthetic and formal and social. It is just this generality, this gesture at transcendence or totality, which is implied in the address of many cultural works and which sets up the 'confusing experience' of reading. It is not then always clear which aspects or determinants of 'identity' critics would invoke in deciding how to specify who the reader, and writer, are; and thus how the dialogic language of the cultural text is supposedly to be closed down into a more particular dyadic interlocution. Above all, it is not clear how such closures and categorisations are supposed to determine substantive critical assessment. Do we, the present authors, for instance, read Julian Barnes as English and white – which we all are – or as male and female – which all of us are not? If our Englishness is supposed to be the key factor, is it then presumed that we shall somehow feel an affinity with Barnes or accede more readily to his authority? (If this applied in Barnes' case, presumably it would apply equally in the case of every other English writer.) We do not assume that every black reader can sustain an unproblematic relation with the author-in-the-text of Richard Wright's *Native Son*, or that 'race' necessarily trumps gender in negotiating with that novel. Is Zadie Smith's very successful *White Teeth* a British Asian writer's novel and so one that all British Asian readers should presumptively feel at ease with? Or is it rather, or also, a novel by a culturally mobile metropolitan writer which reflects like earlier novels by Wells or Lawrence (though not very self-critically, in our view) the process of self-differentiation through education, and which might thus pose some of the same problems of readability and identification, for less educated and mobile people, that Lawrence's novels putatively pose for a Nottinghamshire miner spending his working life in the pits?

In short, while the irruption of diversity into the scene of 'English literature' subverts unwarranted claims for universality which its texts or critics may have made, the idea that 'identity' offers an adequate intellectual basis for a new critical practice is (to say the least) fraught with difficulties. To advocate (as we do) an evaluative rather than sociological–positivist mode of criticism and teaching, when it comes to culture, is certainly to reject identity readings as insufficient, though of course we recognise their importance as a determinant of critical perspectives. The point is (as Edward Said puts it) to enable 'contrapuntal readings', which respect the internal complexity and cultural quality of texts even as they subject them to directly political questions which may include questions of identity.[40] The 'contingencies of value' at play are likely to involve all these factors, and more.[41]

Against this, criticism from cultural–particularist perspectives sometimes implies that no moment of specifically cultural evaluation exists. Claims and criteria of cultural value, it is said, reflect nothing but the position of the claimant; supposedly abstract evaluative discourses are simply the means by which monolithic high-cultural traditions secure hegemony. Having reminded us that almost all famous composers, painters and writers have been white men, the authors of *Cultural Politics* conclude:

> The institutions which construct and reproduce cultural traditions and the national heritage work with gendered and racially inflected criteria of skill, crafts(wo)manship and exceptional talent or genius. These are defined by excluding what is seen as 'Other' – for example, popular culture, much work by women, the work of Black and Asian writers and artists, and the so-called 'primitive' art of non-Western cultures.[42]

These evaluative criteria (which have promoted the fortunes of artists like Bach, Picasso and Joyce) are now to be rejected, the authors imply, in favour of equally political but oppositional criteria, based in one or another form of identity politics.[43]

This approach to canonical culture is in some ways akin to the media sociology that charts, or speculates about, what popular-cultural texts mean for groups of consumers. John Storey, in his successful text-book *Cultural Theory and Popular Culture*, opts for a moderate version of this 'new revisionism', which abstains from value-judgements: the proper business of his kind of cultural studies is to chart the uses audiences make of texts, rather than to critique the texts themselves. A shortish distance separates this abstentionist position from more partisan approaches, such as Ien Ang's work (discussed by Storey) on female viewers of *Dallas* in the Netherlands, or John Fiske's research on TV and its audiences, which tend positively to valorise the pleasure experienced by the consumer.[44] Fiske's work is often – indeed, canonically – cited as paradigmatic of the 'cultural populism' which proceeds from claims about meaning in use to a valorisation of the cultural productions themselves.[45] Simon Frith comments that when critics '[identify] certain social groups with what we might call "positive mass consumption"', and go on to equate 'the value of cultural goods' with 'the value of the groups consuming them', we have a 'reworking', indeed an inversion, of the fundamentally hostile assessment of mass culture produced by the Frankfurt School[46] (as well as by Leavisite literary and cultural critics). Jim McGuigan, from within media and cultural studies, argues that 'excessively audience-orientated and one-dimensional consumptionist perspectives have led to a lamentable foreclosure on questions concerning both "quality" . . . and . . . "progressiveness", resulting in confused and helpless silence'.[47]

A different and more persuasive case against the privileging of canonical learned culture is made by Anthony Easthope in *Literary into Cultural Studies*. Arguing that high and popular texts should be studied alongside each other (a position in itself very reasonable), Easthope advocates the 'cultural studies' paradigm as in every respect superior to that which treats its object, 'literature', as imaginatively transcendent, authored and canonical. The cultural studies paradigm

> insists on the materiality of the process of its own construction as a discourse of knowledge. It challenges the category of the aesthetic and the canonical, stresses that experience always takes place through a means of representation, recognises how readings of texts are discursively constructed, demands that readers' experiences be interrogated as effects rather than natural causes.[48]

This critical approach is certainly to be preferred to the would-be Arnoldian pontification Easthope points to as exemplary of his opposition: Allan Bloom's claim, for example, that 'men live more fully in reading Plato and Shakespeare than at any other time, because they are participating in an essential being and are forgetting their accidental lives'.[49] But we would question the way *Literary into Cultural Studies* presents its case for the cultural studies paradigm as if that in itself undermined claims for the superiority of works that have gained canonical status. As we have tried to show in our earlier discussion, canonical novels, and complex literary works generally, can often be read for the light they shed on processes of representation, their interrogation of the formative influences on experience, their dialogic approach to subjectivity. We would therefore dispute Easthope's tendency to present the 'transcendent' literary text as always guilty of positioning its readers in subordination to a higher authority of Art and the Author, rather than enabling the assumption of a vantage point from which to consider various claims to authority, including those of the prevailing aesthetic logic.

The resistance to evaluation appears defensible if one's approach to culture is purely sociological, or aims only to contextualise cultural works and to chart their signifying practices, the ways they 'construct' or position the subject, and so on. However it is very difficult to undertake, and justify, such a supposedly neutral approach. Not only do critics inevitably bring political and ethical values to bear in any sociology of culture (as in their use of such terms as 'ideology', 'gender', the 'other' and so on); they also, in so doing, make discriminations at the level of representation and semiotics that implicitly concede the superiority of certain kinds of register. The forms of critical sensitivity to the 'construction' and representation of subjectivity that teachers of popular culture seek to instil in students are precisely not registered and reflected upon in most soap operas, romance fictions or advertising images. But they may well be the very stuff of other cultural works, embedded in the logic of their 'signifying practices': works, then, which offer insights and reflect the critic's own sense of the production of meaning, by means of formal properties that it will be difficult therefore not to defend as richer and better.

Political interrogation of cultural texts has been intellectually very productive; but judgements of cultural value are not to be evaded, and cannot be reduced to questions of exclusion and identity. To show that valued cultures have been implicated in oppressive social formations (which is obviously true, as a generalisation) is not at all the same as to show that culturally evaluative discourses, let alone all literary and artistic works, are just a means of speaking for power. Once we contextualise 'canonical texts', Sinfield concedes, they 'may then be respected as serious attempts to comprehend and intervene in the world, and we may quarrel with them as questionable constructions made by other people in other circumstances.'[50] Cultural works indeed come, like Hamlet's father's ghost, in such questionable form that reading is always partly a matter of quarrelling. As well as an empirical claim about how people read, this is the advocacy of a critical and pedagogical practice. If 'cultural treasures', in Benjamin's adage, have an origin that we 'cannot contemplate without horror',[51] then treasure and origin, 'great mind' and anonymous toiler, and (in our terms here) culture's totalising or universal value-claims and its particular origins and audiences, need to be thought about together.

To take the full measure of this is indeed to underline the limits of cultural particularism as a practice of textual critique. Mobilising what one critic has called 'noncanonical theories of value',[52] as a tactic to modify traditional canons and re-read their prestigious texts, allows us to reinstate marginalised or oppressed groups in a more central place within learned culture only if they were originally audible or visible there. Until recent times – until not much before the moment of *Culture and Anarchy*, so far as Britain is concerned – even the most fortunate among the anonymous toilers mostly lived happy lives without reading a book, let alone writing one. What then of the plantation slaves, the pregnant women dragging coal-tubs, the Famine dead? What, today, of the lives of street children? Here, in George Eliot's metaphor, is the scream which lies the other side of silence. The conditions of their lives were so harsh that most people, historically, had little chance of leaving their own enduring memorials; their sufferings have been noted only on the margins of the high cultural record made by others. If this is partly a matter of the conscious complicity of some (by no means all) writers and artists with dominant social forces, it is also bound up with the nature of the culture we have instituted as 'the best'. The element of distantiation and pleasure on which the enjoyment of cultural works depends raises hard ethical questions. The representation of agony and humiliation, in texts offered to readers and spectators at a safe remove, is as fraught with difficulties as the decision not to represent them. The representation of repetitive toil is boring. Perhaps learned culture's element of pleasure, of pleasurable aesthetic mediation, and its reliance on complex forms of reasoning and communicative practice, is against such backgrounds already also a betrayal: art is autistic, rather than autonomous, and more simple-minded than it likes to think. This is what the protagonist of *The Tin Drum* deplores, and enjoys, when he notes that in the autumn of 1939, 'while history, blaring special communiqués at the top of its voice, sped like a well-greased amphibious vehicle over the roads and waterways of Europe', his 'own affairs . . . were restricted to the belaboring of lacquered toy drums'.[53]

Grass's hero goes on drumming; and we are glad that Grass went on writing and showed it could still be more than the solipsistic beating of a drum. But cultural particularists, noting culture's exclusions, have sometimes seemed to conclude that wholesale rejection is the proper response to the whole tradition, the whole formal culture, of societies like ours. Gilroy and Sinfield, though they give illuminating accounts of canonical writers, turn ultimately in the books we have cited to historical and contemporary sub-cultures which they see as at least relatively distinct, oppositional, unimplicated in the dominant. David Lloyd declares in the Introduction to *Anomalous States*: 'To the monopoly of violence claimed by the state . . . corresponds the monopoly of representation claimed by the dominant culture', and he goes on to insist that in postcolonial Ireland the search for 'radical democracy' must go back to whatever traces can be found of half-lost popular cultural forms and practices – 'subordinated, occluded', 'discontinuous, submerged', 'subterranean, marginalized'.[54] Robert Young in *White Mythologies*, though writing as a teacher of English, offers little substantial discussion of literary texts in his demonstration that European culture is complicit through and through with imperialism (in passing he upbraids Edward Said for enjoying conventionally esteemed books): the texts figure mainly just as evidence of the complicity.[55] It is not a frivolous *ad hominem* debating-point, however, to remind these critics where they speak from and to ask them whether, in the terms of Lloyd's rhetoric, such locations would not *a priori* suggest they are at least as closely implicated in the dominant and its supposed 'monopoly of representation' as writers like Austen or Hardy ever were.[56] If the question of intellectual culture's complicity with exploitation and oppression is to be answered by the most general socio-political characterisation of whole societies and epochs rather than also by readings of particular works, then certainly the entire activity of academic criticism, anywhere in the 'west' but especially in privileged locales, could only stand condemned. Our view, however, is that 'horror' (in Benjamin's phrase) should be reserved for culture's 'origins'. Its 'treasures' – including works of cultural criticism which carry forward, even if their inflection is particularist, the project or gesture of 'totality' – are always marked but cannot simply be damned by their genesis. Learned culture, like the education which it presupposes and provides, is implicated in the whole society it belongs to, but can have for all that elements of immanent critique and utopian promise.

Williams was well aware that any idea of culture which accepts, even in modified form, post-Arnoldian criteria of intellectual and artistic distinction will exclude most of what has been made by the subaltern majority: 'What is left [of traditional working-class and popular culture], with what in the new conditions has been newly made, is small in quantity and narrow in range. It exacts respect, but it is in no sense an alternative culture.'[57] The most important forms of 'exclusion' and 'marginalisation', in this socialist perspective, do not result primarily from the operation of discriminatory criteria of value in the institutions which publish and preserve (criteria which, because they are precisely *not* reducible to a judgement of social origin or political inclination, also constantly 'exclude' the vast bulk of soon-forgotten books and symphonies and paintings made by and for the relatively privileged).[58] Most people have been excluded from learned culture from the outset, because the material circumstances of their lives made it impossible for them to acquire the education or to enjoy the time for the making or appreciation of complex and interesting works: they could never even try their hand on equal terms. This was what Arnold himself had to acknowledge, seeing in the East End people with hardly a rag to cover them, and it is what Hardy and other writers addressed in some now-canonical texts.

The making of culture, as well as its enjoyment, has become less exclusive since Arnold's time. In Britain there have been more working-class writers, more women composers, in the last century than in all the centuries before. The learned culture of the past is now transmitted through a generally available public education. Has it then ceased to be 'bourgeois culture'? Williams (in the 1960s) wrote that it was 'very doubtful whether "bourgeois culture" is a useful term' for such works.[59] We prefer to accept the term (and its implicit corollaries in terms of 'race', gender, sexuality); but not because we think that a rival, non-bourgeois 'culture' was made and is awaiting discovery in history's wings: rather, because the epithet should remind us that whatever is universal in learned culture and in its ideal of self-realisation has had to assert itself, and must be tested and made readable, in and against circumstances of inequality, privilege and exclusion. To read in this spirit is to make culture accountable not just to criteria proper to artistic works, but also to the social totality towards which representation always gestures. This is the idea of itself which culture, by Arnold's time, is already articulating and being obliged to articulate.

Notes

Introduction: To relish the sublime?

1 Raymond Williams, *Culture and Society*, London, 1987 (1958), pp. 118f: '*Culture and Anarchy* in fact needs to be read alongside the reports, minutes, evidence to commissions and specifically educational essays which made up so large a part of Arnold's working life.'

2 See Matthew Arnold, *Culture and Anarchy*, ed. and with an introduction by John Dover Wilson, Cambridge, 1971 (this ed. first published 1932), p. 110. Arnold's essay was first published as a book in 1869, and it is this text that is reprinted in Dover Wilson's edition.

3 These are the titles of two films that were massively promoted, and commercially successful, as this book was being written.

4 Two recent examples are Glenn Jordan and Chris Weedon, *Cultural Politics: Class, Gender, Race and the Postmodern World*, Oxford, 1995, pp. 25f., and John Storey, *Cultural Theory and Popular Culture*, 3rd ed., London, 2001, pp. 18–22.

5 We give a summary of some relevant developments in education and politics in Chapter 4 below.

6 Arnold, *Culture and Anarchy*, p. 70.

7 See our discussion in Chapter 1, below.

8 Williams' definition (from *Keywords*) is quoted (in reference to Arnold) by Jordan and Weedon, *Cultural Politics*, p. 7.

9 Plato, *Republic*, Book VII, 514–521.

10 We should also point out that our central category is not 'art', but 'culture' (especially literary culture); whereas many arguments in philosophical aesthetics pertain more (in our view) to the plastic arts

than to the narrative forms of writing that we focus on.

11 Arnold, *Culture and Anarchy*, p. 70.

12 Dates of publication and other bibliographical details of our texts are given at the appropriate points in Chapters 3–5 below.

13 Hardy himself is characteristically evasive about the polemical intentions and possible effects of the book, writing as follows in his 1912 Preface to the Wessex edition of *Jude*: 'The difficulties down to twenty or thirty years back of acquiring knowledge in letters without pecuniary means were used in the same way [i.e., as a good foundation for a tragic fable]; though I was informed that some readers thought these episodes an attack on venerable institutions, and that when Ruskin College was subsequently founded it should have been called the College of *Jude the Obscure*' (Thomas Hardy, *Jude the Obscure*, Harmondsworth, 1987 (1896), p. 42).

14 Raymond Williams, *Culture and Society*, London, 1987 (1958), p. 295.

15 Peter Bürger, *Theory of the Avant Garde*, trans. Michael Shaw, Minneapolis and Manchester, 1984, pp. 19f.

1 Philosophy and self-realisation

1 Matthew Arnold, *Culture and Anarchy*, ed. J. Dover Wilson, Cambridge, 1971, passim, but see esp. pp. 95f. Arnold himself was an admirer of Goethe, von Humboldt and Schleiermacher.

2 Charles Taylor, *Sources of the Self: The Making of the Modern Identity*, Cambridge and New York, 1989, pp. 185f.

3 Arnold, *Culture and Anarchy*, p. 211.

4 For a helpful discussion of the contrasting emphases of Plato and Aristotle on the 'good life', see Martha Nussbaum, *The Fragility of Goodness*, Cambridge, 1986, chapters 1 and 2.

5 Plato, *Republic*, Book III, 412–415.

6 Arthur Schopenhauer, *The World as Will and Idea*, trans. E.F.J. Payne, New York, 1958, Vol. II, pp. 145f. Schopenhauer insists (p. 146) that 'Even in the event of a fairly equal degree of culture, the conversation between a great mind and an ordinary one is like the common journey of two men of whom one is mounted on a mettlesome horse while the other is on foot. It soon becomes extremely irksome for both of them, and in the long run impossible.'

7 The literature on the concept and cult of *Bildung* is very extensive, even more so than that on the *Bildungsroman* (novel of development). For a useful discussion, see Hans Gadamer, *Truth and Method*, London, 1975, pp. 10–19. We have also consulted W.H. Bruford, *The German Tradition of Self-Cultivation: 'Bildung' from Humboldt to Thomas Mann*, Cambridge, 1975; Michael Beddow, *The Fiction of Humanity*, Cambridge, 1982; Franco Moretti, *The Way of the World: The Bildungsroman in European Culture*, London, 1987; Marc Redfield, *Phantom Formations: Aesthetic Ideology and the Bildungsroman*, Ithaca and London, 1996.

8 Arnold, *Culture and Anarchy*, p. 48. The introduction and notes to the edition we cite give a useful account of the historical background to the essay's composition.

9 Ibid., p. 70.

10 To claim this, of course, is not to claim that philosophy has had a monopoly on conceptions of self-realisation at any given time. Religion has also been hugely influential, although how far it should be counted as entirely separate from philosophy on this issue is debatable. Much religious thought on personal well-being, the 'purposes of life' and so on draws on philosophy, and may count as philosophy in the argument of some theologians. Conversely, philosophical teaching has often been rooted in religious convictions and sought to further belief in those. But there is no doubting the specifically secular influence of philosophy on general cultural perceptions of self-realisation until relatively recently, even if today a good part of that function has been taken over by 'self-help' manuals, and even if today there are many competing claims for what can count as the self-realised life (as we note in the Introduction and in Chapter 2).

11 To provide an extended list would be out of place here. We shall confine ourselves to naming two authors upon whose work we have drawn in the writing of this chapter. Despite its many virtues, Charles Taylor's *Sources of the Self* tends at times in this direction. So, too, does Martha Nussbaum in her cultural commentary, for example in *Poetic Justice: The Literary Imagination and Public Life*, Boston, 1995.

12 Taylor, *Sources of the Self*, p. 113. Some similar points have also been made in respect of the differing registers of subjectivity in ancient and modern tragedy. See, e.g., S. Kierkegaard, *Either/Or*, trans. Alistair Hannay, Harmondsworth, 1992, pp. 137–161; Nussbaum, *Fragility of Goodness*, chapters 3 and 11; Amelie Rorty (ed.), *Essays on Aristotle's*

Poetics, Princeton, 1992 (see especially Jean-Pierre Vernant on 'Myth and Tragedy' and Martha Nussbaum on 'Tragedy and Self-Sufficiency: Plato and Aristotle on Fear and Pity').

13 Taylor, *Sources of the Self*, pp. 115–126.

14 Ibid., pp. 127–142.

15 Here again, our debt to Taylor's *Sources of the Self* must be acknowledged, and will be obvious to all readers of that book. See especially pp. 175f., but also the whole of Part 1.

16 John Locke, *An Essay Concerning Human Understanding*, ed. P.H. Nidditch, Oxford, 1975 (1690), I. 3. 25.

17 Immanuel Kant, 'What is Enlightenment?', in Lewis White Beck (ed.), *Kant on History*, New York, 1963, p. 3.

18 Ernst Cassirer, *The Philosophy of the Enlightenment*, Boston, 1951, p. 13.

19 We discuss this further in Chapter 2.

20 *Discours de La Méthode, La Dioptrique, Les Météores, La Géometrie* was published in Leyden in 1637, and first appeared in a Latin edition in Amsterdam in 1644.

21 I. Kant, *Critique of Judgement*, ed. W. Pluhar, Indianapolis and Cambridge, 1987 (1790), pp. 319f.

22 Kant, 'What is Enlightenment?', p. 3. Kant proceeds: 'After the guardians have first made their domestic cattle dumb, and have made sure that these placid creatures will not dare take a single step without the harness of the cart to which they are tethered, the guardians show them the dangers which threaten them if they go alone.'

23 E.L. Tuveson, *The Imagination as a Means of Grace*, Berkeley and Los Angeles, 1960, p. 24.

24 Sylvana Tomaselli, entry on 'Reason' in John W. Yolton (ed.), *The Blackwell Companion to the Enlightenment*, Oxford, 1991, p. 446.

25 Baumgarten's aim in his *Reflections on Poetry* was to reform philosophy by bringing it back to its origins in poetics. For a discussion of Baumgarten's argument and its influence on Herder and other followers, see Howard Caygill, *The Art of Judgement*, Oxford, 1989, pp. 148–184.

26 Friedrich Schiller, *Letters On the Aesthetic Education of Man*, ed. Elizabeth M. Wilkinson and L.A. Willoughby, Oxford, 1967, Letter 24, p. 181.

27 Ibid., p. 89.

28 'Wisdom has its excesses and has no less need of moderation',

says Montaigne in his 'On Some lines of Virgil'. See *The Essays of Michel de Montaigne*, trans. and ed. M.A. Screech, Harmondsworth, 1987, p. 948. Cf. Taylor, *Sources of the Self*, pp. 178–184.

29 Terry Eagleton, *The Ideology of the Aesthetic*, Oxford, 1990, p. 75.

30 Kant, *Critique of Judgement*, p. 160. See also the whole of sections 237–240 and 293–296.

31 Without the mutual antagonism bred of the urge to individualise as much as socialise ourselves, life would have remained that of the Arcadian shepherd, says Kant in his 'Idea of a Universal History from a Cosmopolitan Point of View' (1784) (in Hans Reiss, (ed.), *Kant's Political Writings*, Cambridge, 1991).

32 We would dispute, however, Pierre Bourdieu's dismissive account of the Kantian position as simply the snobbish antithesis to a popular aesthetic taste that, by definition, can never relish the sublime but always prefers what is charming to the senses. See P. Bourdieu, *Distinction: A Social Critique of the Judgement of Taste*, trans. Richard Nice, London, 1979, pp. 41f. and pp. 486–492.

33 See Fredric Jameson, *Marxism and Form*, Princeton, 1971, p. 115, and cf. pp. 83–91 (the context is a discussion of Herbert Marcuse's recourse to Schiller's argument on the 'play drive' in the second part of his *Eros and Civilisation*).

34 Schiller, *Aesthetic Education*, p. 7.

35 See Schiller, *On Naive and Sentimental Poetry*; repr. (together with *On the Sublime*) in a single vol. ed. and trans. Julius A. Elias, New York, 1966; cf. Georg Lukács, *Goethe and his Age*, trans. Robert Anchor, London, 1968, pp. 134f.

36 Peter Bürger, *Theory of the Avant Garde*, Minneapolis and Manchester, 1984, p. 45.

37 Jameson, *Marxism and Form*, p. 91.

38 Ibid., p. 90.

39 Ibid., p. 95.

40 'If the aesthetic suggests the form of a wholly different social order, its actual content . . . would seem no more than an indeterminate negation, brimming with nothing but its own inexpressible potential . . . Culture in no sense determines what we should do; it is rather that, in continuing to do whatever we are doing, we act with an equipoise which implies we could just as easily be doing something else. It is thus a question of style or "grace". . .' (Eagleton, *Ideology of the Aesthetic*, p. 111).

41 Ibid., p. 117.

42 Schiller, *Aesthetic Education*, Letter 27, p. 219 (and note his blithe unconcern for the partiality of his remark that in the Greek States 'every individual enjoyed an independent existence but could, when need arose, grow into the whole organism': see p. 35).

43 Eagleton, *Ideology of the Aesthetic*, p. 22.

44 Ibid., p. 97.

45 Lukács, *Goethe and his Age*, p. 133.

46 Samuel Taylor Coleridge, *Biographia Literaria*, ed. George Watson, Oxford, 1953, pp. 173f.

47 Ibid., pp. 72, 173.

48 Cited in Taylor, *Sources of the Self*, p. 37.

49 Friedrich Schlegel, *Ideen*, cit. in Bruford, *The German Tradition*, p. 82.

50 Cf. Bruford, *The German Tradition*, pp. 16f.

51 Arnold, *Culture and Anarchy*, p. 122, pp. 96f. On the tensions in Arnold's 'Continental' view of the State, and in his presentation of a culture based on an 'anarchic' self-direction as salvation from anarchy, see David Weir, *Anarchy and Culture: The Aesthetic Politics of Modernism*, Amherst, 1997, pp. 42–52.

52 From a lecture to a group of republican students in Munich, cit. in Bruford, *The German Tradition*, p. vii. But see also Mann's approving comments on Goethe's *Wilhelm Meisters Wanderjahre* as 'anticipating' German progress from inwardness to republicanism, and Bruford's discussion of this, pp. 88f.

53 See Bruford, *The German Tradition*, pp. 254, 259.

54 Ibid., p. 89.

55 G.W.F. Hegel, *The Philosophy of Fine Art*, trans. F.P.B. Osmaston, New York, 1975, Vol. 1, pp. 14f.

56 Ibid., pp. 278f.

57 Schiller, *Aesthetic Education*, Letter 27, p. 219.

58 Lukács, *Goethe and his Age*, p. 135.

59 See Schiller, *Aesthetic Education*, p. 35; Karl Marx, *Capital*, Vol. III, Moscow, 1966, p. 88; and cf. Eagleton, *Ideology of the Aesthetic*, p. 118.

60 See Karl Marx, *Grundrisse*, ed. and introd. Martin Nicolaus, Harmondsworth, 1973, p. 555.

61 Ibid., p. 226; cf. p. 157, and see pp. 456–471. See Kate Soper, *On Human Needs: Open and closed theories in a Marxist perspective*,

Brighton, 1981, chapter 7.

62 Marx, *Grundrisse*, pp. 409f.

63 Ibid., p. 488.

64 Ibid., pp. 487f.

65 Eagleton comments (*Ideology of the Aesthetic*, p. 221) that 'Marx is at his most Romantic–humanist in his apparent assumption that human capacities become morbid only by virtue of their alienation, repression, dissociation or one-sidedness. But this is surely a dangerous illusion; we must count among our capacities the power to torture and wage war'. Cf. Soper, *On Human Needs*, chapters 8 and 9, and Jon Elster, *An Introduction to Karl Marx*, Cambridge, 1986.

66 See Rousseau, *Discourse on Inequality*, London, 1973, p. 66; and cf. Spinoza on our natural envy for those of a similar nature, aspiration and ability, *Ethics*, trans. A. Boyle and introd. G. Santayana, London, 1910, Sect. lv. We return to this theme in Rousseau towards the end of Chapter 2.

67 Theodor Adorno, *Negative Dialectics*, trans. E.B. Ashton, London, 1973, p. 41.

68 In commentary on Adorno's privileging of authentic art and critical philosophy, one of his critics has gone so far as to suggest that in his assumption that genuine praxis is primarily contemplative (a matter of intellectual pursuit rather than geared to self-preservation), he 'perpetuates a problematic legacy of Greek philosophy' – for this is a view of praxis that 'cannot be divorced from the real slavery that first made it possible in classical Greece'. See Lambert Zuidervaart, *Adorno's Aesthetic Theory*, Cambridge, Mass. and London, 1991, pp. 148f. But this is surely to mistake the terms in which Adorno – and Marxism more generally – are arguing. In defending a project of cultural democracy, one is not committed to the view that the only 'genuine' forms of praxis are intellectual; even less is one committed to the division of labour that has hitherto rendered intellectual activity the province of a privileged minority served by the 'slavery' of others. The real question of concern is how to make this form of praxis more generally available.

69 Friedrich Nietzsche, *Twilight of the Idols*, trans. Duncan Large, Oxford, 1998, pp. 39f. Nietzsche is especially despairing of the decline of German culture under Bismarck, and takes a more charitable view of French culture of the same period – but what he approves in the latter is the insight, as he sees it, of French writers on their own cultural malaise (cf. Large's introduction, pp. xvii f.). Nietzsche links progressive

politics, we might note, with the advance of science and its supposed de-intellectualizing influence. Cf. Eagleton, *Ideology of the Aesthetic*, p. 256.

70 F. Nietzsche, *Beyond Good and Evil*, trans. R.J. Hollingdale and introd. Michael Tanner, Harmondsworth, 1973, para. 258, p.193.

71 See J.-J. Rousseau, *Emile*, trans. Allan Bloom, Harmondsworth, 1979, esp. Books I and II and pp. 79–82 and 157–161. Cf. Leslie F. Clayton (ed.), *Rousseau on Education*, London, 1969; E. Cassirer, *The Question of Jean-Jacques Rousseau*, trans. and ed. Peter Gay, New York, 1956, pp. 73–75, 107 and 119–121.

2 Cultural self-realisation: countervailing forces and sceptical voices

1 See Jürgen Habermas, *The Theory of Communicative Action*, trans. Thomas McCarthy, Cambridge (Mass.), 1984–89. esp. Vol. II.

2 See Karl Marx, 'Wages, Price and Profit', in Karl Marx and Friedrich Engels, *Selected Works*, London, 1968, pp. 185–221, esp. sections VIII and IX.

3 The first option makes use of an Althusserian account of the relations between base and superstructure in terms of 'metonymic' or structural causality, according to which ideology is functionally necessary to the successful reproduction of the infrastructural economic relations (see Louis Althusser and Etienne Balibar, *Reading Capital*, London, 1970, pp. 186–188); the second is found in so-called 'vulgar' Marxist accounts, that tend to present ideology as a false – and potentially removable – reflection of the 'base'. For a useful survey and critical discussion of the literature on the Marxist theory of ideology, see Michèle Barrett, *The Politics of Truth: From Marx to Foucault*, Cambridge, 1991.

4 Theodor Adorno, *Minima Moralia*, trans. E.F.N. Jephcott, London, 1974, p. 44; cf. F. Jameson, *Late Marxism: Adorno, or, the persistence of the dialectic*, London, 1990, pp. 46–48.

5 Adorno, *Aesthetic Theory*, trans. and introd. Robert Hullot-Kentor, London, 1997, pp. 182f.

6 See ibid., p. 42 and Jameson, *Late Marxism*, p. 163. Cf. the nuanced and influential account of art as suffering 'aesthetic alienation' in virtue of its separation in the modern period from truth (scientific

cognition) and morality in Jay Bernstein, *The Fate of Art*, Cambridge, 1992. Bernstein argues that the modern experience of art as aesthetical is the experience of art as having lost its power to speak the truth – 'whatever truth will mean when no longer defined in exclusive ways'. Art is thus presented as the 'site of beauty bereaved' and the 'critical self-reflection of truth-only cognition and its conscience' (pp. 4f). There is much in Bernstein's argument that is congruent with our presentation of culture as a site of critique of instrumental rationality. However, his book in our view exemplifies a point we make in our Introduction (in our comment in footnote 9) on the greater relevance of much work in philosophical aesthetics to the plastic arts than to the narrative writing we concentrate on here. We would also question its overall philosophical coherence: in insisting that all experience has been so deformed by the separation of spheres that we cannot make intelligible what we are missing, Bernstein not only – as he recognises – plunges art into an aporia (it must either fall silent or speak in deformed terms), but also – as he is less prepared to acknowledge – undermines the terms of his own theorisation . For if there are elements of the deformation of reason in all terms of philosophical analysis, how do we know of it or acquire its concept?

7 Richard Rorty, 'Feminism and Pragmatism', *Radical Philosophy*, 59, Autumn 1991, pp. 3–14.

8 Longinus, 'On the Sublime', trans. and introd. T.S. Dorsch, in *Aristotle, Horace, Longinus: Classical Literary Criticism*, Penguin, 1965, p. 107.

9 This is not to deny, however, that critics of the existing order and its social division of labour have discerned, at least in Kant's case, the aspiration to transcend that order and even some of the elements for doing so. See Bernstein, *Fate of Art*, chapters 1 and 2, esp. pp. 5–8; and cf. our discussion in Ch. 1 above. Eagleton has claimed that Habermas's ideal speech community can be viewed as an update of the Kantian *sensus communis*: see *Ideology of the Aesthetic*, Oxford, 1990, p. 405.

10 Christopher Lasch, *The Culture of Narcissism*, London, 1982, p. 95.

11 Anthony Easthope, *Literary into Cultural Studies*, London, 1991, pp. 94f.

12 Charles Taylor, *Sources of the Self*, Cambridge, 1989, pp. 465f.

13 Cf. Taylor's remark that 'it is amazing how much art in the twentieth century has itself for its subject, or is at one level at least

thinly disguised allegory about the artist and his work': *Sources of the Self*, p. 481.

14 Sigmund Freud, *Introductory Lectures on Psychoanalysis*, Vol. 1, Harmondsworth, 1973, p. 424. Cf. Easthope, *Literary into Cultural Studies*, pp. 68f.

15 See Althusser, 'Ideology and the Ideological State Apparatus' and 'Freud and Lacan', trans. Ben Brewster, in *Lenin and Philosophy and other Essays*, London, 1971. The position is associated with *Tel Quel* in France and *Screen* in Britain. The lingering 'humanism' of the Althusserian position was targeted by Paul Hirst in 'Althusser and the Theory of Ideology', *Economy and Society*, 5 (4), 1976, and *On Law and Ideology*, London, 1979; cf. Michèle Barrett, 'Subjectivity, Humanism, Psychoanalysis', in *The Politics of Truth*, Ch. 5, pp. 81–119.

16 This argument has been influentially developed in the work of Seyla Benhabib. See her chapter in Drucilla Cornell and Seyla Benhabib (eds), *Feminism as Critique*, Cambridge, 1990; and her book *Situating the Self: gender, community and postmodernism in contemporary ethics*, Cambridge, 1992. See also Jean Grimshaw, *Feminist Philosophers*, Brighton, Harvester, 1987, Ch. 6; Pauline Johnson, 'Feminism and Images of Autonomy', *Radical Philosophy*, 50, Autumn 1988.

17 Jean Grimshaw, 'Practices of Freedom', in Caroline Ramazanoglu (ed.), *Up Against Foucault*, London, 1993, p. 60.

18 See Michel Foucault, 'Afterword on the Subject and Power', in Hubert Dreyfus and Paul Rabinow, *Michel Foucault: Beyond Structuralism and Hermeneutics*, Hemel Hempstead, 1982.

19 Benhabib, *Situating the Self*, p. 16.

20 Seyla Benhabib, in Linda Nicholson, (ed)., *Feminist Contentions*, New York and London, 1995, p. 20.

21 Judith Butler, *Gender Trouble: Feminism and the Subversion of Identity*, New York and London, 1990, p. 143.

22 Butler, in Nicholson (ed.), *Feminist Contentions*, p. 136.

23 Ibid., p. 135.

24 Ibid., p. 135.

25 Ibid., p. 36; p. 42.

26 See Peter Dews, *Logics of Disintegration*, London, 1987, p. 222.

27 Jean-François Lyotard, *Libidinal Economy*, trans. Iain Hamilton Grant, London, 1993 (published in France 1974).

28 Michel Foucault, *Discipline and Punish*, trans. Alan Sheridan, London and New York, 1977 (published in France 1975).

29 Seminal works in the development of post-colonial theory include Franz Fanon, *Black Skin, White Masks*, New York, 1964, and *The Wretched of the Earth*, New York, 1961; and Edward Said, *Orientalism: Western Conceptions of the Orient*, Harmondsworth, 1978. We refer here primarily to later arguments developed under the influence of post-structuralism and deconstruction. For a powerful and influential defence of the anti-essentialist position see Gayatri Spivak, *In Other Worlds*, London, 1988; and *The Spivak Reader*, London, 1996. Spivak argues for what she terms 'strategic essentialism' in later writings (see in particular *Outside in the Teaching Machine*, London, 1993), though subsequently she is also critical of the 'identitarian' use made of the idea: see her interview, 'Setting to Work (Transnational Cultural Studies)', in Peter Osborne (ed.), *A Critical Sense: Interviews with Intellectuals*, London and New York, 1966, pp. 163–177 (this also contains relevant interviews with Edward Said, Cornel West and Judith Butler). Recent anthologies of postcolonial criticism and theory include Padmini Mongia (ed.), *Contemporary Postcolonial Theory: a reader*, London, 1996, and Peter Childs (ed.), *Post-colonial theory and English literature: a reader*, Edinburgh, 1999.

30 See for example Nancy Fraser, 'Foucault on modern power: empirical insights and normative confusions', in *Unruly Practices: Power, Discourse and Gender in Contemporary Social Theory*, Cambridge, 1989; and cf. Grimshaw, 'Practices of Freedom', p. 55.

31 Gayatri Spivak, 'Remembering the limits: difference, identity and practice', in Peter Osborne (ed.), *Socialism and the Limits of Liberalism*, London, 1991, pp. 227f. We here draw on Kate Soper, 'Realism, Postmodernism and Cultural Value', in Ronald Barnett and Anne Griffin (eds), *The End of Knowledge in Higher Education*, London, 1997, pp. 48f.

32 Marc Redfield, *Phantom Formations: Aesthetic Ideology and the Bildungsroman*, Ithaca and London, 1996, pp. 26f.

33 For a succinct discussion see Dews, *Logics of Disintegration*, pp. 216–219; and cf. the chapters by Soper and Grimshaw in Ramazanoglu (ed.), *Up Against Foucault*.

34 See Dews, *Logics of Disintegration*, pp. 229f. Dews brings out in this context the contrast with Adorno – who refuses to eliminate subjectivity, but who also sees the limits of any identification of subjectivity with the self-understanding subject of the philosophy of consciousness.

35 Eagleton, *Ideology of the Aesthetic*, p. 414.

36 Cf. Adorno, *Aesthetic Theory*, p. 275

37 Paul Ricoeur, 'Life: a story in search of a narrator', in Mario J. Valdés (ed.), *A Ricoeur Reader: Reflection and Imagination*, Hemel Hempstead, 1991, pp. 426–437 (the phrase quoted is on p. 437).

38 Adorno, *Aesthetic Theory*, p. 276.

39 Ibid., p. 247.

40 Zygmunt Bauman, *Life in Fragments*, Oxford, 1995, p. 79; cf. pp. 223–240.

41 Rousseau opposes *amour propre* to *amour de soi*, or the self-love associated with instincts to self-preservation. See Rousseau, *Discourse on Inequality*, London, 1973, p. 66.

42 This has been rightly emphasised by Habermas and the advocates of 'Discourse Ethics'. See Seyla Benhabib's useful discussion in *Situating the Self*, pp. 74f.

3 'A tendency to set the mind in motion': novel-reading and self-realisation

1 Mary Hays, *The Memoirs of Emma Courtney*, introd. Sally Cline, London and New York, 1986, p. vii.

2 For a general discussion of some of the matters at stake here, see Martin Ryle, 'Long Live Literature?', *Radical Philosophy*, 67, Summer 1994.

3 The phrase 'symbolic act' is taken from a paragraph of Fredric Jameson quoted and discussed below (see footnote 10). The direct affirmation of an *aesthetic* transcendence in fictional modernism – not our present concern – is discussed in Chapter 5; and we make some further general comments on 'identity' as the basis for cultural critique in the Conclusion.

4 Raymond Williams, *Culture and Society*, London, 1987 (1958), p. 295.

5 Joyce Tompkins, *The Popular Novel in England 1770–1800*, Lincoln (Nebraska), 1967 (1932), p. 3.

6 See, for instance, John Holmstrom and Laurence Lerner (eds), *Thomas Hardy and his readers: a selection of contemporary reviews*, London, 1968; or Pierre Coustillas and Colin Partridge (eds), *Gissing: the Critical Heritage*, London and Boston, 1972.

7 Clara Reeve, *The Progress of Romance*, facsimile edition, New

York, 1970 (1785), Vol. I, p. 111.

8 Mary Hays, *The Memoirs of Emma Courtney*, ed. Eleanor Ty, Oxford, 1996 (1796), p. 3. Tompkins, esp. pp. 70, 329, states that moralistic and didactic conceptions of fiction predominated in the later eighteenth century, even though Fielding had set an example of conscious novelistic art.

9 Ty's exemplary Explanatory Notes identify dozens of allusions, most of which are explicitly indicated (and some of which are footnoted) in Hays' text. On Hays' use of her letters to Godwin and to William Frend, see Ty's introduction.

10 There is a large and growing secondary literature on virtually all the novelists and other writers mentioned in this Chapter, as well as on the literature and culture of the Revolutionary period generally. We are particularly indebted to the following surveys and studies: Marilyn Butler, *Jane Austen and the War of Ideas*, Oxford, 1990 (a reprint of the 1987 republication, with a new introduction; the book was first published in 1975); Gary Kelly, *Women, Writing and Revolution 1790–1827*, Oxford, 1993; Mary Poovey, *The Proper Lady and the Woman Writer: Ideology as Style in the Works of Mary Wollstonecraft, Mary Shelley and Jane Austen*, Chicago and London, 1984; Jane Spencer, *The Rise of the Woman Novelist: from Aphra Behn to Jane Austen*, Oxford, 1986. Earlier studies we have found useful include Frank Bradbrook, *Jane Austen and her Predecessors*, Cambridge, 1966 and Tompkins, *Popular Novel in England* (cit. above). We are also indebted to the following scholarly editions and to their introductions and other editorial matter: William Godwin, *Caleb Williams* (1794), ed. and with an introduction by David McCracken, London, 1970; Mary Hays, *The Memoirs of Emma Courtney* (ed. cit. above); Mary Hays, *The Victim of Prejudice* (1799), ed. and with an introduction by Eleanor Ty, Ontario, 1984; Charlotte Lennox, *The Female Quixote* (1752), ed. Margaret Dalziel with an introduction by Margaret Anne Doody, Oxford, 1989; Henry MacKenzie, *The Man of Feeling* (1771), ed. and with an introduction by Brian Vickers, London, 1967; Clara Reeve, *The Progress of Romance* (1785), ed. cit. (which includes both original volumes, separately paginated, in a single volume); Sarah Scott, *Millennium Hall*, ed. and with an introduction by Jane Spencer, London, 1986 (1762); Mary Wollstonecraft, *Mary* (1788) and *The Wrongs of Woman; or, Maria* (1798), published in a single volume ed. and with an introduction by Gary Kelly, Oxford, 1987 (this ed. first published 1976).

Historical and critical generalisations, in what follows, may be taken to reflect the scholarly consensus. We give references only for specific points of detail and to indicate the sources of quoted material.

11 Jean-Paul Sartre, *What is Literature?*, trans. Bernard Frechtman, New York, 1965 (1949), p. 75.

12 Wollstonecraft, *Mary*, 'Advertisement'.

13 Fredric Jameson, *The Political Unconscious:*, London, 1983 (1981), pp. 80ff., and see the whole of this chapter, 'On Interpretation: Literature as a Socially Symbolic Act'.

14 Robert Bage, *Man as he is*, 1792; William Godwin, *The Adventures of Caleb Williams, or things as they are*, 1794; Robert Bage, *Hermsprong or Man as he is Not*, 1796; and for the works by Hays and Wollstonecraft (1798 and 1799), see note 7 above. On Bage, see Tompkins, *Popular Novel*, pp. 193–205.

15 This remark is among the observations and questions that Booth raises in the discussion with Wolfgang Iser printed in Iser, *Prospecting: From Reader Response to Literary Anthropology*, Baltimore and London, 1989, p. 59.

16 Geoffrey Chaucer, *Works*, ed. F.N. Robinson, London, 1970: see p. 167.

17 Tompkins, *Popular Novel*, p. 329; Reeve, *The Progress of Romance*, p. 139.

18 Letter to Cassandra Austen, 1807, quoted by Bradbrook, *Jane Austen and her Predecessors*, p. 90.

19 Lennox, *Female Quixote*, p. 7.

20 Austen, *Mansfield Park*, Vol. 3, Ch. XVII.

21 Butler, *Jane Austen and the War of Ideas*, p. 164.

22 Peter Widdowson, 'Introduction: the Crisis in English Studies', in Widdowson (ed.), *Re-Reading English*, London and New York, 1982, p. 3.

23 Hays, *Emma Courtney*, pp. 20, 21.

24 Ibid., p. 25.

25 Ibid., pp. 59, 60.

26 See Ty's introduction to *Emma Courtney*, p. xiv; Kelly, *Women, Writing and Revolution*, pp. 101f. However, if the letters to Harley are in part transcripts of Hays' to Frend, they must also contain amendments and additions to fit them to the fictional circumstances of *Emma Courtney*, such as the fact of Harley's secret marriage, which had no counterpart in biographical fact.

27 Hays, 'Advertisement to the Reader' in *The Victim of Prejudice*, p. 1.

28 Hays, *Emma Courtney*, pp. 190–192.

29 Tompkins, *Popular Novel*, pp. 317f. Cf. Butler, *Austen and the War of Ideas*, pp. 43f. Both Tompkins ('her short, unlovely form') and Butler ('a humourless, passionate, evidently neurotic woman') display a surprising animosity towards Hays. Kelly's *Women, Writing and Revolution* devotes two substantial chapters to Hays and her work.

30 On *Young Werter* (as it was spelt), see Tompkins, *Popular Novel*, p. 84: the English version, which was done from the French, appeared in 1779 and soon led to the appearance of a number of novels directly in Goethe's debt. Rousseau's *Julie, ou la Nouvelle Héloïse* appeared in 1761.

31 Tompkins, *Popular Novel*, p. 99; and see her discussion of sensibility on pp. 92ff. On Austen, Jacobinism and anti-Jacobinism generally, see especially Butler and Poovey. The parallel between West and Austen has been mentioned by many subsequent critics since Tompkins first observed it.

32 'There is no reference in Jane Austen's novels or letters to [Wollstonecraft], though she was probably acquainted with the novels of Godwin' (Bradbrook, *Jane Austen and her Predecessors*, p. 34). While both Butler and Poovey show that Austen can be categorised as an anti-Jacobin novelist, neither claims that she had read Hays or Wollstonecraft.

33 Wollstonecraft, *Mary*, p. 53; Hays, *Emma Courtney*, p.156; Austen, *Sense and Sensibility*, Ch. 1.

34 Hays, *Emma Courtney*, p. 79.

35 Both Butler (*Austen and the War of Ideas*, p. 196) and Poovey, *Proper Lady* (pp. 185, 193f.) offer accounts of *Sense and Sensibility* which claim that Austen seeks but fails to produce a consistent critique of sensibility, and that this is undermined by our sympathy for Marianne.

36 Butler, *Austen and the War of Ideas*, p. 181.

37 But Spencer, *Rise of the Woman Novelist*, p. 77, suggests that 'the true "man of feeling" was . . . seen as "feminine"'.

38 Margaret Anne Doody, Introduction to Lennox, *Female Quixote*, p. xxi.

39 On fictional treatments of the marriage-choice and of the relative rights of parents and daughters, see Tompkins, *Popular Novel*, p. 147. For the historical development of opinion, see Lawrence Stone, *The Family, Sex and Marriage in England 1500–1800*, London, 1977.

40 See esp. Spencer, *Rise of the Woman Novelist*, p. 4, and passim; and Tompkins, *Popular Novel*, pp. 116–171 ('The Female Novelists'), 285f, 99f, 317f. Tompkins' book covers a great deal of material, clearly indicates its nature, and has been an invaluable bibliographical quarry for later scholars and critics.

41 The first quotation is from Rousseau, *Emilius; or, an Essay on Education*, trans. Nugent, London, 1763, cited in Eleanor Ty's notes to Hays, *Emma Courtney*, p. 203: Ty points out that both Hays and Wollstonecraft of course disagreed with Rousseau's views on female intellectual capabilities. The second quotation is from Fordyce, cited in Kelly, *Women, Writing and Revolution*, pp. 11f: see Kelly's general discussion of the issue. Spencer (pp. 15f.) reminds us that Mr Collins (in *Pride and Prejudice*) was among Fordyce's admirers, and that Fordyce was one of many who produced 'female conduct-books' in the latter half of the eighteenth century.

42 On women's employment see especially Spencer, *Rise of the Woman Novelist*, pp. 14–22, and the authorities she cites. On 'domestic woman' and the novel see also Kelly, *Women, Writing and Revolution*, pp. 9–13. See Wollstonecraft, *Wrongs of Women*, p. 114; Hays, *Victim*, pp. 138ff: Mary seeks 'INDEPENDENCE' (capitalised in original) in working at 'drawing and colouring plants and flowers', until the proprietor of the workshop begins making sexual advances. Cf. also *Emma Courtney*, pp. 162f.

43 On this see John Tosh, *A Man's Place: Masculinity and the Middle-Class Home in Victorian England*, New Haven and London, 1999, esp. p. 4.

44 Poovey, *Proper Lady*, Preface, p. ix.

45 Hays, *The Memoirs of Emma Courtney*, introd. Sally Cline, p. vii. Cline continues: 'Emma is a woman after my own heart. Indeed her heart could be mine. Or yours.' Ty's 1996 edition is the first scholarly reprint. A facsimile ed. (as opposed to a republication) was published by Garland, New York, 1974; and a New York ed. came out in 1802, six years after the original London ed. (see Ty's 'Select Bibliography').

46 Hays, *Emma Courtney*, p. 85.

47 Austen, *Sense and Sensibility*, Ch. 21.

48 Hays, *Emma Courtney*, p. 117.

49 Ibid., p. 156.

50 The *Appeal* was published anonymously in 1798: see Eleanor Ty's introduction to *Emma Courtney*, p. xxxiv. The same few years saw

the publication of Priscilla Wakefield's *Reflections on the Present Condition of the Female Sex* (1798), Anne Frances Randall's *Letter to the Women of England, on the injustice of mental subordination* (1799) and Anne Radcliffe's *The female advocate* (1799): these are noted in Spencer, *Rise of the Woman Novelist*, pp. 108f. The founding text, and the one whose influence is evident in *Emma Courtney*, was of course Wollstonecraft's *A Vindication of the Rights of Woman* (1792).

51 Poovey, *Proper Lady*, p. 98.

52 Introduction to *Emma Courtney*, p. xvii. Ty takes the term and concept 'autonarration' from Tillotama Rajan, 'Autonarration and genotext in Mary Hays' *Memoirs of Emma Courtney*', *Studies in Romanticism*, 32 (2), Summer 1993, pp. 149–176.

53 As well as the melodrama of the final chapters, we might note the provision of a secret wife as an explanation of Augustus' failure to reciprocate Emma's love, which had no counterpart in the biographical case of Frend.

54 Wolfgang Iser, *Prospecting: From Reader Response to Literary Anthropology*, Baltimore and London, 1989, p. 35.

55 Ibid., p. 47.

56 Williams comments on the limitation of Austen's social perspective in *The Country and the City*, London, 1993 (1973), Ch. 11; and see also Ch. 16, 'Knowable Communities'. Edward Said remarks, in *Culture and Imperialism*, London and New York, 1993, pp. 100–116, on the absence in *Mansfield Park* of any direct engagement with the acknowledged fact that the Bertram family is maintaining itself on the profits from slave-worked sugar-plantations. Gayatri Spivak's critique of *Jane Eyre*, in which it is claimed that Jane's integral subjecthood is constructed at the cost of Grace Poole's subjection as an alien racial other, is in 'Three Women's Texts and a Critique of Imperialism', *Critical Inquiry* 12, 1, 1985, repr. in Henry Louis Gates, Jr (ed.), *'Race', Writing and Difference*, Chicago, 1986. For a review of critical approaches to the 'female *Bildungsroman*', see Susan Fraiman, *Unbecoming Women: British Women Writers and the Novel of Development*, New York and Chichester, 1993.

4 Culture and self-realisation: realist engagements

1 Patricia Alden, *Social Mobility in the English Bildungsroman: Gissing, Hardy, Bennett and Lawrence*, Ann Arbor and London, 1986, pp. 1f; and

see Franco Moretti, *The Way of the World: The Bildungsroman in European Culture*, London, 1987, esp. the introductory chapter 'The Bildungsroman as Symbolic Form'.

2 Jack London, *Martin Eden*, Harmondsworth, 1984 (1909), p. 37 (chapter 1).

3 Thomas Hardy, *Jude the Obscure*, ed. C.H. Sisson, Harmondsworth, 1987 (1896), II, vii, p. 169.

4 George Gissing, *In the Year of Jubilee*, ed. Paul Delany and with notes by Jon Paul Henry, London, 1994 (1894), V, 1, p. 249.

5 Matthew Arnold, *Culture and Anarchy*, ed. John Dover Wilson, Cambridge, 1971 (1869), p. 70.

6 Our texts in this chapter are as follows (in chronological order): Thomas Hardy, *The Hand of Ethelberta*, ed. P.N. Furbank and introd. Robert Gittings, London, 1975 (1876); Walter Besant, *All Sorts and Conditions of Men*, London, 1882 (3 vols.); George Gissing, *New Grub Street*, ed. John Goode, Oxford, 1998 (1891), and *In the Year of Jubilee*, ed. cit. (1894); Thomas Hardy, *Jude the Obscure*, ed. cit. (1896); H.G. Wells, *The Wheels of Chance*, London, 1896; George Gissing, *The Whirlpool*, with an introduction by Gillian Tindall, London, 1984 (1897); George Gissing, *The Private Papers of Henry Ryecroft*, London, 1930 (1903); H.G. Wells, *Kipps*, with an introduction by A.C. Ward, London, 1960 (1905) and *Tono-Bungay*, London, 1926 (1909); Jack London, *Martin Eden*, Harmondsworth, with an introduction by Andrew Sinclair, 1985 (1909); E.M. Forster, *Howards End*, ed. Oliver Stallybrass, Harmondsworth, 1992 (1910).

Among the numerous surveys and general critical studies that discuss these novelists (and quite apart from the extensive monographic literature, which we have not attempted to consult systematically), we would mention especially Alden's *English Bildungsroman* and Peter Keating, *The Haunted Study: A Social History of the English Novel 1875–1914*, London, 1991 (1989).

7 'I.L.P.': Independent Labour Party. 'S.D.F.': Social Democratic Federation. See J.F.C. Harrison, *Learning and Living 1790–1860: A Study in the History of the English Adult Education Movement*, London, 1961: the quotation from Moulton is on p. 227, the reference to Fabian and socialist publications on pp. 259f. For our period, see esp. chapter VI and chapter VII. On school education, see also John Carey, *The Intellectuals and the Masses: Pride and Prejudice among the Literary Intelligentsia, 1880–1939*, London and Boston, 1992, pp. 5f. and fn., and Alden, *English*

Bildungsroman, pp. 6f. See also Richard Altick, *The English Common Reader: a social history of the English reading public 1800–1900*, Chicago, 1985 (1957), esp. chapters 8 and 9; Keating, *Haunted Study*, pp. 182f.

8 For Lowe's epigram, see Altick, *English Common Reader*, p. 155.

9 For the franchise, the terminal dates are 1867 (when for the first time a significant number of men outside the professional and gentry classes gained the vote) and 1928 (when women finally gained the vote on equal terms with men). Only seven years after the Second Reform Bill, the 1884 Reform Bill extended the vote to a further 2 million male citizens. See Alden, *English Bildungsroman*, p. 8; Altick, *English Common Reader*, chapters 7–9; Keating, *Haunted Study*, p. 138.

10 J. Walvin, *Leisure and Society 1830–1950*, London, 1978, pp. 64, 80f; and see the whole of chapter 5. See also Altick, *English Common Reader*, p. 87.

11 Walvin, *Leisure and Society*, p. 60.

12 Alden, *English Bildungsroman*, p. 6 (citing and paraphrasing the conclusions of Brian Simon, *Studies in the History of Education: 1780–1880*, London, 1969).

13 See (for example) Wells' description of 'Cavendish Academy' (*Kipps*, I, i, pp. 9f.) and Gissing's of the school in which Waymark teaches in *The Unclassed* (1884). Both of these are supposedly genteel establishments. *The Unclassed* opens with a more positive schoolroom scene (depicting the elementary school attended by Ida Starr). See Raymond Williams' criticisms of 'apocalyptic' pessimism about the cultural tastes of the newly educated, in 'A Kind of Gresham's Law' (1958, repr. in John McIlroy and Sallie Westwood (eds), *Border Country: Raymond Williams in Adult Education*, Leicester, 1993, pp. 84–88).

14 *Martin Eden*, chapter 11, p. 133.

15 *Kipps*, I, ii, pp. 35–40 (the quotation is from p. 40: ellipsis in the original).

16 Forster, *Howards End*, p. 67.

17 The phrase, describing Sophocles, is from Arnold's sonnet 'To a Friend': see Oliver Stallybrass's note to *Howards End*, ed. cit., p. 67.

18 The phrase is from Hardy's preface to the first ed. of *Jude*.

19 *Jude*, VI, i, p. 398.

20 The phrase is Francis Mulhern's: see his *Culture/Metaculture*, London, 2000.

21 Altick, *English Common Reader*, pp. 82f. Cf. Carey, *Intellectuals and Masses*, pp. 5f., 58.

22 See Altick, *English Common Reader*, chapter 13.

23 See the useful chronology in *Jubilee*, ed. cit., pp. ix–xv. On developments of the bicycle, see R. Watson and M. Gray, *The Penguin Book of the Bicycle*, Harmondsworth, 1978, pp. 111–122.

24 See Altick, *English Common Reader*, p. 63; *New Grub Street*, chapter XIII, p. 459, and Goode's note.

25 See Walvin, *Leisure*, chapters 6, 7 and 8, on seaside holidays, sport and popular music respectively. On shopping, and on commodities as 'culture', see Rachel Bowlby, *Just Looking: Consumer Culture in Dreiser, Gissing and Zola*, London and New York, 1985.

26 *Martin Eden*, chapter 40, p. 409.

27 This is implied in Zygmunt Bauman's brief but suggestive commentary on the Arnoldian and post-Arnoldian intellectual in his *Life in Fragments. Essays in Postmodern Morality*, Oxford, 1997 (1995): see pp. 232 ff. Bauman refers here to John Carey's *The Intellectuals and the Masses*, the definitive and definitively one-sided statement of the case against the intelligentsia.

28 Arnold, *Culture and Anarchy*, p. 70 (italics in original).

29 See Pierre Bourdieu, *Distinction: A Social Critique of the Judgement of Taste*, 1979, p. 317 of the English translation by Richard Nice, London, 1992. See also Mike Featherstone, *Consumer Culture and Postmodernism*, London, California and New Delhi, 1991, pp. 89f.

30 The novels (with dates of first publication) are listed in footnote 6, above.

31 *Jubilee*, I, 6, p. 45. Cf. III, 2, p. 122: 'From chambers in Staple Inn, Lionel Tarrant looked forth upon the laborious world with a dainty enjoyment of his own limitless leisure.' The first reviewers mostly disliked Tarrant: see the reviews collected in *Gissing: The Critical Heritage*, ed. Pierre Coustillas and Colin Partridge, London and Boston, 1973, esp. pp. 229, 233, 235, 237, 246.

32 *Jubilee*, VI, 3, p. 335.

33 Ibid., III, 2, pp. 123f.

34 Ibid., I, 8, p. 63. Adrian Poole argues in his study of Gissing that Crewe 'turns out to be extraordinarily likeable, and both he and Beatrice French, whom he encourages in business, have a brash, resilient charm that . . . Tarrant singularly lacks': see Adrian Poole, *Gissing in Context*, London, 1975, p. 195. For favourable responses from early reviewers, see *Gissing: Critical Heritage*, pp. 229, 231 (reviews in the *Telegraph* and the *Sketch*).

35 *Jubilee*, V, 4, pp. 276f; *Howards End*, chapter VI (that the Basts' flat is in Brixton can be inferred from the route Leonard takes towards it, an inference confirmed in Oliver Stallybrass's note, ed. cit., pp. 59, 347).

36 *Gissing: Critical Heritage*, p. 238 (from *The Spectator*, 9 February 1895). The *Telegraph* review is dated 21 December 1894; see p. 229.

37 *Gissing: Critical Heritage*, p. 229. See also pp. 233, 238. John Carey devotes a chapter to Gissing on suburbia in *The Intellectuals and the Masses*.

38 C.F.G. Masterman, *The Condition of England*, ed. J.T. Boulton, London, 1960 (1909), p. 75.

39 Aldous Huxley, *Brave New World*, Harmondsworth, 1965 (1932), p. 200. See Andreas Huyssens, 'Mass Culture as Woman: Modernism's Other', in Tania Modleski (ed.), *Studies in Entertainment*, Bloomington, 1986, pp 188–207.

40 Huyssens, p. 191.

41 *Jubilee*, II, 3, p. 83.

42 See Andrew Sinclair's introduction to *Martin Eden*, ed. cit. We have also consulted Carolyn Johnston, *Jack London: An American Radical?*, Westport (Connecticut), 1984.

43 *Martin Eden*, chapter 37, p. 385.

44 Ibid., chapter 45, p. 464.

45 See ibid., Andrew Sinclair's introduction (p. 11); Johnston, *Jack London*, pp. 30, 49f.

46 See Altick, *English Common Reader*, pp. 287–293 (sensation fiction and anxieties about it); p. 299 (Bulwer Lytton); pp. 368–373 (optimism and pessimism about mass reading).

47 *New Grub Street*, chapter XXVIII, pp. 390 ff. The episode is something of a space-filler, and may be based on Gissing's own experiences in the USA, where he went after being expelled from Owens College. (There are a number of Gissing biographies: we have used Jacob Korg, *George Gissing: A Critical Biography*, Seattle, 1993.)

48 See *Guardian Saturday Review*, 6 January 2001, p. 10.

49 See Andrew Sinclair's introduction to *Martin Eden*, ed. cit., p. 17 ('the most intense male friendship of London's life').

50 *Martin Eden*, chapter 32, p. 345 and chapter 36 (which is devoted to Martin's evening in the ghetto).

51 Ibid., chapter 43, pp. 441f.

52 Carolyn Johnston (*Jack London*, p. 170) concludes: 'It is difficult

to prove whether he committed suicide or not.' She refers readers, for a full account of his death, to Andrew Sinclair, *Jack: A Biography of Jack London*, New York, 1977.

53 Raymond Williams, *Culture and Society*, London, 1987 (1958), p. 295.

54 Ibid., p. 34 (in reference to Wordsworth).

55 The phrase 'separate body of moral and intellectual activities' is from the introduction to *Culture and Society* (p. xviii).

56 In the longer term, since his and Helen's child will inherit Howards End, Leonard is included rather than excluded; but it remains unclear whether 'culture' has been an aid, an obstacle, or an irrelevance.

57 James Joyce, *A Portrait of the Artist as a Young Man*, Harmondsworth, 1992 (1916), p. 220.

58 *Martin Eden*, chapter 36, p. 377; chapter 38, pp. 390ff.; chapter 39 (pp. 396ff.).

59 Johnston, *Jack London*, p. 104, n. 78.

60 See ibid. for a detailed account of London's involvement – always as a high-profile public advocate, rather than an activist – in American socialism, and also of his contradictory political views during his life as a whole. See p. 125 for the admiration of Lenin and Trotsky.

61 Carey gives a full picture of Wells' anti-democratic attitudes in *Intellectuals and Masses*, while showing that overall his positions are incoherent and contradictory with themselves: see pp. 118–181. For Wells' political publications and opinions, see Norman and Jeanne MacKenzie, *The Time Traveller: The Life of H.G. Wells*, London, 1974, esp. Part Three, 'Prophet and Politician', and the Bibliography of Wells' writings.

62 See *Kipps*, II, iv, pp. 196ff. ('The Bicycle Manufacturer'); Harrison, *Living and Learning*, pp. 259f: 'In 1894 Blatchford reprinted some of his articles on socialism . . . as *Merrie England*, and sold 75,000 copies at once and over 2,000,000 during the next fifteen years. The circulation of Clarion rose to 80,000.' See also Watson and Gray, *Book of the Bicycle*, esp. chapter 4.

63 See *Kipps*, II, vii, 'London', pp. 257–266.

64 Alden, *English Bildungsroman*, p. 9.

65 *Kipps*, p. 383 (the penultimate page).

66 Andy Medhurst, 'Negotiating the Gnome Zone: Versions of Suburbia in British Popular Culture', in Roger Silverstone (ed.), *Visions of Suburbia*, London and New York, 1997; see p. 249.

67 Space does not allow us to give any adequate account of the political themes of Gissing's novels. *Demos* (1886) is perhaps the most obviously interesting, but in terms of our theme of culture and self-realisation both *Thyrza* (1887) and *Born in Exile* (1892) would repay the extended discussion we cannot give them here. The books and chapters we cite by Alden and Goode should also be consulted by anyone interested in Gissing's political imagination, as should Fredric Jameson's chapter on Gissing in *The Political Unconscious*, London, 1983.

68 See George Gissing, *Charles Dickens: A Critical Study*, London and Glasgow, 1929 (1898). John Goode's comments on the essay (in his *George Gissing: Ideology and Fiction*, London, 1978) are full of insight, and we draw on them here; but they do not exhaust the interest of Gissing's discussion.

69 David Grylls, *The Paradox of Gissing*, London, 1986, p. 56.

70 See Michael Levenson, *A Genealogy of Modernism: A Study of English Literary Doctrine 1908–1922*, Cambridge, 1894, pp. 52–54, 68, for the effect that the collapse of the progressive consensus had on writers.

71 See Peter Keating, *Into Unknown England 1866–1913: Selections from the Social Explorers*, Manchester, 1976, for an anthology of documentary writing about the East End in our period. Keating, *Haunted Study*, surveys documentary and sociological writing (see especially chapter 5) and points out that the National Association for the Promotion of Social Science was founded in 1858 and the Anthropological Society of London in 1863 (p. 303, p. 164).

72 'To write a novel in a spirit of antagonism to all but a very few of his countrymen,' Gissing declares (*Dickens*, p. 62), 'would have seemed to [Dickens] a sort of practical bull; is it not the law of novel-writing, first and foremost, that one shall aim at pleasing as many people as possible?' Here Gissing is evidently drawing a contrast with his own situation and practice.

73 Goode argues for the pertinence of Gramscian concepts ('incipient class hegemony', 'organic'): see *Gissing: Ideology and Fiction*, pp. 23, 57f.

74 Gissing, *Dickens*, pp. 77f, 73f.

75 In a letter to his brother Algernon soon after the appearance of his first novel, *Workers in the Dawn* (1880), Gissing discussed the social aims of the novel (it will 'attack . . . the criminal negligence of governments which . . . neglect . . . terrible social evils') and adds: 'Herein

I am a mouthpiece of the advanced Radical party'. See Korg, *Gissing*, p. 28. For Waymark's dictum, see *The Unclassed*, London, 1911 (1884), p. 165.

76 Gissing, *The Unclassed*, p. 212. On p. 46 Waymark tells Casti 'prose is the true medium for a polemical egotist'; later he promises that by 'digging deeper' socially, he will write a novel such as Dickens never dared to publish, because 'his monthly numbers had to lie on the family tea-table' (p. 116).

77 See Keating, *Haunted Study*, p. 317; and the whole of chapter 5 (on social documentary and fiction); and also Bowlby, *Just Looking*, esp. pp. 9f.

78 Bowlby, *Just Looking*, pp. 9f: 'Their work [i.e., that of the naturalists] was researched as thoroughly as a sociologist's, and recorded for the most part in an objective, impersonal language. The period of naturalism (1880–1920, approximately) is contemporary with the rise of the social sciences, and there are significant parallels between the two practices.' The claim of 'impersonality' hardly applies to most of Gissing's fiction.

79 Ibid., p. 95.

80 A strongly political (as opposed to documentary and/or sentimental) approach to 'the social question' is characteristic of Gissing's early naturalist fictions of working-class life (*Workers in the Dawn* [1880], parts of *The Unclassed* [1884], *The Nether World* [1889]). *Demos* (1886) is a hostile assessment of the plausibility of a post-Owenite socialism, and includes quasi-portraits of William and May Morris as well as of the fictional socialist artisan Richard Mutimer. His novels of social and cultural mobility, especially *Thyrza* (1887) and *Born in Exile* (1892), have political implications that are less explicitly drawn. *The Odd Women* (1893) engages directly with patriarchy and proto-feminist politics. There is a striking, though ambiguous and patchily sustained, treatment of imperialist psychology in *The Whirlpool* (1897).

81 *Jubilee*, I, 7, p. 50.

82 Ibid., V, 2, pp. 256f.

83 Altick, *English Common Reader*, pp. 205f.

84 *Jude*, V, vi, p. 374.

85 Korg, *Gissing*, pp. 24f. (meeting at Paddington); pp. 45f: 'Two articles on socialism . . . published in the *Pall Mall Gazette* in the early part of September, 1880, show Gissing to have been sympathetic, at

that time, with the rational approach to social reform advocated by responsible socialists and by the Positivists . . . Early in November he went to a meeting of the Positivist Society.'

86 *Jubilee*, IV, i, p. 180.

87 Ibid.

88 His experiences there are reflected in *Born in Exile* (1892), which is Alden's main text in her discussion of Gissing in *English Bildungsroman.*

89 Arnold, *Culture and Anarchy*, p. 91. Critics of Arnold who fail to acknowledge the reality of popular ignorance in 1869 include John Storey, *Cultural Theory and Popular Culture*, London, 2001(3rd. ed) (see pp. 18–22) and Glenn Jordan and Chris Weedon, *Cultural Politics: Class, Gender, Race and the Postmodern World*, Oxford, 1995 (see pp. 25ff.).

90 Gissing, *The Nether World*, Brighton, 1974 (1889), p. 107.

91 Gissing, *Whirlpool*, III, xiii, p. 449.

92 See *Howards End*, VI, p. 67; *Jude*, I, v; *Tono-Bungay*, I, 2, 6, pp. 54f.; *Jubilee*, II, 3, p. 83; *Martin Eden*, chapter 1, p. 34.

93 *Howards End*, V, pp. 44ff.; VI.

94 John Goode argues for this view; Adrian Poole sees the novel as mere regressive conservatism. Harvey Rolfe's return in *The Whirlpool*, after the death of his problematical wife, to the small midland town where he grew up and to the company of his old friend, the bluff pipe-smoking amateur classicist Morton, is another instance of this image.

95 *New Grub Street*, chapter XXXI, p. 426.

96 *Martin Eden*, chapter 35, p. 364.

97 Besant's novel was several times reprinted in the first year after its publication, and Besant, the first chairman of the Society of Authors, was one of the most popular writers of the 1800s. John Goode discusses his work and contrasts it with that of Gissing in chapter 6 of David Howard, John Lucas and John Goode (eds), *Tradition and tolerance in nineteenth-century fiction: Critical essays on some English and American novels*, London, 1966.

98 William Morris, *Hopes and Fears for Art*, lectures published in pamphlet form 1878–1880 and as a book in 1882: see May Morris (ed.), *Collected Works of William Morris*, London, 1914, Vol. XXII, pp. 62f., 25.

99 *Jude*, I, iii, p. 61.

100 Ibid., VI, i, p. 399; George Lukács, *The Meaning of Contemporary Realism*, London, 1963, p. 40.

101 *Tono-Bungay*, III, 2, 10, p. 247; III, 1, 5, p. 207.

102 'The Waste Land', 430.

103 *Kipps*, II, ii, pp. 164f.

104 Bennett would repay more detailed discussion than we are able to give him here. There is an interesting chapter on him in Alden's *English Bildungsroman*, and much praise for him in Carey, *Intellectuals and Masses*.

105 For instance, the boy Jude's pain when he realises that the itinerant pill-vendor, Vilbert, has forgotten to bring him the promised Latin and Greek grammars is not the less real to us because we (unlike him) have already understood the narrator's clues and realised the truth he is discovering: 'what shoddy humanity the quack was made of'. See *Jude*, I, iv, pp. 69f.

106 Thomas Hardy, *The Return of the Native*, ed. Amanda Hodgson, London, 1995 (1878), III, ii, p. 174. When Jude catches himself dreaming of ecclesiastical preferment, he condemns this as 'mundane ambition masquerading in a surplice' (*Jude*, III, 1, p. 181).

107 See Gittings' introduction to *Ethelberta*, ed. cit., esp. pp. 24–27. On the wider context, see (although he does not discuss *Ethelberta*) Bruce Robbins, *The Servant's Hand: English Fiction from Below*, New York, 1986.

108 *Jude*, I, iii, pp. 64, 65.

109 Ibid., II, ii, p. 131.

110 Ibid., VI, i, p. 401.

111 Ibid., II, iv, p. 145.

112 Ibid., V, vii, p. 379.

113 The comment was made in the 1912 preface to *Jude*: see ed. cit., p. 41.

114 Ibid., II, ii, p. 131.

115 Ibid., III x, p. 154.

116 Ibid., V, ii, p. 335.

117 Ibid., V, v, p. 359.

118 Ibid., V, v, pp. 358, 365, 366.

5 Culture and self-realisation: modernist distances

1 Peter Bürger, *Theory of the Avant Garde*, trans. Michael Shaw, Minneapolis and Manchester, 1984, pp. 19f.

2 All the phrases quoted occur in the first two paragraphs of the chapter. See James Joyce, *Ulysses*, with notes and introduction by Declan Kiberd, London, 1992 (1922), p. 45: the pagination reproduces that of the standard Bodley Head edition of 1960.

3 John Carey, *The Intellectuals and the Masses: Pride and Prejudice among the Literary Intelligentsia, 1880–1939*, London and Boston, 1992, p. 16.

4 See (for the terms and phrases we use here) Malcolm Bradbury and James McFarlane (eds), *Modernism 1890–1930*, Hassocks (Sussex), 1978 (1974), p. 24: 'In any working definition of [modernism] we shall have to see in it a quality of abstraction and highly conscious artifice . . .'; Bürger, *Theory of the Avant Garde*, pp. 19f; Andreas Huyssens, 'Mass Culture as Woman: Modernism's Other', in Tania Modleski (ed.), *Studies in Entertainment*, Bloomington, 1986, pp. 188–207, esp. pp. 187f. (the ideal-type modernist artwork is 'self-referential, self-conscious . . .'); Allon White, *The Uses of Obscurity: The Fiction of Early Modernism*, London, 1981, p. 16: 'The obscurity of modernism is not susceptible to simple de-coding . . . Modernist difficulty signifies in and by the very act of offering resistance. The formal, structural difficulties of a text, the kinds of de-formation that it uses, are inseparable from the way it produces significance, from its mode of signification.'

Other chapters and books we have consulted in preparing our discussion of modernism include: Ernst Bloch, Georg Lukács, Bertolt Brecht, Walter Benjamin, Theodor Adorno, *Aesthetics and Politics*, ed. New Left Review, with an Afterword by Fredric Jameson, London, 1980 (1977); Marshall Berman, *All that is Solid Melts into Air: The Experience of Modernity*, London, 1983 (1982); Marshall Berman, 'Why Modernism Still Matters', chapter 1 of Scott Lash and Jonathan Friedman (eds), *Modernity and Identity*, Oxford, 1986 (1982); Andreas Huyssens, *After the Great Divide: Modernism, Mass Culture and Postmodernism*, London, 1988 (1986) (which includes, as chapter 3, 'Mass Culture as Woman', first published in Modleski, *Studies in Entertainment*); James F. Knapp, *Literary Modernism and the Transformation of Work*, Evanston, 1988; Michael H. Levenson, *A Genealogy of Modernism: A Study of English Literary Doctrine 1908–1922*, Cambridge, 1984; Peter Nicholls, *Modernisms: a literary guide*, London, 1995. Nicholls' book gives by far the fullest documentary and analytical account of literary modernism as an international movement.

On modernist painting (which we do not attempt to discuss here), see T.J. Clark, *Farewell to an Idea: Episodes from a History of Modernism*, New Haven and London, 1999, for a recent assessment of modernist works in their time, and of the idea of 'modernism' within art-historical and cultural-theoretical argument.

5 Adorno, in Bloch and others, *Aesthetics and Politics*, pp. 159f. (from Adorno's review of Lukács' *The Meaning of Contemporary Realism*, 1958).

6 The heterogeneity of modernists' political views is evident from any reasonably detailed survey (e.g. those cited above by Nicholls and Williams). Despite this there has been a tendency to assume that modernists were generally progressive. In the case of anglophone literary modernism (Yeats, Eliot, Pound, Faulkner, Wyndham Lewis . . .), such a view is quite untenable. Williams points out (*Politics of Modernism*, pp. 53f.) that modernist movements invariably 'claimed to be anti-bourgeois' whatever their general political orientation. On Joyce's political views (unsystematic, broadly democratic and pacifistic), see Dominic Manganiello, *Joyce's Politics*, London and Boston, 1980.

7 The phrase is used by the editors of *Aesthetics and Politics*: see p. 66.

8 Peter Bürger identifies, and criticises, ideas about 'the detachment of art from practical contexts', insisting that this is 'a *historical process*, i.e . . . socially conditioned'. See *Theory of the Avant Garde*, p. 46.

9 Knapp, *Modernism and Work*, pp. 135f.

10 Bloch and others, *Aesthetics and Politics*, p. 66: this is from the editorial comment ('Presentation II') by Rodney Livingstone, Perry Anderson and Francis Mulhern.

11 The experiential aspect of the contradiction between his allegiance to art and to 'ordinary' people is the theme of Williams' early (1958) essay 'Culture is Ordinary', repr. in John McIlroy and Sallie Westwood (eds), *Border Country: Raymond Williams in Adult Education*, Leicester, 1993, pp. 89–102.

12 White, *Uses of Obscurity*, pp. 31f.

13 See John Goode, 'The art of fiction: Walter Besant and Henry James', in David Howard, John Lucas and John Goode (eds), *Tradition and tolerance in nineteenth-century fiction: critical essays on some English and American novels*, London, 1966, esp. pp. 244f.

14 George Gissing, *Charles Dickens: A Critical Study*, London, 1929 (1898), p. 43.

15 See Nicholls' introduction (*Modernisms*, pp. 2–4). His example is Baudelaire's poem 'To a Red-Haired Beggar Girl'. He concludes: 'Is it

too much to say that this grounding of the aesthetic in an objectification of the other would constitute *the* recurring problem of the later modernisms?' On the 'gender of modernism', which is one aspect of this 'problem', see the critical anthology of that title edited by Bonnie Kime Scott (Bloomington, 1990); and see also Kate Soper, 'Stephen Heroine', in *Troubled Pleasures*, London, 1990.

16 George Gissing, *New Grub Street*, Oxford, ed. John Goode, 1998 (1891), pp. 485f. (chapter XXXV).

17 On *Household Words*, see Richard Altick, *The English Common Reader: A Social History of the Mass Reading Public, 1800–1900*, Chicago, 1984 (1957), p. 347. On *The Egoist*, see Levenson, *Genealogy*, p. 70.

18 See Andreas Huyssens, 'The Politics of Identification: "Holocaust" and West German Drama', in Huyssens, *Great Divide*, esp. pp. 108f., 114.

19 This is a failing of the way Bourdieu presents his thesis of the intelligentsia as 'the dominated fraction within the dominant class' (of which the subcultural split between modernist and realist writers is an integral element). See Pierre Bourdieu, *Distinction: A Social Critique of the Judgement of Taste* (1979) p. 317 of the English translation by Richard Nice, London, 1992; and our reference to this in Chapter 4.

20 John Carey explains modernism as 'exclusion of the masses' and shows that many pre-modernist writers too – but not only those given to more exacting forms – were snobs: see *Intellectuals and Masses*, passim.

21 From Ford's essay 'The Passing of the Great Figure', quoted in Levenson, *Genealogy of Modernism*, pp. 51f.

22 Glenn Jordan and Chris Weedon, *Cultural Politics: Class, Gender, Race and the Postmodern World*, Oxford, 1995, p. 11.

23 As we argued in Chapter 2, a world without power is in any case hard to imagine and not obviously desirable. Moreover, the 'power' of writers and artists in relation to their audiences is surely benign, since we choose to read, listen or look because we seek pleasure and knowledge.

24 See Bürger, *Theory of the Avant Garde*, esp. pp. 34, 46, 87.

25 James Joyce, *A Portrait of the Artist as a Young Man*, Harmondsworth, 1992 (1914–1915), pp. 240, 276; the reference to Shelley is on p. 231 ('This supreme quality [the *quidditas* of the object] is felt by the artist when the esthetic image is first conceived in his imagination. The mind in that mysterious instant Shelley likened beautifully to a fading coal.')

26 Williams, *Politics of Modernism*, p. 53.

27 We emphasise: now-canonical art and writing. Our generalisation would not apply to the very different artefacts and performances of Russian futurism and constructivism, and would apply only with qualifications to Dada and surrealism (which some accounts would include as variants of modernism). It does not in any case mean that in the broadest historical perspective we should not conceptualise and analyse 'modernism' and 'mass culture' in relation to one another, as Huyssens does, as well as seeing 'modernism' as a split between arty and middlebrow bourgeois culture.

28 'Mr Bennett and Mrs Brown' was a revised version of an essay first published in the *Nation and Athenaeum*, given as a talk in Cambridge in 1924 and published in that revised version in the *Criterion* before appearing as a pamphlet from the Hogarth Press. See the note in Woolf, *A Woman's Essays*, ed. and annotated Rachel Bowlby, Harmondsworth, 1991, p. 69. See also for further background (though the book is critically unreliable) Ulysses L. D'Aquila, *Bloomsbury and Modernism*, New York, 1989.

29 Nicholls, *Modernisms*, p. 14.

30 See Carey's discussion in *Intellectuals and Masses*, pp. 19–21.

31 White, *Uses of Obscurity*, p. 43.

32 This is the argument of Peter Keating in his 'Epilogue' to *The Haunted Study*, London, 1991 (1989): see pp. 446f.

33 For a non-polemical summary of the development of academic English studies in England, see Keating, *Haunted Study*, 'Epilogue', esp. pp. 452–456. The crucial period was the turn of the nineteenth and twentieth centuries.

34 Douglas Crimp, 'On the Museum's Ruins', in Hal Foster (ed.), *Postmodern Culture*, London, 1985 (1983); see pp. 49f.

35 Alan Sinfield, *Faultlines: Cultural Materialism and the Politics of Dissident Reading*, Oxford, 1992, p. 287. (Sinfield writes: '. . . to keep the idea of Man and literary culture relevant and persuasive'. This association of 'Man' with literary culture raises a question beyond our concerns at this point, though we discuss it elsewhere in the book, especially in Chapter 2.)

36 F.R. Leavis, *Mass Civilisation and Minority Culture*, Cambridge, 1930.

37 Zygmunt Bauman, *Life in Fragments. Essays in Postmodern Morality*, Oxford, 1997 (1995), p. 232. Peter Nicholls, in a prefatory

note to his *Modernisms*, observes that Carey has mounted a challenge to which modernism's defenders need to reply.

38 Lukács, 'Realism in the Balance' (1937), reprinted in Bloch and others, *Aesthetics and Politics*: see esp. pp. 44f., 53f., 57; Carey, *Intellectuals and Masses*. The issues with regard to Lukács are more complex than can be registered here, of course.

39 Berman, *All that is Solid*, pp. 127f. (the specific reference is to Marx – one of Berman's modernists – but the idea of 'complex development' draws on Berman's key general idea that in modernism, romantic self-development and material-technological development come together: see p. 62).

40 Berman, *All that is Solid*: on 'development', see pp. 127f., p. 62; on 'autocracy' and 'expressway modernism', see pp. 125, 313. Perry Anderson criticises Berman's periodisation and historical specification of modernism in 'Modernity and Revolution', *New Left Review*, 144, March–April 1984.

41 Williams, *Politics of Modernism*, p. 77.

42 This point is well made by Carey: see *Intellectuals and Masses*, pp. 19–21.

43 But see the discussions cited in note 15 above.

44 *Ulysses*, p. 838.

45 See Carey, *Intellectuals and Masses*, esp. chapter 3, 'The Suburbs and the Clerks' (pp. 46–70); Paul Oliver, Ian Davis and Ian Bentley, *Dunroamin: the Suburban Semi and its Enemies*, London, 1981; Andy Medhurst, 'Negotiating the Gnome Zone: Versions of suburbia in British popular culture', pp. 240–268 in Roger Silverstone (ed.), *Visions of Suburbia*, London and New York, 1997.

46 But Carey writes: 'This novel embraces mass man but also rejects him. Mass man – Bloom – is expelled from the circle of the intelligentsia, who are incited to contemplate him, and judge him, in a fictional manifestation' (*Intellectuals and Masses*, p. 21). In our view Bourdieu is guilty of the same misreading when he presents Joyce as mocking Bloom's petty-bourgeois tastes in *Distinction*, pp. 321–323.

47 Adorno, in Bloch and others, *Aesthetics and Politics*, p. 162 (from his review of Lukács' *Meaning of Contemporary Realism*, first publ. 1958). Adorno writes: 'by reflecting it photographically or "from a particular perspective"'. We omit the second phrase because it is primarily directed against Lukács' preference for socialist-realist 'perspectives', not relevant to our concerns here.

48 *Ulysses*, p. 777.

49 Ibid., p. 798.

50 Here we are obviously indebted, in general terms, to Colin MacCabe's influential *James Joyce and the Revolution of the Word*, London, 1979. See also the discussion of this in Knapp, *Modernism and Work*, pp. 135f. We make no pretence here of having drawn on the vast monographic and specialist literature on Joyce.

51 Fredric Jameson, *The Political Unconscious*, London, 1983 (1981), pp. 80ff., and see the whole of this chapter, 'On Interpretation: Literature as a Socially Symbolic Act'.

Conclusion: Culture and self-realisation in postmodern times

1 Jim McGuigan, *Cultural Populism*, London, 1992, p. 82.

2 For a report on Indian call centres, see Luke Harding, 'Delhi Calling', *The Guardian, G2*, 9 March 2001, pp. 2f.

3 Max Weber, *The Protestant Ethic and the Spirit of Capitalism*, trans. Talcott Parsons, with an introd. by Anthony Giddens, London, 1984 (1930), pp. 181f.

4 The argument of Adorno and Horkheimer in *Dialectic of Enlightenment*, London, 1979, can be read as an extended reflection on this theme. Cf. Kate Soper, 'The Politics of Nature: Reflections on Hedonism, Progress and Ecology', *Capitalism, Nature, Socialism*, 10 (38), 1999.

5 Lucio Magri, 'The Peace Movement and Europe', in *Exterminism and Cold War*, New Left Review (ed.), London, 1982, pp. 124, 132. In his concluding essay, E.P. Thompson commented: ' [Magri's] definition of the matter is superb and I urge readers to return to it again and again' (ibid., p. 347).

6 André Gorz, *Ecology as Politics*, Boston, 1980; *Farewell to the Working Class: an Essay on Post-Industrial Socialism*, London, 1982; *Paths to Paradise: On the Liberation from Work*, London, 1985; *Critique of Economic Reason*, London, 1989; *Capitalism, Socialism, Ecology*, London, 1994; *Reclaiming Work: Beyond the Wage-Based Society*, Cambridge, 1999. For an excellent commentary and full bibliography, see Finn Bowring, *André Gorz and the Sartrean Legacy*, London and New York, 2000; cf. Finn Bowring, 'Misreading Gorz', *New Left Review*, 217, May–June 1996; C. Lodziak and J. Tatman, *André Gorz: A Critical*

Introduction, London, 1997; Sean Sayers, 'Gorz on Work and Liberation', *Radical Philosophy*, 55 Summer 1981, pp. 16–19; Martin Ryle and Kate Soper, 'Future Work' (review of *Reclaiming Work* and books by Jeremy Rifkin and Vivienne Forrester), *Red Pepper*, September, 2000, pp. 28f.

7 Cf. Harry Braverman's argument that the 'social division of labour' which subdivides society should not be confused with the 'detailed division of labour' within the work-place: the former, unlike the latter which subdivides individuals without regard to human capabilities and needs, may enhance the individual and the species (Braverman here has in mind the kinds of development of skill possible to the craftsman and other socially 'divided' but skilled labourers). See *Labour and Monopoly Capital: the Degradation of Work in the Twentieth Century*, New York and London, 1974, esp. p. 73.

8 This form of accounting has its origins in the exclusive focus of the Marxist theory of alienation on the travails of the waged worker, and is responsible for the gender inflection of much subsequent socialist discussion of work and the public–private divide. For a survey and critique, see Linda Nicholson, 'Feminism and Marx', in Seyla Benhabib and Drucilla Cornell, *Feminism as Critique*, Cambridge, 1987, pp. 16–30. In 'What's Critical about Critical Theory?' in the same work (pp. 31–55), Nancy Fraser offers a critical discussion of the gender blindness of Habermas' theorisation of the 'systemic'/'symbolic' divide. Gorz is subject to a similar charge of abstracting from the negative effects for women of the gender division of labour through the emphasis he places on the inalienable nature and existential value of the household chores of self-maintenance. (But see also the exposition and defence of Gorz' position in Bowring, *André Gorz*, pp. 128–136.) One can agree that the invasion of the 'life world' by commercial pressures is to be resisted, and that much that gives its special value to the work performed in the sphere of reproduction is sacrificed in the process of commodification. But what also needs to be recognised by any serious opponent of patriarchy is the onus this places on men to participate as fully and freely as women in the inalienable activities of nurturing and self-maintenance. What also needs stressing is the desperate situation of many carers of the ill and elderly, who require far more state support than they currently receive.

9 See, for example, Herbert Marcuse, *Eros and Civilisation*, Boston, 1966, Part II. On the influence of Schiller on Marcuse's utopian

conceptions, see Chapter 1 of the present work. On Walter Benjamin's development of Fourier's utopian view of work as a form of play, see Susan Buck-Morss, *The Dialectic of Seeing: Walter Benjamin and the Arcades Project*, Cambridge (Mass.), 1989, pp. 261–266 and 273–280.

10 G.W.F. Hegel, *Phenomenology of Spirit*, trans. A.W. Miller, Oxford, 1977, pp. 115–19.

11 Leo Tolstoy, *Anna Karenin*, Harmondsworth, 1970 (1878), pp. 268–277.

12 This summative phrase is taken from the title of the first volume of Manuel Castells' major three-volume study, *The Information Age: Economy, Society and Culture*. Volume 1, *The Rise of the Network Society*, Oxford and Malden (Ma), 1996, contains an extensive bibliography of recent work on the social impact of new IT: of particular relevance to our discussion here are chapters 5–7.

13 Douglas Rushkoff, *Cyberia: Life in the Trenches of Hyperspace*, London, 1994, p. 19 ('rechoosing reality'); pp. 72f. (quotation from Leary).

14 Michael Benedikt (ed.), *Cyberspace*, Cambridge (Ma.), 1991, p. 3, cit. in Julian Stallabrass, *Gargantua: Manufactured Mass Culture*, London, 1996, p. 65 (Stallabrass's chapter 3, 'Empowering Technology', is an incisive mockery of the wilder claims of cyberphiles).

15 Bruce Mazlish, *The Fourth Continuity: The Co-Evolution of Humans and Machines*, New Haven, 1993, p. 182, pp. 2l8f., cit. in Mark Slouka, *The War of the Worlds*, London, 1996, p. 65.

16 On the invasive impact of technoculture on sensory perception and motor capacity, see Paul Virilio, *Lost Dimension*, New York, 1991; Virilio, *The Art of the Motor*, Minneapolis, 1995; Virilio, *Open Sky*, London, 1997; and cf. Bowring, *André Gorz*, pp. 183–185.

17 See Sadie Plant, 'Coming Across the Future', in Joan Broadhurst Dixon and Eric J. Cassidy (eds), *Virtual Futures: Cyberotics, Technology and Posthuman Pragmatism*, London, 1998, pp. 30–36.

18 Relevant critiques include those in Stallabrass, *Gargantua*, esp. pp. 40–83; Stephen Doheny-Farina, *The Wired Neighbourhood*, New Haven, 1996, esp. Part Two; Andrew Ross, *Strange Weather: Culture, Science and Technology in the Age of Limits*, London, 1991; Theodore Roszak, *The Cult of Information. A Neo-Luddite Treatise on High-Tech, Artificial Intelligence and the True Art of Thinking*, Berkeley, 1994.

19 See Rushkoff, *Cyberia*, pp. 196–199.

20 See Stallabrass, *Gargantua*, pp. 56–58, 49.

21 William Burroughs likes it, he says, because there 'you' can 'lay Cleopatra, Helen of Troy, Isis, Madame Pompadour, or Aphrodite. You can get fucked by Pan, Jesus Christ, Apollo or the Devil himself. Anything you like likes you when you press the buttons' (*The Adding Machine*, London, 1985, p. 86, cit. Plant, 'Coming Across the Future', p. 35).

22 The first phrase is from M. Schudson, 'The new validation of popular culture: sense and sentimentality in academia', *Critical Studies in Mass Communication*, 4, March 1987, quoted by McGuigan in *Cultural Populism*, p. 80; the second is from Zygmunt Bauman, *Life in Fragments. Essays in Postmodern Morality*, Oxford, 1997 (1995), pp. 239f.

23 Although it has brought pressures that make it more difficult for academics to pursue research and scholarship – above all in the very institutions that have been most open to less privileged students.

24 On current opportunities and constraints in the academic teaching of culture, see the essays in N. Aldred and M. Ryle (eds), *Teaching Culture*, Leicester, 1999. The leading recent advocate of a pragmatic, policy-oriented turn in cultural studies has been Tony Bennett: see the thoughtful review of Bennett's *Culture: A Reformer's Science*, London, 1998, by Calvin Taylor in *Key Words*, 3, 2000, pp. 135–138. On the genesis of cultural studies within adult and popular education, see Tom Steele, *The Emergence of Cultural Studies 1945–65: Cultural Politics, Adult Education and the English Question*, London, 1997. (A sometimes idealised image of radical adult education as the site of renegotiations of knowledge needs to be tempered by the recognition that a one-dimensional emphasis on class tended to prevail there: contemporary departments of cultural and literary studies are much more likely than their extra-mural precursors to acknowledge the cultural and political importance of gender, sexuality and 'race'.)

25 Terry Eagleton, *The Idea of Culture*, Oxford, 2000, p. 130; Francis Mulhern, *Culture/Metaculture*, London and New York, 2000, pp. 173f. See the review of both books by Martin Ryle in *Radical Philosophy*, 103, September/October 2000, pp. 46–48. Cf. Bruce Robbins' 1996 aside to the effect that the term 'politics' has become 'inflated' in literary studies (in his review of Harold Bloom's *The Western Canon*, in *Radical Philosophy*, 79, September/October 1996, p. 46).

26 If Eagleton and Mulhern say relatively little about the direct

social uses and impact of cultural criticism and teaching as this has borne on matters of gender, sexuality and ethnic/'racial'/national identity, this reflects their commitment – which we share – to a definition of 'politics' that refers also to the economic.

27 See Bennett, *Culture: A Reformer's Science*, and the review by Taylor cit. above.

28 Jameson's reference was to the capacity of realist fiction to invoke and realise the 'category of totality which [has been] systematically undermined by existential fragmentation on all levels of life and social organization': see his Afterword to Ernst Bloch and others, *Aesthetics and Politics*, London, 1980 (1977). (Bruce Robbins suggested, in a reply to this, that modernism too had its modes of invoking 'totality': see Robbins, 'Modernism in History, Modernism in Power' in Robert Kiely (ed.), *Modernism Reconsidered*, Cambridge (Ma) and London, 1983, pp. 229–246.)

29 See Andrew Robinson, *Satyajit Ray: The Inner Eye*, London, 1989, pp. 74ff.

30 Ibid., pp. 42f.

31 Ibid., pp. 83–87.

32 Walter Benjamin, 'Theses on the Philosophy of History', Thesis VII, in Benjamin, *Illuminations*, ed. and introd. H. Arendt and trans. H. Zohn, London, 1970, p. 258.

33 Raymond Williams, *The Long Revolution*, London, 1961, pp. 42f.

34 In E.P. Thompson's two-part review of *The Long Revolution*; see *New Left Review*, 9 and 10, May–June and July–August, 1961.

35 The dismissive and inaccurate reference to Charlotte Bronte in *The Long Revolution* (p. 67) is especially striking: 'The novels of Charlotte and Anne Bronte are, in terms of plot and structure of feeling, virtually identical with many stories in the periodicals: the governess-heroine, the insane wife or alcoholic husband, the resolution through resignation, duty, and magic.'

36 Paul Gilroy, *The Black Atlantic: Modernity and Double Consciousness*, London, 1999 (1993), pp. 10f., 14. It is certainly extraordinary that Williams contrives to say nothing of Carlyle's 'Occasional Discourse on the Negro Question' (1848), later retitled 'On the Nigger Question'. See Catherine Hall, 'Competing Masculinities: Thomas Carlyle, John Stuart Mill and the Case of Governor Eyre' for a summary (with extensive bibliography) of the way that Victorian

intellectuals divided over the brutal handling by the British Governor of the riot in Morant Bay, Jamaica in 1865: Eyre's defenders included Ruskin, Dickens, Kingsley and Tennyson (Catherine Hall, *White, Male and Middle-Class: Explorations in Feminism and History*, Cambridge, 1992, pp. 255–295).

37 Marc Redfield, *Phantom Formations: Aesthetic Ideology and the Bildungsroman*, Ithaca and London, 1996, 'Preface', pp. viiif. (and cf. pp. 25f.).

38 Alan Sinfield, 'Cultural Imperialism', in *Faultlines: Cultural Materialism and the Politics of Dissident Reading*, Oxford, 1992 (the sentence quoted is on pp. 290f.).

39 Janet Batsleer, Tony Davies, Rebecca O'Rourke and Chris Weedon, *Rewriting English: Cultural Politics of Gender and Class*, London and New York, 1985, p. 21. Later (p. 38), it is acknowledged that this is also an enabling form of education.

40 Edward Said, 'Orientalism and After' (interview with *Radical Philosophy*, 1992), reprinted in Peter Osborne (ed.), *A Critical Sense: Interviews with Intellectuals*, London, 1996, pp. 65–86; see p. 68.

41 See Barbara Herrnstein Smith, *Contingencies of Value: Alternative Perspectives for Critical Theory*, Cambridge (Ma), 1988.

42 Glenn Jordan and Chris Weedon, *Cultural Politics: Class, Gender, Race and the Postmodern World*, Oxford, 1995, p. 11. Cf. the arguments of Anne Ardis against what she calls 'traditional' criteria of value in *New Women, New Novels: Feminism and Early Modernism*, New Brunswick and London, 1990, pp. 7f.

43 This is exemplified in subsequent chapters of *Cultural Politics*: e.g. Part III, chapter 8, 'Gender, Racism and Identity: Black Feminist Fiction', which deals with fiction by Black and Asian women in the USA and Britain.

44 John Storey, *Cultural Theory and Popular Culture*, London, 2001 (3rd ed.). The discussion of Ang's work is part of the useful account of the 'meaning in use' mode of analysis in feminist cultural studies, and its contrast with critical readings that draw on a notion of ideology: see pp. 113–138. Storey's approach had earlier been criticised by (amongst others) Jim McGuigan, in his *Cultural Populism*, London, 1992.

45 'In a book such as [Fiske's] *On Television*', writes Francis Mulhern, 'the complex relations between "containment" and "resistance" in viewing experience undergo euphoric simplification, and the audience takes control of the broadcast text': Mulhern, p. 140 (the

reference is to John Fiske, *Television Culture*, London, 1987). See also Simon Frith, *Performing Rites: Evaluating Popular Music*, Oxford, 1998, pp. 14f.

46 Frith, *Performing Rites*, p. 13.

47 McGuigan, *Cultural Populism*, p. 82. On some related questions, see Frank Kermode, *History and Value*, Oxford, 1988, especially chapters 6 and 7.

48 Anthony Easthope, *Literary into Cultural Studies*, London, 1991, pp. 174f. See Martin Ryle's review of the book (and others) in *Radical Philosophy*, 70, Summer 1993, pp. 50f; and also Martin Ryle, 'Long Live Literature?', *Radical Philosophy*, 67, Summer 1994 and the debate between Easthope and Ryle in *Radical Philosophy*, 70, March–April 1995. Easthope's recent early death was a great loss to cultural and literary studies in Britain.

49 Easthope, *Literary into Cultural Studies*, p. 173.

50 Sinfield, *Faultlines*, p. 22.

51 Walter Benjamin, 'Theses on the Philosophy of History', Thesis VII, in Benjamin, *Illuminations*, p. 258.

52 Ardis, *New Women, New Novels*, pp. 7f.

53 Günter Grass, *The Tin Drum*, trans. Ralph Mannheim, London, 1998 (first publ. 1959; this trans. 1961), p. 240 (opening lines of 2, 5, 'Maria').

54 David Lloyd, *Anomalous States: Irish Writing and the Post-Colonial Moment*, Dublin, 1993, pp. 6f.

55 Robert Young, *White Mythologies: Writing History and the West*, London, 1990. On p. 133 Young writes: 'Said's culture, for all his reservations, resembles nothing so much as that of Arnold, Eliot or Leavis – there seems no irony intended at all when Said, the great campaigner against racism and ethnocentrism, laments in Leavisite tones the loss of culture's "discrimination and evaluation".' Said's 1992 interview with *Radical Philosophy*, in which he explains the grounds for his literary humanism, is reprinted in Peter Osborne (ed.), *A Critical Sense*, London, 1996: see pp. 65–86, esp. pp. 67–70.

56 The empirical answers, at the time the relevant books were first published, being London University (Gilroy: however when he began work, Gilroy was in a marginal post in the then Polytechnic sector); Sussex University (Sinfield); University of California at Berkeley (Lloyd); Wadham College, Oxford (Young).

57 See Raymond Williams, *Culture and Society*, London, 1987

(1958), pp. 319ff. On the uses of learned culture to British working-class audiences, especially in the first half of the twentieth century, see now Jonathan Rose, *The Intellectual Life of the British Working Classes*, New Haven and London, 2001, an important work of scholarship which however appeared too late for us to make use of it in the present book. For some reservations about Rose's perspective, see the review by Martin Ryle in *Radical Philosophy*, 112, March–April 2002.

58 Almost all the writers (for instance) discussed in Joyce Tompkins' survey *The Popular Novel in England, 1770–1800*, Lincoln (Nebraska), 1967 (1932), on which we draw in Chapter 3 above, are now forgotten.

59 Of course Williams' subsequent work often shows – as, clearly, in his dealings with 'high' literature in *The Country and the City*, London, 1973 – a less acquiescent and more critical temper.

Index